THE HIDDEN PLACES OF
CORNWALL

By Jim Gracie

© Travel Publishing Ltd.

Regional Hidden Places

Cornwall
Devon
Dorset, Hants & Isle of Wight
East Anglia
Gloucs, Wiltshire & Somerset
Heart of England
Hereford, Worcs & Shropshire
Lake District & Cumbria
Lancashire & Cheshire
Northumberland & Durham
Peak District
Sussex
Yorkshire

National Hidden Places

England
Ireland
Scotland
Wales

Hidden Inns

East Anglia
Heart of England
Lancashire & Cheshire
North of England
South
South East
South and Central Scotland
Wales
Welsh Borders
West Country
Yorkshire
Wales

Country Living
Rural Guides

East Anglia
Heart of England
Ireland
North East of England
North West of England
Scotland
South
South East
Wales
West Country

Published by: Travel Publishing Ltd, 7a Apollo House,
Calleva Park, Aldermaston, Berkshire RG7 8TN

ISBN 1-904-43429-0

© Travel Publishing Ltd

First published 1989, second edition 1992, third edition 1996,
fourth edition 1998, fifth edition 2000, sixth edition 2003,
seventh edition 2005

Printing by: Scotprint, Haddington

Maps by: © Maps in Minutes ™ (2005)
© Crown Copyright, Ordnance Survey 2005

Editor: Jim Gracie

Cover Design: Lines & Words, Aldermaston

Cover Photograph: Mullion Harbour, Cornwall
© www.britainonview.com

Text Photographs: © www.britainonview.com

Foreword

The **Hidden Places** is a collection of easy to use travel guides taking you in this instance on a relaxed but informative tour of *Cornwall*. This county has been described as "an isolated beauty that contains some of the most dramatic and spectacular scenery in the country". It is surrounded by rugged coastlines and has often been referred to as the 'English Riviera' encompassing pretty fishing ports, secluded scenic villages, narrow winding lanes and strong, romantic seafaring traditions. This is a land of strong Celtic heritage and ancestry, a place that is dotted with monuments such as crosses, holy wells and prehistoric sites and where legends of old still hold their romance amongst the Cornish people.

This is the 7th edition of a **Hidden Places** title covering Cornwall and the guide has been fully updated. In this respect we would like to thank the many Tourist Information Centres in Cornwall for helping us to update the editorial content.

Our books contain a wealth of interesting information on the history, the countryside, the towns and villages and the more established places of interest. But they also promote the more secluded and little known visitor attractions and places to stay, eat and drink many of which are easy to miss unless you know exactly where you are going.

We include hotels, inns and bed and breakfast accomodation, restaurants, public houses, teashops, historic houses, museums, gardens, and many other attractions throughout the area, all of which are comprehensively indexed. Most places are accompanied by an attractive photograph and are easily located by using the map at the beginning of each chapter. We do not award merit marks or rankings but concentrate on describing the more interesting, unusual or unique features of each place with the aim of making the reader's stay in the local area an enjoyable and stimulating experience.

Whether you are visiting the area for business or pleasure or in fact are living in Cornwall we do hope that you enjoy reading and using this book. We are always interested in what readers think of places covered (or not covered) in our guides so please do not hesitate to use the reader reaction forms provided to give us your considered comments. We also welcome any general comments which will help us improve the guides themselves. Finally if you are planning to visit any other corner of the British Isles we would like to refer you to the list of other **Hidden Places** titles to be found at the rear of the book and to the Travel Publishing website at **www.travelpublishing.co.uk.**

Travel Publishing

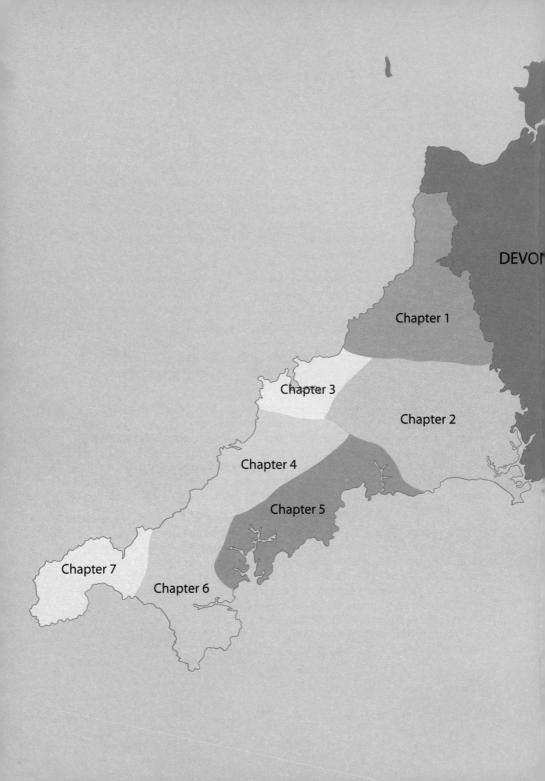

DEVON

Chapter 1

Chapter 3

Chapter 2

Chapter 4

Chapter 5

Chapter 7

Chapter 6

Contents

PLACES TO STAY, EAT AND DRINK

● Denotes entries in other chapters

1 North Cornwall

For all that it is part of England, Cornwall has held onto its Celtic heritage tenaciously. Even North Cornwall - separated for most of its length from Devon by the River Tamar, and therefore at most risk from English influences - has hung on to its traditions, and people still talk of "crossing the Tamar into England". The most common reminders of this heritage are the place names beginning with Tre (a town or settlement), Pol (a pool, pit or headland) and Pen (head, end or summit). There are also many ancient monuments to be discovered, such as crosses, holy wells and prehistoric sites.

Tales of the Arthurian legend abound in Cornwall, the most famous site being at Tintagel, a small coastal village where, on a rocky headland known as The Island, stand the romantic remains of Tintagel Castle. Said to be the birthplace of King Arthur, this ancient village has certainly embraced the legend and there is plenty for the King Arthur hunter to enjoy. One of the most interesting buildings here is the Old Post Office in Fore Street, built in the 14th century as a private house, centuries before the Penny Post came into being.

Further up the windswept and dramatic coastline of north Cornwall lie the sheltered beaches of Bude. The birthplace of British surfing (often referred to by Australian surfers as the 'Bondai of Britain'), this traditional seaside resort has been a favorite holiday destination for many years after

Coastline at Tintagel

CROOKLETS INN

Crooklets Beach, Bude, Cornwall EX23 8NF
Tel: 01288 352335

Sitting on an imposing corner site, the **Crooklets Inn** is only yards from the beach and a short stroll from Bude town centre. It has recently been upgraded, turning it into one of the best small hotels in the area. There are five fully en-suite rooms with sea views, all extremely comfortable and spacious. The bar offers five lagers and four real ales, as well as the usual range of wines, spirits and soft drinks. The new conservatory houses the restaurant, where the menu includes many home-cooked dishes that are both delicious and filling. This place represents real value for money, and you can't afford to miss it!.

thriving as a port handling slate from the inland quarries. It also boasts a castle, modest by Tintagel's standards, and decidedly more modern, but renowned for being the first building in the country to be constructed on sand, its foundations resting on a concrete raft. Cornwall is particularly well endowed with beautiful gardens, and in this northern part Lanhydrock and Pencarrow are outstanding. Cornwall's churches are among the most distinctive in the land, some of them quite modest, others contrastingly grand. Many of the county's churches are distinguished by magnificent woodcarving.

Bude

This traditional seaside resort, with its three miles of sandy beaches, rock pools and Atlantic breakers rolling in from the west, has numerous facilities for beach lovers, surfers and coastal walkers. It first developed as a resort in Victorian times, and in the 1880s the completion of the branch line from the main GWR line started to attract holidaymakers seeking fresh, bracing air. Since the 1950s Bude has had a new lease of life as the premier British surfing centre, due to its exposed position on the Atlantic coast. During a winter gale this can be a remote and harsh environment but in

EDGCUMBE HOTEL

19 Summerleaze Crescent, Bude,
Cornwall EX23 8HJ
Tel: 01288 353846 Fax: 01288 355256
e-mail: info@edgcumbe-hotel.co.uk
website: www.edgcumbe-hotel.co.uk

The **Edgcumbe Hotel** is an elegant, whitewashed building with extensive views, two minutes walk from the town centre. It has 15 spacious room, all are completely en-suite, and all have been tastefully furnished with TV, radio alarm clock, tea/coffee making facilities and radio intercom to reception. The cuisine in the dining room is all home cooked using local produce wherever possible, making dining here a culinary experience not to be missed. Plus there is a well-stocked residents bar - just right for a relaxing drink after a hard day exploring or lying on the beach!

THE CLIFF HOTEL

Crooklets Beach, Bude, Cornwall EX23 8NG
Tel/Fax: 01288 353110
website: www.cliffhotel.co.uk

Set in five acres and looking down onto the beach and sea, **The Cliff Hotel** offers some of the best accommodation, food and drink in Northwest Cornwall. It is owned and personally managed by Rosalind and John Jeffs, a young, energetic couple who have had plenty of experience in the hotel and catering trades.

The building dates back to the gentler days of the 1920s, with later additions, when style, comfort and relaxation were all. These qualities still remain, combined with modern standards of service and great value for money, earning it four diamonds from the AA, the RAC and the English Tourist Board. The hotel boasts 15 fully en suite rooms that are spacious and well decorated and furnished, each with colour TV, tea/coffee making facilities, radio, hair dryer and direct dial phone.

You can book on a bed and breakfast or dinner bed and breakfast basis, and children are more than welcome. The food, of course, is outstanding and you can have freshly prepared bar snacks at lunchtime, either in the bar or on the sun terrace. Dinner in the evening comprises three course, with the produce used being fresh and local wherever possible, As well as sizzling steaks, there is roast beef, steak and kidney pies and freshly caught seafood. Each dish is beautifully cooked and presented.

The hotel has an indoor swimming pool, bowling green, putting green, hard surface tennis court and games room. And only two minutes walk away is a challenging 18-hole golf course.

summer, with a gentle breeze blowing in off the sea and the possible sighting of dolphins, there can be few more exhilarating places in Cornwall.

Originally a busy north Cornwall port, Bude developed rapidly after the **Bude Canal** to Launceston was opened in the 1820s. The canal was an ambitious inland waterway project that was intended to connect the Atlantic with the English Channel via the River Tamar. The only stretch to be completed was that between Bude and Launceston and it was, in many ways, remarkable as the sea lock at the entrance to the canal was the only lock on the whole length of the canal - although it ran for 35 miles and rose to a height of 350 feet in six miles.

To achieve the changes in levels, inclined planes, or ramps, were used between the different levels and a wheeled tub boat was pulled up the ramps on metal rails. The longest such canal when it opened in 1823, Bude Canal carried lime-rich sea sand that was ideal for fertilizing inland farmland, and on the journey back towards Bude, cargoes of oats and slate were taken to the ships in Bude harbour. The advent of the railway and the discovery of more efficient fertilizers combined to make the canal redundant and it has not been in commercial use since 1891. The canal today has a new use as a resource for fishing, boating and walking, and the **Bude Canal Trail** follows this tranquil backwater into the heart of Cornwall.

The Beach at Bude

The first two miles, to Helebridge, remain in water.

Close to the entrance to the canal stands **Bude Castle** overlooking Summerleaze Beach, an unusually small fortification designed as his home by the 19th century engineer and prolific inventor, Sir Goldsworthy Gurney (1793-1875), a local man who was probably the greatest inventor Cornwall - a place renowned for its inventors - has ever produced (see also Launcells). What makes this building particularly interesting is that it is thought to be the first in Britain to be constructed on sand; it rests on a concrete raft - a technique developed by Gurney. Among his other inventions were a steam jet, a musical instrument consisting of glasses played as a piano, and the Bude Light, an intensive light obtained by introducing oxygen into the interior

flame and using mirrors. He used this to light his house and to light the House of Commons, where his invention replaced 280 candles and gave rise to the expression 'in the limelight'. This earned the inventor his knighthood and served the House of Commons for 60 years. He also introduced the world's first town-to-town carriage service using self-propelled steam carriages. To celebrate the Millennium, Carole Vincent and Anthony Fanshawe designed the **Bude Light 2000**, the first large-scale public sculpture to combine coloured concrete with fibre optic lighting. The 30 feet beacon stands close to the castle, and uses the latest-fibre optic techniques to 'reconstruct' the constellations at the time of the 2000 Millennium.

The history of the town and its canal can be explored in the **Bude-Stratton Museum**, which stands on the canal side near the sea lock in the Canal Company's former smithy, where the old forge can still be seen. From shipwrecks, railways, farming and local geology, the story of Bude and the surrounding area is told in a vivid series of displays, including life in the town during the Second World War. There are also displays honouring Sir Goldsworthy Gurney, and another local worthy, the giant Anthony Payne (see under Stratton).

One of the high spots in the Bude calendar is the annual Jazz Festival, which takes place in August and September each year. This is when 'New Orleans comes to Britain', and with over 20 venues in and around the town, it is one of the leading festivals of its kind in Britain.

The **South West Coast Path** passes through the town. To the north is **Duckpool Beach**, at the shore end of the Coombe Valley, and a favourite with surfers.

Around Bude

Poughill
1 mile NE of Bude off the A39

The thatched cottages of the old village of Poughill (pronounced Poffle) stand around the **St Olaf's Parish Church**. Though its foundations are Norman, the church as you see it now, dates largely from the 14th century, and is dedicated to a Norwegian king and martyr. Noted for its late 15th century carved oak bench ends, keen eyed visitors will also spot that the Royal Arms of Charles II have been incorrectly dated 1655. The mid-15th century wall paintings depict St Christopher. Over the church door is a tablet commemorating Sir Goldsworthy Gurney, a gift, along with the church clock, of his daughter.

In the churchyard is a huge granite slab, placed there in about 1890 when a landslide on a nearby cliff revealed an ancient burial mound. The vicar had the remains buried in the churchyard and also placed the great covering slab there. Opposite the church lies the **Church House** (now three houses), which was built in 1525. It is unusual in that it is built of stone, as cob was generally used at that time.

Morwenstow
5½ miles N of Bude off the A39

Located on the harshest stretch of the north Cornwall coast, this village has been used to taking the full brunt of Atlantic storms through the years and, though at times rather storm-lashed, this is a marvellous place from which to watch the changing moods of the ocean. Not surprisingly, shipwrecks have been common down the ages along this stretch of coast and, though many floundered as a result of storms, it was also not unknown for local criminals to lure unsuspecting ships on to the rocks by lighting lanterns from the cliff tops or the shore.

The village's most renowned inhabitant was the eccentric vicar and poet, the Reverend Robert Stephen Hawker, who came here in 1834 and stayed among his congregation of 'smugglers, wreckers and dissenters' until his death in 1875. A colourful figure dressed in a purple frock coat, a fisherman's jersey and long fisherman's boots, he would spend much of his time walking this area of his beloved county or writing verse and smoking - some accounts say it was opium - in the driftwood hut - known as **Hawker's Hut** (NT) - which he built himself 17 steps down from the top of the precipitous **Vicarage Cliff**. From the hut there are great views along the coastline and, on clear days, out to Lundy Island.

One of the first people to show concern for the number of merchant vessels that were coming to grief along this perilous stretch of coastline, Hawker would spend much of his time monitoring the sea and would often climb down the cliff to rescue shipwrecked crews or recover the bodies of those who had not survived. After carrying the bodies of the dead mariners back to the village he would give them a Christian burial. It is estimated that he recovered the bodies of over 40 mariners. One of the many ships wrecked off Sharpnose headland was the *Caledonia*, a Scottish ship of 500 tons, whose figurehead stands above the grave of her captain in Morwenstow churchyard.

Hawker's other contribution to Morwenstow was the rectory which he built at his own expense and to his own design. As individual as the man himself, the chimneys of the house represent the towers of various churches where he had been vicar; the broad kitchen chimney is in remembrance of his mother, and is modelled on her tomb.

His lasting contribution to the church was to reintroduce the annual Harvest Festival and his most famous poem is the rousing Cornish anthem, *The Song of Western Men*, which contains the well-known line 'And shall Trelawney die?'.It

was first published anonymously in a Plymouth newspaper. Many people thought it was a traditional Cornish song composed in the 17th century about Bishop Jonathan Trelawney, imprisoned with six other bishops during the reign of James II. Hawker's first wife was half his age, and when she died he married a woman a third his age, who bore him three children. Eccentric to the end, Hawker became a Roman Catholic on his deathbed, even though he had written an anthem to Trelawney, who was a staunch Protestant. The National Trust-owned land, between the church and the cliffs, is dedicated to this remarkable man's memory.

Another interesting gentleman of Morwenstow was David Coppinger, a Dane who settled near the village in the 18th century. Based as much on fact as fiction, the story begins when, during a terrible storm, Coppinger dived from a sinking foreign ship and swam through the waves to shore. He then leapt up on to a horse belonging to a young girl called Dinah Hamlyn, who had come to see the storm, and rode it hard inland to Dinah's house. Here he stayed and, upon her father's death, he married the girl. Coppinger turned the house into the headquarters for his ruthless gang of smugglers and, with neither the local people or the authorities prepared to take action against him, he began to terrorise the area, even taking control of the local roads, which became known as 'Coppinger's Tracks'. His schooner, the Black Prince, regularly took contraband goods from France and the Channel Islands to Cornwall, and soon he was a rich man. At home, he was equally violent, treating his wife with great cruelty. Eventually the revenue men took control and, realising his days were numbered after many members of his gang had been killed, Coppinger fled from the country on a strange boat that mysteriously appeared at the point where he first arrived. Some people claim that Coppinger was an invention of Robert Hawker, but this is unlikely.

To the north of the village, and close to the Devon border, lies **Welcombe Mouth**, a graveyard for many ships which foundered on the jagged rocks and now a good spot for surfing. **Welcombe and Marsland Valleys Nature Reserve**, set in the forested valley slopes, is a haven for butterflies.

At Higher and Lower Sharpnose Points, to the south of Morwenstow, the erosion caused by the constant bombardment of the sea can be seen clearly as there are boulders strewn along the bottom of these crumbling cliffs; some of the outcrops of harder rocks have begun to form tiny islands.

Kilkhampton
4½ miles NE of Bude on the A39

This small village sits 600 feet above sea level, and claims to be Cornwall's most northerly village of any size. Sitting astride the A38, it is thought to have been an important settlement in Saxon times, as the surrounding area is littered with ancient burial grounds. In 1088, the manor of Kilkhampton, along with that of Bideford, was awarded to Robert FitzHamon (who went on to found

BROCKLANDS ADVENTURE PARK

West Street, Kilkhampton, Nr Bude, Cornwall EX23 9QW
Tel: 01288 321920
website: www.brocklands.com

Five miles from Bude, just off the A39 road to Bideford, **Brocklands Adventure Park** provides a memorable day out for all the family. The number and range of the attractions, both inside and outside, is truly bewildering, ranging from crazy golf, archery and pony rides to  roller races, paddle boats, bumper boats, racing cars, a steam railway and a mega tube slide laid into a 30ft embankment. A recent major addition was a top of the range 4 lane bowling alley.

The educational Click-On Centre is filled with computerised information on West Country wildlife, and a viewing gallery tells visitors all about the local animal and bird life. A 200-seat restaurant offers plenty of space to relax and take on fuel for another round of fun. There are also picnic areas in and out of doors, and gifts, toys and souvenirs can be bought in the shop.

Tewkesbury) by William Rufus in recognition of his support during Odo's Revolt. The village's tall and elegant **St James's Parish Church** was built in the 15th century on the site of the previous Norman church, of which only the splendid doorway remains. St James's Day (July 25th) is still celebrated in the village. The church contains many monuments to the local Granville family, many of them made by Michael Chuke, a local man and a pupil of Grinling Gibbons. Equally notable are the magnificent carved bench-ends, and the organ is the one played by Purcell when it was in Westminster Abbey. The Grenvilles at one time lived in the very grand Stowe House, which no longer stands but is described vividly by

Charles Kingsley in his *Westward Ho!*. With its entrance on West Street, **Brocklands Adventure Park** (see panel on page 9) is one of the most popular family attractions in the region. It features exhibitions on local wildlife, nature walks, a slide called the 'Smarties Tube' and a bowling alley.

Two miles north of the village is **Killarney Springs,** another family fun park with rides, boating, nature trails and so on.

Stratton
1½ miles E of Bude on the A3072

Believed to have been founded in Roman times, this old market town predates its much larger neighbour of Bude. In fact, when it's ancient **St**

TREE INN

Stratton, North Cornwall EX23 9DA
Tel: 01288 352038

The whitewashed **Tree Inn** at Stratton dates back to the 13th century, so when you call in, you're also visiting a piece of Cornwall's long and fascinating history. At one time it was the HQ of Sir Beville Grenville, the Royalist captain who led his troops to a magnificent victory at nearby Stamford Hill in 1643. One of Grenville's greatest supporters was Anthony Payne the Cornish giant, who stood over seven feet tall, and the inn was his actual birthplace.

Nowadays the inn is a firm favourite with locals and visitors alike, and has recently been taken over by Bob and Emma Semple and Emma's mother Beth. who have lived in the village for over 18 years. This means that they regard it not just as a business venture, but as an advertisement for the local hospitality. The inn offers three real ales, as well as a wide range of wines and spirits, and the inside is as picturesque as the outside, with old oak beams, dark wood and framed prints

on the wall. The whole ambience is one of comfort, tradition and friendliness. The accommodation is currently being refurbished to provide spacious and comfortable rooms.

Food is available daily, served from 12 · 2 pm and from 6 · 9 pm. There's a printed menu and a daily specials board, and meals can either be eaten in the bar or in the separate restaurant, which opens every evening and Sunday lunchtimes in summer and on Fiday and Saturday evenings and Sunday lunchtimes in winter. The food is always freshly cooked from good, local produce wherever possible.

Andrew's Parish Church was first being built, Bude was simply an unimportant part of the town. The church is well worth a visit, its main feature being a tomb with a cross-legged knight, thought to be that of a member of the Blanchminster family. Originally from Shropshire, their manor house was at Bien Amee, now a moated site near Binhamy Farm.

Situated on a hill, the steeply sloping main street is lined with fine Georgian houses and cottages, many of which are still thatched today. During the Civil War, the town was a stronghold of the Royalists and their commander, Sir Bevil Grenville, made The Tree Inn (see separate advert) his centre of operations. In May 1643, at the Battle of Stamford Hill, Grenville led his troops to victory over the Parliamentarians, who had been holding an Iron Age earthwork just northwest of the town. The dead of both sides were buried in unmarked graves in Stratton churchyard. The Battle is re-enacted in mid-May each year.

The Tree Inn was also the birthplace of the Cornish Giant, Anthony Payne. Also known as the 'Falstaff of the West', he was seven feet four inches tall and weighed 38 stones. He was an excellent choice as Sir Bevil's bodyguard and they fought together at Stamford Hill and later at Lansdown Hill near Bath. At this second encounter with the Parliamentarians Grenville was killed and Payne helped the General's son lead the King's Army to victory before carrying his master's body back to Stratton. After the Civil War, Payne continued to live at the Grenville manor house until his death, and when he died the house had to be altered to allow his coffin in and out. The Tree Inn, whose beams are made from the timbers of wrecked ships, still remembers Stratton's most famous son and a life-size portrait hangs in the inn's courtyard.

Launcells
2½ miles E of Bude off the A3072

Set in a delightful wooded combe lies St Swithin's Parish Church, a 15th century building that is remarkable as it has managed to escape the ravages of enthusiastic Victorian restorers, prompting John Betjeman to declare it 'the least spoilt church in Cornwall'. The church is notable for its fine Tudor bench-ends and for over 1400 15th century Barnstaple floor tiles, with raised griffins, lions, pelicans and flowers. In the churchyard lies the grave of the remarkable Sir Goldsworthy Gurney (see also Bude). Up until 1321 the church was dedicated to St Andrew.

Marhamchurch
2 miles SE of Bude off the A39

This hilltop village was founded as a monastic settlement in the early 6th century, and the 14th century St Marwenne's Parish Church is dedicated to its founder. It was originally a Norman structure, but nothing remains of it. The church has a magnificent 15th century oak door and

BULLERS ARMS

Marhamchurch, Bude, Cornwall EX23 0HB
Tel: 01288 361277 Fax: 01288 361541
e-mail: aperry1224@aol.com
website: www.bullersarms.co.uk

Marhamchurch sits a short drive due east of the A39, and only two miles from the unspoilt beaches of the wonderful resort of Bude. The village is small and picturesque, noted mainly for the beautiful St Marwenne's Church. But it is also noted for something else as well - the **Bullers Arms**, one of the best inns in the whole of North Cornwall.

It became an inn in 1856, when it was called the King's Arms, But the building itself goes back ever further than that, as it used to be a typical Cornish "long house". This gives a delightful feeling of olde worlde charm to the place. After the Boer War its

name was changed to the Bullers Arms, after General Sir Redvers Buller, who relieved Ladysmith during the war and became a local hero, as he was born just over the border in Devon.

The inside of the inn is a delight - everything an inn should be! There are cosy corners, old stone and brick, dark wood, brass and framed prints adorning the walls, and plenty of those charming knickknacks that add so much colour and character to a place. It's no wonder that the place is popular both with locals and tourists, who return again and again to sample the delights of such a special, friendly place.

Good, honest food is available every day at lunchtime (12 noon - 2.30pm) and in the evenings from 6 pm until 9.30 pm, except for Christmas Day. The Sunday carvery is especially popular (with a vegetarian option always available), and even though there is a separate dining room that can seat up to 120 in absolute comfort, you are well advised to book just in case you can't get a table! Only the finest and freshest of produce is used to prepare the meals wherever possible, and as well as a tempting menu, there is also a daily specials board that is bound to contain something to please your palate.

The Bullers Arms has a well stocked bar, with a wide range of real ales, spirits and wines on offer. And if you're looking for a place to stay in the Bude area, then the Bullers Arms is the place for you! It has eleven fully en suite rooms on offer, all keenly priced, and all well furnished and decorated to a high standard. Full English breakfasts are served, though lighter options are available, and the B&B tariffs stay the same throughout the year.

All credit cards, with the exception of Diners and American Express, are accepted in this shining example of a Cornish inn - one that will draw you back again and again!

a 'sanctuary knocker' which allowed fugitives to seek 40 days protection in the church. The surviving stretch of waterway on the Bude Canal lies just below Marhamchurch; this was also the site of one of the canal's ramps which carried the barges on to the continuation of the canal at the top of the hill.

Week St Mary
6 miles SE of Bude off the B3254

This small village was the site of a Norman fortress, and has the 15th century **St Mary's Parish Church**. The 'week' part of the name comes from the old English 'wic', meaning a dairy farm. It was the birthplace of Thomasine Banaventure, who was born in humble circumstances, but who later, as **Dame Percyval**, founded a school in the village and rose to become Lady Mayoress of London. To the west lies **Penhallam**, the grass-covered ruins of a 12th to 14th century moated manor house which has been excavated, revealing low walls on a central 'island' and a flat-bottomed moat, which was 5.5 metres wide and over 1.5 metres deep.

Poundstock
4½ miles S of Bude off the A39

The unusual **Guildhouse**, found here in a wooded hollow, was constructed in the 14th century, probably to house the masons working on the building of **St Winwaloe's Parish Church**. It remains a fine example of a once common style of non-secular building. It was restored in the 19th century, and is the only one still in use in Cornwall. After the church had been built the guildhouse became a meeting place and the festivities held here were so great that they were suppressed by the Puritans. Over the years it has also acted as a poorhouse and a village school. The Atlantic coast is only a mile west of Poundstock and from the top of the 400-foot cliffs there are views across to Lundy in the north and Trevose Head in the south.

Penfound Manor is said to be the oldest inhabited house in England, with parts of it dating from Saxon times. It is said that William the Conquerer gave it to his half brother Robert. It is also said to be haunted by the ghost of Kate Penfound, who was killed by her own father (a Royalist) while trying to elope with John Trebarfoot, a Parliamentarian. Her father and John then fought, each dying from wounds they received.

Widemouth Bay
3 miles S of Bude off the A39

Ever since the 1930s, this little village has been a seaside resort catering to visitors attracted by the wide curving bay of flat sand. Its north and south beaches are both backed by low cliffs and grassy fields. There is a car park, as well as toilets, shops and surf hire, so it is a popular holiday beach.

WIDEMOUTH MANOR

Widemouth Bay, Bude, Cornwall EX23 0DE
Tel: 01288 361263 Fax: 01288 361615
e-mail: paul-whyle@btconnect.com

With eight fully en-suite rooms, **Widemouth Manor** is one of the best small hotels in the Bude area. It is situated a couple of miles south of the town and has a wonderful outlook over the bay. It is currently undergoing a complete refurbishment which will improve it even further. The hotel serves fine English cuisine in its spacious restaurant, though quick snacks are also available, and the bars serve a wide range of real ales, beers, wines and spirits. The atmosphere is relaxed and the staff are efficient and friendly, making this your ideal base for exploring Cornwall or having a relaxing seaside holiday!

KENNACOTT COURT

Widemouth Bay, Bude, Cornwall EX23 0ND
Tel: 01288 362000 Fax: 01288 361434
e-mail: phil@kennacottcourt.co.uk
website: www.kennacottcourt.co.uk

Kennacott Court is a unique collection of self catering cottages set in 70 acres of quite outstanding countryside near Bude. The view over the rolling fields to Widemouth Bay is truly stunning, and for this alone a stay here would be worth while.

Of course there is so much more to Kennacott Court's cottages. They have been converted from old stone barns to exacting standards, and many retain some original features. In recognition of this they have been given five stars by the English Tourism Council - the highest accolade available. All are comfortable, fully centrally heated, spacious and fully equipped to make your stay as enjoyable as possible, with a range of accommodation that can sleep from two up to ten people.

For the benefit of guests, there is a magnificent leisure building that has a large indoor heated swimming pool, sauna, solarium, fitness room, snooker room and an under-fives playroom with plenty of soft toys. Also there is a games barn that has a badminton and soft-tennis court, skittle alley, pool table and table tennis. As you would expect, being set within 70 acres, there is a wealth of outdoor activities to take part in, from walking to outdoor tennis, a 6 hole par-22 golf course, a putting green and plenty of healthy activities for children.

This makes it the ideal base from which to explore the Bude area, which is steeped in history. Kennacott Court has it all, and if you visit, you're sure to return again and again!

Tintagel

The romantic remains of **Tintagel Castle** (English Heritage - see panel on page 17), set on a wild and windswept headland that juts out into the Atlantic, are, perhaps, many people's main image of Cornwall. These ruins were a stronghold of the Earls of Cornwall, but the reason for most people clambering up the wooden stairway of some 300 steps to **The Island** is that the castle is the legendary birthplace of King Arthur. Along with Caerleon in Wales, South Cadbury in Somerset, Camelford in

Widemouth Bay

revealing even more remains, most of which predated Rosnant. Artefacts from as far away as Asia Minor were unearthed, showing that it was an important place of trade.

The castle remains on the mainland which the visitor sees today are those of a castle built by Earl Reginald of Cornwall, the earliest parts dating from the mid 12th century. Reginald was the brother of the Earl of Gloucester, who encouraged Geoffrey of Monmouth to write his *History of the English Kings*, a chronicle that mentions Tintagel as being Arthur's birthplace. So maybe Reginald saw Tintagel as the natural site for his new castle.

The town naturally owes much of its

Cornwall, Greenan in Ayrshire and Kelso in Roxburgh (and a few more besides!), Tintagel also lays claim to being the site of Camelot, the mythical headquarters of the Knights of the Round Table.

In the 5th and 6th centuries, the place was certainly occupied by a Celtic monastery. There are still some Dark Age remains, and when they were excavated, a medieval monastery was uncovered as well. This led some people to conjecture that, rather than being the headquarters of Arthur, Tintagel was the site of the mythical Rosnant monastery, mentioned in many Irish chronicles. However, Whithorn in Scotland seems a more likely location. In 1983 a fire swept The Island,

Tintagel Castle

YE OLDE MALTHOUSE

Props: B. J. Stephens, FBII &
Mrs C. M. Stephens
Fore Street, Tintagel, Cornwall PL34 0DA
Tel: 01840 770461 Fax: 01840 779234
e-mail: info@yeoldmalthouseinn.com
website: www.yeoldemalthouseinn.com

One look at **Ye Olde Malthouse** tells you that you've found one of the oldest and best inns in Cornwall! Set right in the historic village of Tintagel, with its many Arthurian legends, it is a mellow old white washed building that originally dates from the 14th century. Over the years it has retained much of its olde worlde charm and original features, while still keeping up with modern day standards of service, hospitality and great value for money.

The inn is open all day, every day, and caters especially for real ale enthusiasts. Up to four real ales are available during the holiday season, mainly local brews such as Sharpe's, Skinner's St Austell and others from smaller micro breweries. Having a name like Ye Olde Malthouse, you might suspect that the inn once brewed its own ale, and an old well over 40 feet deep in the grounds might be where the brewer drew his water!

Being so old, the inn abounds with antiquity. A tunnel was once discovered connecting the inn to the nearby vicarage, and it is still there, though boarded up and underneath the drive up to the car park. Maybe a vicar at one time enjoyed his ale a bit too much, and used the tunnel to get his supplies without the villagers suspecting?

The inn has seven guest rooms on offer - four fully en suite, one with private bathroom and two with shared facilities. Each one is cosy and extremely comfortable, and the very reasonable tariff includes a full Cornish breakfast, or a lighter option if required. They are available all year round, making this the ideal place for a winter's break in Cornwall, which usually avoids the worst of the winter weather! Special rates are available.

The non-smoking restaurant seats up to 30 in absolute comfort and you can also sit outside on warm days. The superb food is served from 10.30 am until 9 pm but you are well advised to book in the evenings, as word of the food's excellence has gotten around. Being so near the sea, seafood is a speciality, with the produce being brought in daily from nearby Port Isaac. So you know that what you are getting is local and as fresh as possible. There's also a good choice of vegetarian dishes, and great care is taken in the preparation of all the food served in the inn, with diabetic and special dietary needs catered for.

All credit and debit cards except American Express and Diners are taken.

popularity to its Arthurian connections and one of its most interesting attractions, **King Arthur's Great Halls** in Fore Street, continues to draw visitors. These vast halls tell the story of the King and the chivalrous deeds which he and his Knights of the Round Table performed. The Great halls claim to be the largest attraction in the world dedicated to Arthur, and were founded by a millionaire in the 1930s. Among the many sights are numerous carved slates and stones, one of only seven Pillow Swords, and 72 stained glass windows which bear the Knights' Coats of Arms and depict some of their adventures. And in the Arthurian Experience Merlin takes his audience on a journey through time, telling Arthur's story in laser lights, music and sound. The halls are open daily, all year round, and in the shop is a vast selection of Arthurian, Celtic and Anglo-Saxon books, postcards, jewellery, gifts and swords.

Also on the High Street, though this

TINTAGEL CASTLE

Tintagel, Cornwall
Tel: 01840 770328
website: www.english-heritage.org.uk

For over 800 years the tale has been told that **Tintagel Castle** was the birthplace of King Arthur, born to the beautiful Queen Igerna and protected from evil by the magician Merlin, who lived in a cave below the fortress. But the history of the site goes back even further. Fragments of a Celtic monastic house dating from the 6th century have been unearthed on the headland and their origins certainly coincide with the activities of the Welsh military leader on which the Arthurian legends are thought to be based. The castle was, in fact, built in the 12th century, some 600 years after the time of King Arthur, by Reginald, Earl of Cornwall, the illegitimate son of Henry I. Whatever the truth behind the stories, the magic of this site, with Atlantic breakers crashing against the cliffs, certainly matches that of the tales of chivalry and wizardry.

In 1998 the discovery of a 6th century slate bearing the Latin inscription 'Artognov' · which translates as the ancient British name for Arthur · renewed the belief that Tintagel was Arthur's home. The cave, found at the foot of The Island, is known as **Merlin's Cave** and is said still to be haunted by a ghost. Tintagel is also of great interest to nature-lovers: the cliffs are at the heart of a Site of Special Scientific Interest, providing breeding grounds for sea birds, lizards and butterflies. Tintagel Castle is one of over 400 historic sites in the care of English Heritage.

Old Post Office, Tintagel

15th century tower has long been used as a landmark by sailors. St Materiana is also known as St Madryn, a princess from Gwent, and the originally Norman building displays some Saxon fragments in its structure, and still retains its Norman font.

time not connected with King Arthur, is the weather-beaten **Old Post Office** (National Trust), housed in a small manor house dating from the 14th century and still retaining the stone-paved medieval hall complete with its ancient fireplace. At the time of the introduction of the penny post in 1840, Tintagel had no post office, and with the increase in the volume of letters the trek from Camelford became too much of a burden. A post office was set up in a rented room in the house, and in that role it served the village until 1894. It was then sold to an artist, Miss Catherine Jones, who with the help of other artists raised money to repair the building. In 1903, it was purchased for £100 by the National Trust. One of their very first acquisitions, it has remained in the Trust's care ever since. **St Materiana's Parish Church** is set some distance away from the centre of the village on an exposed cliff and its early

To the north of the village lies the mile-long **Rocky Valley**, a curious rock strewn cleft in the landscape which has a character all of its own. In the wooded upper reaches can be found the impressive 60-feet waterfall known as **St Nectan's Kieve** - named after the Celtic hermit whose cell is believed to have stood beside the basin, or kieve, at the foot of the cascade. The tranquil kieve has been a place of worship and reverence since pre-Christian times, and the waterfall is in a designated Site of Special Scientific Interest. Here too can be seen the **Rocky Valley Carvings**, on a rock face behind a ruined building. It has been suggested that the carvings date from early Christian times, around the same time that St Nectan was living here. However, it is impossible to be accurate and other suggestions range from the 2nd century BC to the 17th century.

Around Tintagel

Bossiney

½ mile N of Tintagel off the B3263

Bossiney was once one of Cornwall's many 'rotten boroughs', and among those sent to Parliament by the corruptible was no less a person than Sir Francis Drake, who addressed his "electorate" from **Bossiney Mound**, beneath which is supposed to lie Arthur's Round Table. If Arthur ever returns, a legend says that the table will rise from the mound to accommodate him and his knights once more. Cornwall was always a leading villain in the rotten borough stakes: at the beginning of the 19th century it had 21 boroughs and 44 MPs. Reached by a short signposted footpath from the village, **Bossiney Haven** is a beautiful, sheltered beach surrounded by a semi circle of cliffs. The views from the cliff top are spectacular but only the fit and agile should try to scramble down on to this small and secluded beach.

Boscastle

3 miles NE of Tintagel on the B3263

On 16th August 2004 a 12-feet high wave of mud and water swept down the valley of the River Valency and destroyed many historic and picturesque buildings in this delightful little port. No one will ever forget the horrific TV pictures of cars being swept along the main street and into the harbour. It is now doing its best to return to normal, though it will be a long time before all the damage is repaired - indeed some things may never be the same.

The straggling village grew up around, and takes its name from, the now demolished Bottreaux Castle that the de Botterell family built in Norman times. The picturesque inlet, between the cliffs, is the only natural harbour between Hartland Point and Padstow and is formed by the rivers Valency and Jordan. The harbour's inner jetty was built by the renowned Elizabethan seafarer, Sir

Boscastle Harbour

Lobster Pots at Boscastle

century, when Boscastle had grown to become a bustling commercial port handling coal, timber, slate and china clay. Because of the dangerous harbour entrance, ships were towed in by rowing boats and a blowhole in the outer harbour sometimes still sends up plumes of spray.

Next to the slipway where the River Valency meets the sea was Boscastle's **Museum of Witchcraft** (see panel below), which suffered a lot of damage during the floods. The owner,

Richard Grenville, in 1584, at a time when the village was prospering as a fishing, grain and slate port. The outer jetty, or breakwater, dates from the 19th

Museum of Witchcraft

The Harbour, Boscastle, Cornwall PL35 0HD
Tel: 01840 250111
e-mail: museumwitchcraft@aol.com
website: www.museumofwitchcraft.com

The **Museum of Witchcraft** in Boscastle houses the world's largest collection of witchcraft related artefacts and regalia. The museum has been located in Boscastle for over forty years and despite severe damage in recent floods, it remains one of Cornwall's most popular museums.

The fascinating displays cover all aspects of witchcraft and inlcude Divination, Sea Witchcraft, Spells and Charms, Modern Witchcraft, Herbs & Healing, Ritual Magic, Satanism and Hare & Shapeshifting

One exhibit features the burial of Joan Wytte who was born in Bodmin, Cornwall, in 1775 and died of bronchial pneumonia in Bodmin Jail in 1813. She was a renowned clairvoyant and healer but became aggressive and impatient due to an untreated abscess in her tooth and people came to believe she was possessed by the devil. She became

known as 'The Fighting Fairy Woman' and was imprisoned for Grievous Bodily Harm.

Her skeleton came into the possession of the Museum of Witchcraft and was exhibited there for many years. When Graham took over 8 years ago he and the museum team believed she deserved a proper burial and Joan was finally laid to rest in 1998.

Among the other artefacts to be seen here are an amazing collection of figures and dolls, carved plates and stones, jewellery, cauldrons, weapons and unpleasant devices used for extracting confessions! A stair lift is available for those with limited mobility.

Graham King, is determined to restore it to its former glory. It is claimed to be the largest museum of its kind in the world, and was originally opened in 1951 by a man called Cecil Williamson on the Isle of Man. He moved it first to Windsor and then to Boscastle in 1961. It is claimed that Williamson knew so much about witchcraft and the occult that his knowledge helped Britain's war efforts during World War II, as some of the leading Nazis were steeped in the occult as well.

Thomas Hardy was a regular visitor to Boscastle, which appears as Castle Boterel in his early novel *A Pair of Blue Eyes*. Much of the land around Boscastle, including Penally Point and Willapark cliffs, is owned by the National Trust and provides some excellent if sometimes quite demanding walking. The **South West Coast Path** at Boscastle has now reopened after suffering substantial damage during the flooding.

architect. and also where, in 1870, he met his future wife, Emma Gifford, the rector's sister-in-law. Emma later professed that the young architect had already appeared to her in a dream and wrote how she was 'immediately arrested by his familiar appearance'. Much of the couple's courtship took place along the wild stretch of coastline between Boscastle and Crackington Haven and, when Emma died, over 40 years later, Hardy returned to St Juliot to erect a memorial to her in the church. Following his death in 1928, a similar memorial was erected to Hardy himself.

Crackington Haven
7½ miles NE of Tintagel off the B3263

One of the most dramatic places along this remarkable stretch of coastline, the small cove at Crackington Haven is overlooked by towering 400-feet cliffs and jagged rocks. The small and narrow sandy cove is approached, by land, down

St Juliot
4 miles NE of Tintagel off the B3266

Tucked away in the wooded valley of the fast flowing River Valency, this hidden hamlet is home to **St Juliot Parish Church**, upon which Thomas Hardy worked when an

View over Crackington Haven

a steep-sided wooded combe which has a few houses, an inn and a village shop at the bottom, while, from the sea it is difficult to see how sizeable vessels once landed here to deliver their cargoes of limestone and Welsh coal. So dramatic is the scenery that some episodes of the TV series *Poldark* were filmed around here. Beyond **Penkenna Point** (430 feet) to the north is **St Genny's Parish Church**, with its sloping graveyard which gives wonderful views out towards Lundy.

Some of the most spectacular coastal scenery can be viewed by walking the cliff top path from Crackington Haven to Cambeak to the south, but, though impressive, the cliff rock is often loosely packed and care should be taken at all times when close to the cliff edge. Just to the south of Crackington Haven a difficult path (so take care) leads to **The Strangles**, a remote beach with a rather curious name. Although, at low tide, large patches of sand are revealed among the rocks, the undercurrents here are strong and swimming is always unsafe. During one year alone in the 1820s, some 20 ships were said to have come to grief in this cove. Above the Strangles is **High Cliff**, the highest point on the Cornwall coast. On the coast road a mile and a half south of Crackington Haven is the National Trust's **Trevigue** working livestock farm, where the wildlife includes badgers, deer, foxes, rabbits, birds of prey, bats and glow worms.

Camelford

4 miles SE of Tintagel on the A39

Situated on the banks of the River Camel, this small and historic old market town lies on the northern fringes of Bodmin Moor, and is one of the many places that lays claim to being the site of Arthur's Camelot. It built its prosperity on the wool trade, and the central small square is lined with 18th and 19th century houses; the early-19th century town hall has a camel for a weathervane. The town name has nothing to do with camels. It comes from the word "cam", meaning crooked, "alan" meaning beautiful and "ford". The name of the river, the Cam, comes from the Celtic for "cooked stream". A bridge has spanned the river since 1511, and at one time had a chapel attached to it. **North Cornwall Museum and Gallery**, housed in a building that was originally used for making coaches and wagons, shows aspects of life in this area from the 19th century and includes the reconstruction of a moorland cottage. A full range of tools used by blacksmiths, cobblers and

printers is also on display as well as a large number of items varying from lace bonnets to early vacuum cleaners, and a collection of Cornish and Devonshire pottery. This fascinating place is open from April to September daily except Sundays. A mile north of Camelford on the B3266 Boscastle road is another interesting museum. This is the **British Cycling Museum**, whose exhibits include over 400 cycles, an old cycle repair shop, a gallery of framed cycling pictures, an extensive library and a history of cycling from 1818. The museum is open Sunday to Thursday all year. Nearby is the **Gaia Energy Centre**, which promotes renewable energy and conservation through exhibits and educational programmes. It sits on the site of Britain's first commercial wind farm.

St Thomas's Church in the town dates from 1938, but the much older **St Julitta's Parish Church**, outside the town, has Norman origins. Julitta is thought to be a Turkish saint who was martyred after her son was killed by Alexander, the governor of Seleucia. Close by, on the riverbank at

Trewarmett Inn

Trewarmett, Near Tintagel,
Cornwall PL34 0ET
Tel: 01840 770460 Fax: 01840 779011

Driving along the B3263 a mile or so east of Tintagel, no one can miss one of the best hostelries in the county · the **Trewarmett Inn**. A lively mural on one of its end walls depicts a sailing ship, a pirate and the Greek god of the sea, old Poseiden himself, and it advertises the inn long before you pass it by! The inn itself is over 300 years old, and has been offering hospitality of some kind for all that time. It now offers a warm, friendly welcome to travellers and locals alike, having many original features that add to the overall ambience of the place. There are flag-stoned floors, low-beamed ceilings, knick knacks and plenty of olde worlde framed prints on the walls.

The inn is an ale-lovers' paradise, having

three to five real ales available, depending on the season. Plus, of course, a full range of ciders, lagers, wines (two of them local wines from Cornwall), spirits, and should you be driving, soft drinks. The service is great, and the prices always keenly set.

Food is another of the inn's specialities, served between 12 noon · 2.30 pm and 6 pm · 9 pm (ish). In fact, so good is it that during the summer months you are well advised to book well in advance. Everything is home-cooked on the premises, using only the finest and freshest of local produce (except perhaps for one of the inn's speciality dishes · delicious ostrich fillet with liver and bacon!) The restaurant is non-smoking for the

comfort of the customers, and the inn accepts all credit and debit cards except Diners.

The accommodation comprises five rooms, all spacious and comfortable, and all fully en suite. The décor and furnishings are of the highest standard to make your stay a thoroughly enjoyable one. The Trewamett Inn is close to many of Cornwalls' attractions, such as Tintagel and Bodmin Moor, so you can make the place your base! Car parking is easily available as well.

From 9pm onwards, Wednesday and Saturday nights are folk nights and the good music, the friendly crowd and the excellent drink should set your toes tapping as you listen to the traditional music, much of it from Cornwall itself. If you're a bit of a singer, or can play an instrument, you are welcome to join in and add to the fun! The music sessions have been described as being among the best in the county.

So why not make Trewarmett Inn your base when visiting this lovely part of Cornwall? You're assured of a very warm welcome and an enjoyable stay.

KITTIWAKE COTTAGE

Gull Rock, Treknow, Tintagel,
Cornwall PL34 0EP
Tel: 01840 770438
e-mail: jan@gullrock.eclipse.co.uk
website: www.kittiwake-cottage.co.uk

Sitting high on a cliff overlooking the sea and Trebarwith Strand, **Kittiwake Cottage** has an outstanding location. Dating from the early 20th century, this picturesque cottage was once a coach house, but in 1989 was converted to a superior self-catering cottage that has everything the discerning tourist needs for a fabulous holiday in the heart of

the North Cornwall Heritage Coast. It stands in six acres of unbeatable countryside, and sleeps up to four in absolute comfort.

The ground floor has been divided into two, the old stable now being a well-appointed kitchen/diner and the coach house itself being a spacious lounge with splendid views. It comes fully equipped with a colour TV and a wood burner for a cosy atmosphere in the evenings. You can also sit out on the patio with a quiet drink, taking in the magnificent sunsets. There is also a bathroom with WC on the ground floor.

Upstairs, the hayloft is now two low-ceilinged bedrooms, one with twin beds and one with a double. Imagine sitting at the dormer window in the early morning taking in the view! On the landing is another toilet and wash hand basin.

Many original features have been retained in some rooms, such as beaming and stone walls. Windows and doors are double-glazed, and heating is electric by coin in the slot meter. Duvets and bed linen are provided.

Kittiwake Cottage is the perfect place for a self-catering holiday in Cornwall. There is so much to see and do within a short drive, and the sandy beaches are excellent for surfing. Golf, fishing and sailing are also available locally.

Slaughterbridge, lies a 6th century inscribed stone slab which is said to mark the place where King Arthur fell at the Battle of Camlann in AD 539 with Mordred, ending the fellowship of the Round Table. The **Arthurian Centre** houses the Land of Arthur exhibition and also contains an information room (including brass rubbing and a video presentation), a play area, a refreshment area and a shop stocked with Arthurian books and gifts.

Trewarmett
1½ miles SE of Tintagel on the B3263

This moorland village, like so many

places in this area, has associations with the legend of King Arthur - here an ancient rectangular enclosure surrounded by stone slabs is said to be one of the places where King Arthur held court. More recently, in the 19th century, the Prince of Wales slate quarry employed many men around the Trewarmett area. The quarry is now flooded, but the **Beam Engine House** can still be seen. Another quarry, **Jeffrey's Pit**, has a picnic area beside it.

Trebarwith
1½ miles S of Tintagel off the B3263

A good surfing beach, **Trebarwith**

BEAVER COTTAGES

Tregatta, Tintagel, Cornwall PL34 0DY
Tel/Fax: 01840 770265
e-mail: beaver.cottages@virgin.net

On the Camelford to Tintagel road, the B3263, right in the heart of King Arthur country, you will find **Beaver Cottages**, two magnificent stone-built self-catering cottages that offer the very best in holiday accommodation all year round. The nearest beach is Trebarwith Strand, and if you take the coastal path leading from the stile in the car park, you'll be in King Arthur's Castle in a few minutes.

There are two cottages, both graded three star · the Main Cottage and The Old Smithy.

They have been pro-fessionally converted from an old Cornish farmhouse but have all the modern conveniences you could ask for, including central heating and double glazing for the winter months. The owners stay on the premises, so you are assured of all the help and assistance you need.

Main Cottage sleeps six with one double bedroom and a room with a king-sized or twin beds, each with a shower, toilet and wash basin, and a room with two 30 inch wide bunks. The rooms are comfortable and spacious, with well maintained furnishings and décor. Downstairs there is a dining room, spacious lounge, shower room and a kitchen that comes fully equipped with electric cooker, fridge and microwave. There is a garden at the front for the exclusive use of guests, and parking at the rear.

The Smithy is smaller, sleeping up to four in absolute comfort. It is adjacent to the owners' cottage and has its own entrance and private garden at the back. Upstairs there is one double bedroom and a bathroom with a shower. Downstairs there is a lounge and dining area separated by an elegant archway, and a fitted galley kitchen with electric stove, fridge and microwave. Within the dining area is a sofa bed that sleeps two. There is ample parking at the side of the cottage.

Central heating for both cottages is included in the tariff, and electricity is by a £1 coin meter. Both cottages have a colour TV, bed linen is provided, and the double beds have king size duvets, while single beds have single duvets.

Booking is from Sunday to Sunday in both these excellent properties, with arrival time after 2.30 pm and departure time by 10 am to allow the owners to prepare the cottages for the new guests. Three day minimum short breaks are available out of season, with Christmas and New Year bookings also being taken.

Rocky Coastline near Trebarwith

Strand, some two miles west of this hamlet, is the only easily accessible beach between Polzeath and Crackington Haven. Backed by crumbling cliffs that were once quarried for slate, this sandy stretch of coastline is strewn with rocks and, though popular during the summer, swimmers must be wary of being swept off the rocks - or hit by falling rocks. It's also a popular surfing spot, and has been used as a backdrop by film makers.

Delabole
3 miles S of Tintagel on the B3314

Home to the most famous slate quarry in Cornwall, this village is the third highest in Cornwall, and is, almost literally, built of slate: it has been used for houses, walls, steps and the church. At one time, most of the buildings in the county incorporated roofing slates or flagstones from Delabole and over 500 people were employed blasting and slicing the stone into attractively named standard sizes, such as Ladies, Countesses, Duchesses, Queens and Imperials. The high quality dark blue slate has been quarried here without interruption since Tudor times, making it the oldest continuously worked slate quarry in Europe. It is known that in around 2000 BC the Beaker folk on Bodmin Moor used slate as baking shelves. The huge crater of **Delabole Slate Quarry** is over half a mile wide and 500 feet deep and is the largest man-made hole in the country. Although the demand for traditional building materials declined throughout the 20th century, the quarry is still worked and visitors can join in walkabout tours seeing the sawing of large slate blocks, the hand-splitting of roofing slates and - most impressive of all - watch 600-tonne slate blocks being sawed by diamond wire. A range of old slate quarrying tools is on display in the Visitor Centre, and you can even buy specially made slate signs.

Once known as 'the great slate road', the lanes to the west of Delabole used to carry vast quantities of stone to the harbours at Port Gaverne, Port Isaac, Port Quin and Boscastle until the railways took over the transport of the stone in the 1890s.

Launceston

On the eastern edge of Bodmin Moor and close to the county border with Devon, Launceston is one of Cornwall's most pleasant inland towns and was a particular favourite of Sir John Betjeman, who called it 'the most interesting inland town in Cornwall'. An important regional capital - the capital of Cornwall until 1838 which also guarded the main overland route into the county, it dates originally from Celtic times. It was here, shortly after the Norman Conquest, that William I's half-brother, Robert of Mortain, Earl of Cornwall, built a massive castle overlooking the River Kensey. A place from which Robert tried to govern the fiercely independent Cornish people, **Launceston Castle** was subsequently the base of the Earls of Cornwall. Launceston was the only walled town in the county, and once had a royal mint.

Visited by the Black Prince and seized by the Cornish rebels of 1549, the castle changed hands twice during the Civil

Launceston Castle

War before becoming an assize court and prison that was famous for imprisoning and executing 'on the nod'. It was here, in 1656, that George Fox, the founder of the Society of Friends, was held for several months. Today, the castle is in ruins but the 12-foot thick outer walls of the round keep and the tower can still be seen. The outer bailey is now a public park. During World War II the castle was used as a military hospital.

As well as growing up around the castle, Launceston was also the home of a powerful Augustinian Priory that was founded in 1136 on the northern banks of the river. Though most of the buildings have gone, the priory's chapel of ease, now **St Thomas' Church**, remains. Although this is a small building, it boasts, among other Norman features, the largest font in Cornwall. It stands beside the river Kensey, over which pedestrians can still walk by way of the **Clapper Bridge**. The 16th century **St Mary Magdalene's Parish Church** is almost all the work of a local squire Sir Henry Trecarrel and is noted chiefly for its ornately carved granite façades, the finest of their kind in England. Portraits of Sir Henry and his wife can be seen on the south side of the porch, while under the east window is a recumbent figure of Mary Magdalene; it is said that good luck will come to anyone who can throw a stone or coin on to her back and make it stay there.

The town's medieval **South Gate** is another reminder of the importance placed on the town as a stronghold as this castellated building has served as both a guardhouse and a gaol. Now it houses a fine at gallery. The West and North Gates were demolished in the 19th century, and there never was an East Gate, as the steep land to the east precluded an attack from that direction. During the Napoleonic Wars, Launceston was a parole town holding French prisoners of war. These were mainly French naval officers, and their professional skills came to be much appreciated by the local community. Elsewhere in Launceston, the streets around the castle are filled with handsome buildings dating from Georgian times and earlier and these include the impressive Lawrence House (National Trust) in Castle Street. Built in 1753 and containing some superb plasterwork ceilings, this is home to the **Lawrence House Museum** which dedicates its numerous displays to the history of the area, including the French connection (that connection remains strong, and there are close links between Launceston and its twin town Plestin-lès-greves in Brittany).

To the west of the town, and running through the beautiful Kensey Valley, the **Launceston Steam Railway** takes visitors on a journey back in time. Travelling in either open or closed carriages, passengers can enjoy a round trip along five miles of narrow-gauge track to Newmills and back. The locomotives used to haul the trains were built in the 1880s and 1890s by the

THE TAMAR OTTER SANCTUARY

North Petherwin, Nr Launceston,
Cornwall PL15 8LW
Tel: 01566 785646

A branch of the famous Otter Trust, the **Tamar Otter Sanctuary** is dedicated to breeding otters for release into the wild to save the species from extinction in lowland England. Visitors can watch the otters at play and in their breeding dens (holts), and see orphaned cubs in the rehabilitation centre.

Also here are a dormouse conservation project, a visitor centre, refreshment and gift shop, lakes with waterfowl and an area of woodland where fallow and Muntjac deer roam freely. Pheasants, peacocks and wallabies can also be seen at the sanctuary.

workshops open to the public, a transport museum and a gift shop. Close to the station at Newmills is a riverside farm park with indoor and outdoor games for children.

At Polson is the **Antique Chairs Museum**, where you can not only see a display of chairs from all ages, but see them being restored as well. And to the west of the town, on a minor road but well signposted, is the **Hidden Valley Adventure Park**, a great place for a day out with the children. South of the town, at Kennards House near Trethorne, is the **Trethorne Leisure Farm**, another attraction for children.

Around Launceston

Laneast
5 miles W of Launceston off the A395

The birthplace of John Couch Adams, the astronomer who discovered the planet Neptune, Laneast is also home to one of the many holy wells found in this part of the county. The well is now housed in a 16th century building, close to which stand a tall Celtic cross and **St Sidwell and St Gulvat Parish Church**, which is mainly Norman.

St Clether
6 miles W of Launceston off the A395

An elaborate holy well can be found a few hundred yards northwest of this tranquil village, standing on its own on

famous Hunslet Engine Company of Leeds, and worked on the slate carrying lines high in the mountains of North Wales. In addition to a station buffet (cream teas a speciality), the railway also has a model railway display,

a bracken-covered shelf in the valley of the River Inney. With its adjacent 15th century chapel, this well is the most enchanting of its kind in the county. The village itself has **St Clederus Parish Church**, which is part Norman, but heavily restored by the Victorians; however, a number of earlier features have survived, including the Norman stone pillars and font and the 15th century tower.

North Petherwin

5 miles NW of Launceston off the B3254

Situated above the River Ottery, this village is home to the **Tamar Otter Sanctuary** (see panel opposite), which is a branch of the famous Otter Trust. The sanctuary is open for visits from 1 April (or Good Friday if earlier) to the end of October.

Warbstow

8 miles NW of Launceston off the A39

This village of old slate cottages is overlooked by **Warbstow Bury Hillfort**, one of the largest Iron Age earthworks in Cornwall. There are wonderful views over northern Bodmin Moor from the fort.

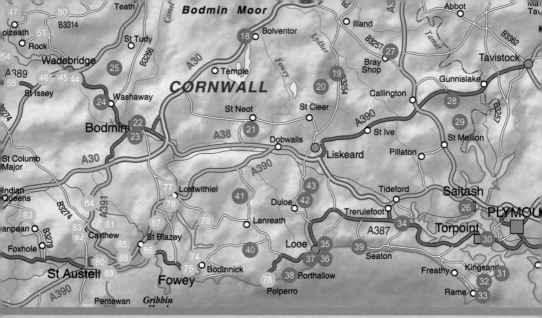

PLACES TO STAY, EAT AND DRINK

● Denotes entries in other chapters

2 Southeast Cornwall

In AD 928 Athelstan used the River Tamar to establish the boundary of his Celtic kingdom and, today, the river still separates Cornwall from its neighbour Devon. To the north the landscape is dominated by a rugged and rocky coastline and bleak Bodmin Moor, a mysterious place and the inspiration for Daphne du Maurier's famous and most popular novel *Jamaica Inn*. Here can be found a wealth of Iron Age and Bronze Age monuments and interesting natural formations that are typified by the curious Cheesewring. Legends abound in such lonely places and the isolated Dozmary Pool is very much linked to the legend of King Arthur; it was here, so many believe, that the great king's sword Excalibur was received by the Lady of the Lake. The south coast has numerous coves and inlets as well as tranquil wooded valleys. Both Saltash, on the south coast, and inland Gunnislake have been gateways into Cornwall for centuries and while

Saltash now has two magnificent bridges - one road, one rail - to carry passengers into the county, Gunnislake is still relying on the 16th century bridge constructed by the influential Earls of Edgcumbe.

Along the coast, numerous picturesque ancient fishing villages can be found that not only prospered from pilchard fishing but also from shipping, first, the minerals mined further north on Bodmin Moor and, later, the china clay industry. However, these many sheltered and often lonely beaches also gave rise to a darker and more sinister trade and many villages were alive with smuggling activity. The romance of this coastline

Bodmin Moor

and its colourful past has lead to many writers settling in the area including Daphne du Maurier, who for a time lived just outside Fowey in a house she immortalised in her novel *Rebecca*.

Of the places to see here, apart from the quaint villages and wonderful coastlines and river valleys, there are two superb country houses, Cotehele and Mount Edgcumbe, both of them owned by the Earls of Edgcumbe. The older, Cotehele, lies in the Tamar Valley and is one of the best preserved late medieval estates in the country, while 16th century Mount Edgcumbe House has been restored to its original glory after being all but destroyed in 1941 during a German bombing raid on Plymouth. Both too have beautiful gardens, full of exotic plants, that benefit from the mild climate that Cornwall enjoys courtesy of the Gulf Stream.

Bodmin Moor

An Area of Outstanding Natural Beauty, the bleak expanse of Bodmin Moor, which lies between 800 and 1400 feet above sea level and covers around 100 square miles, is the smallest of the three great West Country moors. The granite upland is characterised by saturated moorland and weather-beaten tors and from here the rivers Inny, Lynher, Fowey, St Neot and De Lank flow to both the north and south coasts of Cornwall.

At 1377 feet, **Brown Willy** is the highest point of the moor and of Cornwall while, just to the northwest,

lies **Roughtor** (pronounced 'row tor' to rhyme with 'now tor'), the moor's second highest point. Standing on National Trust-owned land, Roughtor is a magnificent viewpoint and also the site of a memorial to the men of the 43rd Wessex Regiment who were killed during World War II. Throughout this wild and beautiful moorland there are the remains left behind by earlier occupiers: there are scattered Bronze Age hut circles and field enclosures, such as **Fernacre Stone Circle**, and Iron Age hill forts. Many villages grew up around the monastic cells of Celtic missionaries and took the name of a saint while others were mining villages where ruined engine houses still stand out against the skyline. In medieval times a chapel dedicated to St Michael was built on the summit of Roughtor, and well into the 19th century the chapel was the setting for enormous Temperance gatherings.

No mention of Bodmin Moor would be complete without mentioning the **Beast of Bodmin Moor**. Lots of people have claimed to have seen this huge, mysterious animal - thought to be a huge cat of some kind - and hazy film of it also exists. Many people, however, including some eminent zoologists. dismissed the beast as a myth. Then a 14-year old boy discovered a mysterious skull in the River Fowey. It had large fangs, and was sent to the Natural History Museum in London for identification. Curiously, it was identified by experts as the skull of a leopard.

Bolventor

In the centre of Bodmin Moor off the A30

Situated at the heart of the moor, this scenic village is the location of the former coaching inn immortalised in Daphne du Maurier's novel, *Jamaica Inn*. Daphne du Maurier made her first journey to Cornwall in 1926, when she travelled to Fowey with her mother and sisters. Crossing Bodmin Moor, she fell in love with the windswept yet romantic landscape and it became the inspiration for many of her novels. **Jamaica Inn** (see panel below) dates from 1750, and is little changed since then. It still welcomes visitors who not only come

here seeking refreshment and comfortable accommodation during a long journey but also to discover the secrets of the moors.

Just to the south of Bolventor lies the mysterious natural tarn, **Dozmary Pool**, another place that is strongly linked with the legend of King Arthur. According to one tale, King Arthur was brought here following his final battle at Slaughterbridge, near Camelford. As he lay dying at the water's edge, he implored his friend, Sir Bedivere, to throw his sword, Excalibur, into the centre of the lake, where it was received by a lady's hand rising up from the water. However, there are several other lakes around the country, notably Looe Pool

JAMAICA INN AND MUSEUMS

Bolventor, Launceston, Cornwall PL15 7TS
Tel: 01566 86250 Fax: 01566 86177
e-mail: enquiry@jamaicainn.co.uk
website: www.jamaicainn.co.uk

Built in the mid 18th century to serve travellers making the journey on the new turnpike road between Launceston and Bodmin, **Jamaica Inn** has become one of the best known hostelries in the country if not the world thanks to novelist Daphne du Maurier. Whilst staying here in the 1920s, she was taken with the romance of the surrounding bleak moorland and fascinated by tales of smugglers and villains who met here.

Today, the inn still serves travellers who can enjoy a drink in the Smugglers bar, dinner in the du Maurier Restaurant or relax by a roaring log fire before retiring to one of the inn's comfortable guest rooms. However, there is much more here than an atmospheric, 300 year old inn. Tales of smugglers and the arch villain, Demon Davey, vicar of Altarnun, are told through a theatrical

presentation at the Smugglers at Jamaica Inn exhibition whilst more can be learnt of Daphne herself in the Daphne du Maurier Room. Many of her novels are based in Cornwall where she came to live with her husband in the 1930s and the room here is filled with memorabilia including her Sheraton writing desk.

Finally, there is Mr Potter's Museum of Curiosity, a fascinating collection of tableaux created by the Victorian taxidermist, Walter Potter. Visitors can see Steptoe and Son's bear and Walter's first tableau, the Death and Burial of Cock Robin, along with smoking memorabilia, Victorian toys and dolls' houses and some curious oddities.

at Mount's Bay and both Bosherstone and Llyn Llydaw in Wales, which also lay claim to being home to the Lady of the Lake and the resting place of Excalibur.

This desolate and lonely place is also linked with **Jan Tregeagle**, a wicked lawyer and steward of Lanhydrock who sold his soul to the devil. His many evil deeds include the murder of the parents of a young child whose estate he wanted. As a punishment, so the story goes, Tregeagle was condemned to spend the rest of time emptying the lake using only a leaking limpet shell. His howls of despair are said to be heard there to this day. This pool is according to legend bottomless, but it did dry up completely during the prolonged drought of 1869. It lies close to **Colliford Lake Park**, centred on Colliford Lake, the county's largest man-made reservoir. At 1,000 feet above sea level, this area is the perfect habitat for long tailed ducks, dippers, grey wagtails and sand martins and on the banks of the lake some rare varieties of orchid can be found. The lake also offers excellent watersports facilities.

Trewint

3 miles N of Bolventor off the A30

This handsome village often played host to John Wesley, the founder of Methodism, while he was on his preaching tours of Cornwall. One day in 1743 two of Wesley's men, John Nelson and John Downs, came to Trewint and called at the house of a stonemason

called Digory Isbell. Digory was at work at the time, so his wife Elizabeth gave the two men refreshment. They then insisted on paying, and fell on their knees to pray without using a prayer book. Digory was told this story on his return, and was so impressed that a year later Wesley himself was entertained in the house. Shortly after this, Digory was inspired by a passage in the Bible to build an extension to his house for the use of Wesley and his preachers. **Wesley Cottage** fell into disrepair down the years until being restored and opened to the public in 1950. The rooms, thought to be the smallest Methodist preaching places in the world, have been maintained in the 18th century style and visitors can see the specially constructed prophets' room and pilgrims' garden. Digory Isbell and his wife are buried in Trewint churchyard. The cottage is open every day from dawn to dusk, apart from Christmas day.

Altarnum

4 miles NE of Bolventor off the A30

Situated in a steep-sided valley of Penpont Water, this charming moorland village is home to a splendid, chiefly 15th century, parish church that is often referred to as the **Cathedral of the Moors**. Dedicated, as is the holy well nearby, to St Nonna, the mother of St David of Wales, the church has a 108 feet pinnacled tower that rises high above the peat-stained river while, inside the unusually light and airy interior, there are various features from Norman times through to the fine 16th century bench end carvings. In the churchyard stands the only relic of St Nonna's time, a Celtic cross which is thought to date from the same time as her journey here from Wales in around AD 527. Also here are fine examples of the work of the Altarnun-born sculptor Nevill Northey Bunard.

Altarnum Church

The waters of St Nonna's well were once thought to cure madness; after being immersed in the waters, lunatics were carried into the church for prayers, and the whole process was repeated until the patient showed signs of recovery from the fury.

The **Old Rectory** of 1842 (not open to the public) lies close to the church, and is featured in *Jamaica Inn*.

Upton Cross

7 miles SE of Bolventor on the B3254

A handsome village that is home to **Sterts Art Centre**, which has one of the few open-air amphitheatres in the country, Upton Cross is also the place to come to for traditional **Cornish Yarg Cheese**. Made at Netherton since 1983 in the beautiful Lynher Valley, this famous cheese, which comes wrapped in nettle leaves, not only has a distinctive taste and appearance, but is a local delicacy that has spread to many of the best restaurants and delicatessen counters in the country. Visitors can watch the cheesemaking process, the milking of the dairy herd, follow the pond and woodland trails, and enjoy

---

CARADON INN

Upton Cross, Nr Liskeard, Cornwall PL14 5AZ
Tel: 01579 362391
e-mail: info@caradoninn.com

If you're looking for a picturesque pub with B&B accommodation and superb food in the Liskeard area, then head for the **Caradon Inn** at Upton Cross! It is popular with visitors and locals alike, and if you want to eat in its superb restaurant, which serves the best of Italian, South African and Cornish food, then you're advised to book. The interior is typically Cornish, with slate floors, old prints on the walls and many traditional features. It has three comfortable rooms for discerning tourists which are very popular with people who appreciate tradition and high standards of service.

cheese tastings, light lunches and cream teas in the barn shop and tea room.

Minions

6 miles SE of Bolventor off the B3254

Boasting the highest pub in the county, this moorland village was, particularly during Victorian and Edwardian times, a thriving mining centre with miners and quarrymen extracting granite, copper and lead. This was also the setting for EV Thompson's historical novel, *Chase the Wind*. Today, a former mine engine house of the Phoenix Mine has become the **Minions Heritage Centre** which covers over 4,000 years of life on the moorland and includes the story of mining as well as the life and times of much earlier inhabitants of this area.

Close to the village stands the impressive **Hurlers Stone Circle**, a Bronze Age temple comprising three circles - the largest being some 135 feet in diameter. The name comes from the ancient game of hurling (a Celtic form of hockey) and legend has it that the circles were men who were turned to stone for playing the game on a Sunday.

Also close to the village lies the **Cheesewring**, a pile of granite slabs caused by natural erosion and glaciation whose appearance is reminiscent of a cheese press. Again numerous legends are attached to this curious monument although the tale of Daniel Gumb, a local stone cutter who was a great reader as well as teaching himself mathematics and astronomy, is undoubtedly true. He married a local girl and they made their home in a cave under the Cheesewring; before the cave collapsed, many of Gumb's intricate carvings could be seen in the granite, including the inscription 'D Gumb 1735'. A local legend tells that the Cheesewring was the haunt of a druid who possessed a golden chalice which never ran dry and provided thirsty passers-by with an endless supply of water. For some, the discovery in 1837 at the nearby **Rillaton Barrow** of a ribbed cup of beaten gold lying beside a skeleton adds credence to the story.

Hurlers Halt

Minions, Liskeard, Cornwall PL14 5LE
Tel/Fax: 01579 363056
e-mail: Symons@hurlershalt,fsnet.co.uk
website: www.hurlers-halt.co.uk

Hurlers Halt, named after the ancient stone circles at Minions on Bodmin Moor, the highest village in Cornwall, has two superb self-catering units on offer to discerning tourists. The Cottage is extremely comfortable, with a single and two interconnecting bedrooms a double and a twin. The Wink, is a tastefully converted barn with a double bedroom and access by loft ladder to a children's twin bedded sleeping area. The units are cosy and furnished to a high standard, with many modern facilities to make a stay here relaxing and enjoyable. Both units are fully centrally heated and are **strictly non-smoking**. The location makes it ideal for exploring Cornwall.

Dubbed the Rillaton Cup, it can be seen on display at the British Museum in London, with a copy in the Royal Cornwall Museum in Truro. The barrow itself dates from about 1500 BC.

St Cleer

6½ miles SE of Bolventor off the B3254

A sizeable moorland village in the heart of bleak former mining country, St Cleer is arranged around its 15th century parish church, and is named after its founder, St Cleer, or Clara, who came to this part of Cornwall in the 8th or 9th centuries. A legend tells of his devotion to celibacy, and how a local woman of high rank wanted to marry him. So he fled to France, where she had him murdered. Just to the northeast of the churchyard lies another 15th century structure: a fine stone building that covers a holy well. One of the many preserved wells to be found in Cornwall, **St Cleer's Holy Well** was thought to have curative powers particularly for those suffering from insanity and, here, the patients were tossed up and down in the waters until they became sane.

Dating from Neolithic times and found a mile east of the village, **Trethevy Quoit**, also known as The Giant's House, is an impressive enclosed chamber tomb which originally formed the core of a vast earthwork mound. The largest such structure (known as a dolmen) in the county, Trethevy Quoit is believed to be over 5,000 years old and, although the rectangular hole cut into the stone blocking the tomb's entrance was thought to allow bodies to be placed inside, the reason for the hole in the capstone is not known with any certainty.

Also close by is **King Doniert's Stone**, a tall stone cross which was erected in memory of King Durngarth, a Cornish king thought to have drowned in the nearby River Fowey in AD 875. The Latin inscription on the cross, which is now sadly in two pieces, reads, after translation, 'Erected for Doniert for the good of his soul'.

Downstream from King Doniert's Stone, the River Fowey descends for half a mile through dense broadleaved woodland in a delightful series of cascades known as **Golitha Falls**. This outstanding beauty spot is also a National Nature Reserve, and the grey wagtail and the great spotted woodpecker are among the rare birds to be seen.

St Neot

6 miles S of Bolventor on a minor road

This tranquil village on the southern edge of Bodmin Moor once thrived on the woollen industry but, today, it is famous for its splendid 15th century **St Anietus's Parish Church.** St Neot is not only the home of a fine 9th century granite cross but it still retains its fabulous early 16th century stained glass windows. In one, God is depicted measuring out the universe during the Creation while, in another, Noah can be seen with his Ark, which takes the shape of a sailing ship of the period. Perhaps the most interesting window of all is that of St Neot, the diminutive saint after whom the village is named. St Neot became famous for his miracles involving animals and one story tells of an exhausted hunted doe who ran to the side of the saint. A stern look from the saint sent the pursuing hounds back into the forest, while the huntsman dropped his bow and became a faithful disciple.

Another tale, and one that can be seen in the church window, tells of an angel giving Neot three fish for his well - saying that, as long as he only eats one fish a day there will always be fish in the well. Unfortunately, when Neot fell ill his servant took two fish from the well, cooked them and gave them to Neot who, horrified, prayed over the meal and ordered the fish to return to the well. As the dead fish touched the water they came alive again. There is some doubt as

CARNGLAZE CAVERNS & THE RUM STORE

St Neot, Liskeard, Cornwall PL14 6HQ
Tel: 01579 320251 Fax: 01579 321571
e-mail: information@carnglaze.com
website: www.carnglaze.com

Carnglaze consists of three underground caverns set in six and a half acres of wooded hillside of the Loveny valley just outside of St Neot, Nr Liskeard. You will be taken on a guided tour which lasts for around 45 minutes through the 3 unique underground caverns of cathedral proportions all amazingly created by local slate miners!

During the tour which goes over 100 meters into the hillside and around 15 meters below ground you will see the famous subterranean lake with it's crystal clear blue/

green water. This combined with the total silence of the surrounding atmosphere and subtle lighting makes it an unforgettable experience.

Set amongst the wooded hillside at Carnglaze is the Enchanted Dell. Within the Dell is a delightful collection of limited edition faeries, fountains, mushrooms and a dragon, reached via a landscaped and illuminated garden incorporating water features.

Also to be found here is The Rum Store, one of the caverns which aquired its name during the second World War, when it was used as a rum store by the Royal Navy. Now it is a 400 seat concert auditorium which has played host to a variety of performances, including choirs and orchestras. The slate walls and roof provide a stunning backdrop and as you would expect, outstanding accoustics!

to whether the St Neot of this village is the same St Noet of the town of St Neots in Cambridge. If he is, then he was a relative and close friend of King Alfred, who certainly visited Cornwall in hunting trips.

Outside the church, and tied to the tower, is an oak branch that is replaced each year on Oak Apple Day. The ceremony was started by the Royalists wishing to give thanks for the oak tree where Charles II hid while fleeing the country.

Just south of the village are the three **Carnglaze Slate Caverns** (see panel opposite), set in six and a half acres of woodland, where visitors can see a subterranean lake. Slate for use in the building trade was first quarried here in these vast man-made caverns in the 14th century. Opencast and underground mining were carried on until the end of the 19th century, and the caverns were opened as a tourist attraction in 1973. The largest chamber is over 300 feet high and was once used as a rum store, first by smugglers and in World War II by the Royal Navy. The lichen on the cavern walls is covered with minute droplets of water which reflect the available light in the most magical way. The slate-roofed, slate-walled cavern is a unique venue for concerts. Visitors can see the remains of the tramway which was built to haul the stone to the surface from the lower levels and, at the deepest level, there is a subterranean pool which is filled with the clearest blue-green water. There is also an Enchanted Dell among the woodland, filled with fairies, fountains and a dragon.

Warleggan
5 miles SW of Bolventor off the A30

The remote location of this hamlet, up a steep wooded lane, has led to its long associations with the supernatural and it has long been acknowledged as a haunt of the Cornish 'piskies'. **St Bartholemew's Parish Church** had, up until 1818, a spire, but in that year it was struck by lightning. However, Warleggan's most eccentric inhabitant was the Reverend Frederick Densham who arrived here in 1931. He immediately began to alienate his parishioners by closing the Sunday School, putting barbed wire around the rectory and patrolling the grounds with a pack of German Shepherd dogs. He even painted the church and rectory in garish colours, but was ordered to remove the paint by the Bishop of Truro. In response to his eccentricity, his congregation worshipped in other churches or became Methodists, and one record in the parish registry of the time reads, 'No fog. No wind. No rain. No congregation'. Unperturbed, Densham fashioned his own congregation from cardboard, filled the pews and preached undisturbed. It does appear that the rector did have a kinder nature, however, as he constructed a children's playground in the rectory garden.. He died in 1953, and people began returning to the church. It is said his ghost still haunts the village.

Bodmin

Situated mid way between Cornwall's north and south coasts and at the junction of two ancient cross country trade routes, Bodmin has always been an important town and was used by traders between Wales, Ireland and northern France who preferred the overland journey between the Camel and Fowey estuaries rather than the sea voyage around Land's End. **Castle Canyke**, to the southeast of the town and with Arthuriam connections. was built during the Iron Age to defend this important trade route and a few centuries later the Romans erected a fort on a site here above the River Camel. One of a string they built in the southwest to defend strategic river crossings, the remains of the earthwork can still be made out today. The waymarked footpath, the **Saints' Way**, follows the ancient cross country route.

In the 6th century, St Petroc, one of the most influential of the early Welsh missionary saints, visited Bodmin and in the 10th century the monastery he had founded in Padstow moved here as a protection against sea raids by the Vikings. The town's **St Petroc's Parish Church** is one of six dedicated to the saint in the county, and indeed the 15th century building is certainly one of the most impressive in all Cornwall. Because of this, when Cornwall became a Church of England diocese in its own right in 1877, Bodmin was one of the places considered for its new cathedral (see also St Germans, St Columb Major and Truro). Building began on the site of the former Norman church in 1469 and, funded by the townsfolk - even the local vicar gave a year's salary - the church was completed in 1472 at a cost of £268. Though remodelled in the 19th century, it has retained its splendid Norman font, whose immense bowl is supported on five finely carved columns, and the ivory casket that is thought to contain the remains of St Petroc. The town is also renowned for its abundance of holy wells; one of them, dating from the 6th

GEORGE AND DRAGON

St Nicholas Street, Bodmin,
Cornwall PL31 1AB
Tel: 01208 72514

Located just outside the town centre, on the Lostwithiel Road, **The George and Dragon** can lay claim to being Bodmin's oldest pub. The traditional 18th-century terraced building is a blaze of colour in summer with the addition of numerous hanging baskets while inside, the many original features have been blended well with the needs of a busy modern pub. In these stylish surroundings customers, both locals and visitors alike, can enjoy locally-brewed ales and receive excellent hospitality from landlords Dave and Dawn

Bramall. Three guest rooms available for bed and breakfast.

PROVIDENCE CAFÉ AND BISTRO

Honey Street, Bodmin, Cornwall PL31 2DN
Tel: 01208 72200

The **Providence Café and Bistro** is truly something special. Situated in the heart of Bodmin, it offers an ultra relaxed ambience and atmosphere for eating, with friendly and laid back staff. The food itself is outstanding and as all the produce is sourced locally, you know that everything you eat is as fresh and wholesome as possible. The menu carries a wide range of dishes, including vegetarian, and you can eat either in the restaurant area where the walls are decorated with the work of local artists, in the garden in the summer months, or have coffee in the small lounge and conference area upstairs. The café's motto is 'nourishment for body and soul', and they're not far wrong!

century, is in the churchyard, along with a little well house. Work started on the Roman Catholic **St Mary's Church** on St Mary's Road in 1937, having first of all been located next to the Anglican church. It finally opened for worship in 1965. It is unusual in that it was founded by the Canons Regular of the Lateran.

The only market town in Cornwall to appear in the *Domesday Book*, Bodmin - the name means the 'house of the monks' - was chiefly an ecclesiastical town until the reign of Henry VIII. By then it had a population of about 1,500, and was a stannary town (which meant assayed tin) and the largest setlement in the county. But it was not always a quiet place of contemplation and, during Tudor times alone it witnessed three uprisings: against the tin levy in 1496, in support of Perkin Warbeck against Henry VII in 1497 and, in 1549, against the imposition of the English Prayer Book. In 1838 the town took over as the seat of the county from Launceston but when the Great Western Railway arrived in the 1840s it was forced to build the station (now Parkway) some distance away, denying the town the instant access that a central station would have provided; the link from the main line to the town had to wait until the 1880s. Of the places and buildings to visit here, **Bodmin Jail**, on Berrycomble Road, is the most interesting. It was the former county prison and dates back to 1776. The last hanging took place here in 1909 and visitors have the chance to view the site. This too was the place where, during the Great War, both the Crown Jewels and the *Domesday Book* were hidden for safe keeping. The Shire Hall, built in 1837, served as the County Court until 1988. Now restored (it was officially re-opened by the Queen in June 2000), it brings to life in **The Courtroom Experience**, the notorious murder in 1844 of Charlotte Dymond on lonely Bodmin Moor and the trial of Matthew Weeks for the crime. Weeks went to the gallows for her murder, but was he guilty? Visitors can hear the evidence and cast their votes as part of the jury, and the 45-minute session also includes a visit to the cells. Charlotte Dymond is also remembered in a ballad by the Cornish poet Charles Causley:

It was a Sunday evening
And in the April rain
That Charlotte went from our house
And never came home again.

Courtroom 2 is now a popular venue for the performing arts, and the Town & Countryside Centre is full of information on what to see and do in the locality. **Bodmin Town Museum** provides, through its numerous displays, an insight into the town's past as well as life in and around Bodmin through the centuries. Housed in The Keep, **The Duke of Cornwall's Light Infantry Regimental Museum** covers the history of the regiment, which was formed as marines in 1702 and played an important part in the capture of Gibraltar in 1704. The museum has two main galleries and its many important exhibits include eight Victoria Crosses and George Washington's bible captured in 1777 during the American War of Independence. The restored GWR station of Bodmin General is the headquarters of the **Bodmin & Wenford Railway**, which runs a mainly steam-operated service to Boscarne Junction in one direction and Bodmin Parkway in the other. There are one-off events throughout the year, including jazz specials, vineyard specials, steam and diesel galas and murder mysteries. In the station, visitors can see the collection of locomotives and carriages and enjoy home-made refreshments in the buffet

and browse through the souvenir shop.

A short distance from the town centre lies **Bodmin Beacon Local Nature Reserve** from which there are splendid views across the town and the moors. On the summit of the beacon stands a 144 feet obelisk, the **Gilbert Memorial**, which is dedicated to Sir Walter Raleigh Gilbert, a local soldier. Also easily reached from Bodmin is the **Camel Trail**, a walking and cycling path along the River Camel to Padstow which follows the track bed of one of Britain's earliest railways.

Around Bodmin

Cutmadoc
2 miles S of Bodmin off the A38

To the west of the village lies the spectacular estate of **Lanhydrock House**, one of the most visited of all the National Trust's properties. Prior to the Dissolution of the Monasteries, this large estate belonged to Bodmin's Augustinian priory of St Petroc, then, in 1620, it was bought by Sir Richard Robartes, who accumulated his fortune in tin and wool, and who was the leading Parliamentarian in Cornwall. He later found favour with Charles II on his restoration, and was created Earl of Radnor. The house was laid out on four sides of a square, but the east wing was removed in 1780, creating the present U-shaped house. The family lived here until it passed into the hands of the National Trust in 1953 along with 400 acres of grounds. It was probably the grandest house in Cornwall, set in a superb position in the Fowey Valley, the surrounding estate including formal and woodland gardens, woods and parkland.

However, a fire in 1881 destroyed most of the building, except the north wing and the Long Gallery, and brought about the

Lanhydrock House

death from shock of its owners, Viscount Clifden and his wife. Their son rebuilt the place in the shell of the original, retaining all the splendour while adding the very latest Victorian amenities such as central heating, plumbed bathrooms and modern kitchens. Forty nine rooms, most of them 'downstairs', are open to the public, and as well as admiring the magnificent plaster barrel-vaulted ceiling in the Long Gallery visitors can also see the kitchen complex, the nursery wing and the grand dining room. One special bedroom belonged to Tommy Agar-Robartes, who was killed at the Battle of Loos in 1915; it contains many of his personal belongings. Catering outlets in the servants' quarters and old stable block offer a variety of menus, and the shop sells a wide range of goods, many of them locally produced. Plants grown in the Lanhydrock nurseries are on sale in the main car park, next to which are a picnic area and adventure playground. The grounds are a pleasure to wander around and here there are fabulous displays of rhododendrons, magnolias and camellias in the spring, a superb avenue of ancient beech and sycamore trees, a cob-and-

Lanhydrock Gardens

thatch summer house and a photogenic formal garden that is overlooked by the small estate church of St Hydroc. In the woods are many unusual flowers and ferns, as well as woodpeckers, owls and other birds.

Lanhydrock is possibly the most complete grand Victorian house in Britain, and you should allow at least one and a half to two hours for a compelete tour.

Cardinham

3 miles NE of Bodmin off the A30

A small village on the western slopes of Bodmin Moor. **St Meubred's Parish Church** is 15th century, and in its churchyard stands a worn 10th century cross richly decorated with intricate spirals and rings. It was damaged during the war by bombs intended for Bodmin. St Meubred was one of those obscure Cornish saints about whom very little is known. It is thought that he was in fact Irish, and came to Cornwall to preach. He was later beheaded in Rome, and his body was sent back to Cardinham for burial.

Now a peaceful backwater that is enjoyed by both walkers and cyclists, the 650 acre **Cardinham Woods** was in medieval times the site of **Cardinham Castle**, a Norman motte and bailey castle. Belonging to the Cardinham family, under-lords of Robert of Mortain, Earl of Cornwall, the structure was abandoned in the 14th century and today only an earthwork mound remains on which a few traces of the original

keep have been preserved. There are also the remains of an old silver mine. This attractive and varied woodland was acquired by the Forestry Commission in 1922 and is managed by Forest Enterprise for commercial forestry, producing, among others, a high quality Douglas fir for the British timber industry. It is a haven for a wide variety of wildlife, with otters on the river, red and roe deer, ravens and buzzards. The site has several waymarked woodland trails, and cycling is allowed on some of them. Visitors will also find a café and a picnic area with barbecue facilities. Close by, surrounded by woodland, is **Pinsla Garden & Nursery**, a romantic 1½ acre garden of herbaceous and shrub borders, alpines and cottage garden beds, jungle planting, paths lined with granite boulders, a tree tunnel and a stone circle in the meadow. The owners grow and stock a wide range of plants in the nursery.

St Bellarmins Tor lies to the north of the village, with, on top, the remains of a small chapel dedicated to St Bartholomew, whom legend tells us lived there as a hermit.

Nanstallon

2 miles W of Bodmin off the A389

Close to this village, on sunny slopes above the River Camel, are **Camel Valley Vineyards**, where red, white and sparkling wines are produced from 8,000 vines. Bob and Annie Lindo's vineyard is open to visitors from Easter week to the end of September, with guided tours at

2.30 Monday to Friday and out of hours group tours by arrangement.

Blisland

6 miles NE of Bodmin off the A30

Found down a maze of country lanes, at the centre of this moorland village is the tree-lined village green which has stayed faithful to its original Saxon layout - an uncommon sight on this side of the River Tamar. Fine Georgian and Victorian houses, a rectory and an inn complete the picture but it is the uniquely dedicated **St Protus and St Hyacinth Parish Church** that takes the attention of most visitors. A favourite of Sir John Betjeman, who described it as 'dazzling and amazing', the part-Norman building has a bright whitewashed interior, a good wagon roof, an unusual mock-Renaissance altar and two fonts, one Norman and the other dating from the 15th century.

On the moorland to the north of the village are numerous ancient monuments including the 108-feet diameter stone circle of **Blisland Manor** Common and, a couple of miles further away, **Stripple Stone Henge Monument** on Hawkstor Down.

Washaway

5 miles NW of Bodmin on the A38

Lying just north of the village is one of Cornwall's most attractive manor houses, the lovely **Pencarrow House**. Hidden within a 50 acre wooded estate which encompasses an Iron Age encampment, Italian gardens and lovely lawns, this historic Georgian house at the end of a mile-long drive was built in the 1770s by the Molesworth-St Aubyn family and, still living here, they have over the years, remodelled the house on two separate occasions. Of the many beautiful items to be seen on a visit to this award winning house the series of family portraits, many by eminently fashionable painters of the time, are particularly superb.

Excellent furniture and exquisite porcelain are also on show, along with a collection of antique dolls. Sir Arthur Sullivan was a guest at the house in 1882

ST MABYN INN

St Mabyn, Bodmin, Cornwall PL30 3BA
Tel:01208 841266
e-mail: gjstmabyn@aol.com

St Mabyn is a picturesque village east of Wadebridge off the A39, named after St Mabyn, (AD474 · AD550) a saintly lady who was one of 24 children of a 5th century Welsh King called Brychan Brycheiniog. The **St Mabyn Inn** dates from the 17th century, and began life as a farmhouse, then became an alehouse before becoming the cosy, popular inn it is today.

The place is a real ale lover's paradise. It is open all day ever day for the sale of four real ales, which rises to six in the summer months. Here you can sample Sharpe's Doom Bar, Cornish and Special, plus Bass. There is also a fine range of wines, spirits, ciders, lagers and soft drinks. The bar itself is full of cosy, old world charm, with plenty of dark wood and framed prints. There is also a pool table.

Mine hosts are Jane and Gary, who have created a pub that would be a

credit to any village. Food is served between 12 noon and 2.30 pm and 6 pm until 9.30 pm daily and there is a separate, no smoking restaurant that seats 45 in absolute comfort. Jane is a great cook and you can chose from the menu or a daily specials board. Children are always welcome if you're dining, and most credit cards are accepted. Lunchtime favourites include steak and kidney pie, lamb chops and lasagne, while sizzling steaks with all the trimmings are popular. A Sunday roast is added to the Sunday menu, and you should always book in advance for this.

So call in at the St Mabyn Inn · you won't be disappointed!

and during his stay wrote the music for *Iolanthe*. It was Sir William Molesworth, the Secretary of State for the Colonies, who, during Parliamentary recesses in the mid 19th century, began the ambitious remodelling of the gardens and grounds. Today's visitors benefit from his splendid plans as this internationally renowned garden contains over 700 different species of rhododendron, camellia, blue hydrangea and specimen conifers. The gardens and plant sales area are open daily from early March, the house, tea rooms and craft shop Sunday to Thursday from the end of March to the end of October. Children are very welcome, and their imaginative play area includes a Wendy House in Cornish slate.

Saltash

A small medieval port on the River Tamar, and once the base for the largest river steamer fleet in the southwest, Saltash has gone through a number of names in its 1000-year history. It's been called Villa de Esse, Ash, and Assheburgh over the eyars. With narrow streets that rise up steeply from the riverbank, the town has long been the 'Gateway to Cornwall' for many holidaymakers, who cross the Tamar River into Cornwall at this point via one of the town's mighty bridges. Designed by Isambard Kingdom Brunel in 1859, the wrought-iron **Royal Albert Bridge** carries the railway while, alongside, is the much more slender

Tamar Bridge, opened in the early 1960s. This modern suspension road bridge replaced the ferry service which had been in use since the 13th century. A tunnel was also constructed to ease the ever-increasing flow of cars through the town.

Though older than Plymouth, on the other side of the Sound, Saltash, particularly with the construction of the road bridge, is now becoming almost a suburb of the city. However, though heavily influenced by its neighbour, Saltash has retained much of its charm and Cornish individuality, and Saltash people still talk of 'going over into England' when crossing one of the bridges. From the old quayside, there are river trips up stream to Calstock and there are also several interesting buildings to discover. The mainly 17th century **Guildhouse** stands on granite pillars and close by is **Mary Newman's Cottage**, a quaint old building that was the home of Sir Francis Drake's first wife. Dating from the 15th century, the cottage and gardens are occasionally

open to the public. **Trematon Castle** (not open to the public) was built by Reginald Vautorte, a Norman who came over to England with William the Conqueror. The walls are over 15 feet thick, and so secure was it that the treasures collected by Sir Francis Drake after his trips abroad were stored here.

Around Saltash

Callington
7½ miles N of Saltash on the A388

This old market town, which lies at the foot of Kit Hill (to the north), began life as a Celtic settlement called Celliwic, and was then settled by the Saxons. It is situated on the fertile fruit-growing land between the Rivers Tamar and Lynher. However, during the 19th century, the countryside around Callington, from Dartmoor in the east to Bodmin Moor in the west, prospered from frantic mining activity. The area's heritage, landscape and character can be seen by wandering around the town

HIGHER MANATON FARMHOUSE BED & BREAKFAST

Bray Shop, Nr Callington, Cornwall PL17 8PX
Tel/Fax: 01579 370460
e-mail: dtrewin@manaton.fsnet.co.uk
website: www.cornwall-devon-bandb.co.uk

Walkers, tourists and nature lovers enjoy the peace, comfort and hospitality of **Higher Manaton Farmhouse**, which David and Wendy Trewin have run as a B&B since 1976. Their 18th century farmhouse, which stands off the B3257 north of Callington, has three non-smoking bedrooms, a family room and a double room en suite, and a twin bedded room with private bath-room. Guests have the use of a lovely lounge with games, books and local maps. David is a farmer and master woodturner and many of his pieces are on display around the house. ETB 4 Diamonds

where, through the interesting and unusual **Mural Project**, local scenes have been painted on the walls of the town's buildings by professional and amateur artists. A booklet explains where the murals are, who painted them and what they depict. **Callington Museum** is housed in an old cemetery chapel on Liskeard Road. The town is the headquarters of Ginsters, the well-known firm of pasty makers.

Overlooking the River Lynher, to the southwest of the town, lies **Cadsonbury Hillfort** - a massive Iron Age bank and ditch encompassing a hill that are thought to be the remains of the home of a local chief. To the east of Callington lies the attractive early 16th century **Dupath Chapel**, a granite building that houses Dupath Well. The waters of the well were thought to cure whooping cough, and weer also used in baptisms held in the chapel.

Kit Hill

8 miles N of Saltash off the B3257

On the summit of this 1,096 feet granite peak is a reminder of the area's old industry in the form of a 80 feet chimney stack that was built in 1858 to

CROSS HOUSE INN

School Road, Harrowbarrow, Callington
Cornwall PL17 8BQ
Tel: 01579 350482

The family-owned **Cross House Inn,** which sits off the A388, is well worth seeking out for its warm and friendly atmosphere. Originally an old farmhouse dating from 1783, it has recently been refurbished to a high standard, making it a popular place for visitors and locals alike. The bar/lounge has a roaring fire in the colder months, and sells a fine range of beers, wines, spirits and soft drinks if you're

driving. In the spacious restaurant you can choose from the menu or the daily special board. Everything is beautifully cooked and represents amazing value for money.

serve one of the area's mines. Providing a dramatic outline for many miles, this 500 acre site was donated to the county of Cornwall by Prince Charles in 1985 and is a country park that is also rich in old industrial remains. From the summit there are outstanding views across southeast Cornwall to Plymouth Sound. Three viewing tables have been placed at the top of peak so that distant features can be identified . There are also many Neolothic and Bronze Age barrows and earth mounds dotting the hillside. It was at Kit Hill in AD 835 that the **Battle of Hingston Down** took place, where King Egbert of Wessex defeated Cornish and Danish forces. In the 18th century a man called Sir John Call built a folly to commemorate the battle, and its remains can still be seen.

St Ann's Chapel

7½ miles N of Saltash on the A390

Found close to the Cornwall-Devon border, and in the heart of glorious countryside, the **Tamar Valley Donkey Park** is just the place for a family day out. This is a very friendly establishment offering a fun-packed day, and as well as the donkeys and donkey rides, there are many other animals to see, a children's adventure play ground and a café.

WRECKERS MORRIS DANCERS

St Dominic, Cornwall
website: www.wreckers-morris.co.uk

Morris dancing is alive and kicking in Cornwall. One of the newest sides on the scene is Wreckers Morris, based at St. Dominic.

Now in its fifth season, Wreckers is a vibrant, vigorous side which dances in the Border style.Border dances originate from those English counties bordering Wales and generally feature much clashing of sticks.

Dressed in long tattered coats of black and gold (the Cornish colours), Wreckers make an impressive sight wherever they perform. The dancers make a lot of noise, as do their bells and sticks.

The band often features around half a dozen musicians.The melodeon is the traditional morris instrument and the Wreckers band frequently musters four or more. Then there are guitars, mandolin, percussion of various kinds and sometimes flute and trombone!

Most performances are usually followed by a song and music sessions and Wreckers has also been known to provide a full range of entertainment for weddings – that includes a ceildih as well as the standard performance.

Wreckers make an effort to get the audience involved and as many people find out – morris dancing is not as easy as it looks! Most performances take place from May onwards – with a special start-of-season appearance at dawn on 1st May when Wreckers greet the sunrise at the Hurlers stone circles on Bodmin Moor.

St Mellion

5 miles N of Saltash on the A390

Named after St Melaine, a 6th century bishop of Rennes in France, the village is now best known for the **St Mellion Golf and Country Club**, which owns some of the finest golf courses in Europe. Jack Nicklaus has named the Nicklaus Course potentially the finest in Europe, and the Old Course has hosted the Benson and Hedges International on six occasions.

Gunnislake

8 miles N of Saltash on the A390

Often referred to as the first village in Cornwall, Gunnislake is a charming community that is set in the beautiful wooded valley of the River Tamar. In the 1520s, Sir Piers Edgcumbe of Cotehele House built the **New Bridge**, a striking 180 feet long, seven-arched granite structure which continues to serve as one of the major gateways into the county. In fact, this remained the lowest crossing of the river by road until the early 60s when the massive suspension bridge linking Plymouth with Saltash was opened. The river crossing at Gunnislake meant that the village was a place of strategic importance, a feature

which made it the centre of bitter fighting during the Civil War.

Like many other villages of the Tamar Valley, Gunnislake, during the 18th and 19th centuries, was alive with mining, although one of the first mines here had been worked from the 14th century. Now the mines have closed and many of their buildings have been left to be reclaimed by nature. One of Turner's great paintings, *Crossing the Brook*, takes in a view of Gunnislake and the surrounding valley and, as well as the beautiful countryside, a miners' lodging house is also immortalised. The place was also greatly admired by Sir John Betjeman.

Calstock

6 miles NE of Saltash off the A390

The parish of Calstock has the second largest population of any parish in Cornwall, and measures 5 miles east to west and four miles north to south. Well known for its splendid views of the

Railway Viaduct, Calstock

Tamar valley, the village itself lies 14 miles upstream from Plymouth, and has been an important river port since Saxon times. It was mentioned in the *Domesday Book*, and was part of the Earldom of Cornwall in the 13th century. It became even more important in the 19th century when vast quantities of tin, granite and copper ore were brought here for loading on to barges to be transported down the Tamar to the coast and beyond. In the countryside surrounding Calstock the remains of old mine workings, along with the spoil heaps, can still be seen along with the remains of the village's boat-building industry. Earlier, in the 18th century, the Tamar Valley was renowned for its fruit growing and, in particular, its cherries, and today the springtime blossom is still a beautiful sight if not quite as spectacular as it once was.

The decline of the town as a port came with the construction of the huge **Calstock Railway Viaduct** which carries the Tamar Valley Line southwards to Plymouth. Completed in 1908, the giant 11-arched viaduct, the first in the country to be constructed of concrete blocks, stands 120 feet above the River Tamar. Probably one of Britain's most picturesque branch lines, the Tamar Valley Line can still be taken down to the coast and, though the river has lost most of its commercial traffic, it is still used by a lot of pleasure craft.

Southwest of Calstock on the steep wooded slopes of the Tamar Valley is **Cotehele House**, one of the best preserved and most romantic late medieval estates in the southwest of England. Largely built in late 15th and early 16th centuries by Sir Piers Edgcumbe and his son Richard, this low granite manor house is surrounded first by grounds that contain exotic and tender plants that thrive in the mild valley climate and, then, by an estate that has retained its ancient network of paths which allow exploration of the valley.

The estate came into the Edgumbe family in 1353, when Hilaria de Cotehele married William Edgcumbe, son of a Devon squire. When the present house was being built, the Cornish aristocracy was moving away from the basic, heavily fortified dwellings they once lived in. Most of England by this time was building houses that owed more to elegance than defence, and it is no accident that Cotehele - the first in the county to show touches of real elegance - should be right on the Devon border. But Sir Piers was taking no chances, and added some defensive features to his manor house, such as crenellations, just in case.

In the 1550s, the Edgcumbe family moved their main residence from here southwards to Mount Edgcumbe overlooking Plymouth Sound and, since then, Cotehele has remained relatively untouched save for some additions to the northwest tower in 1627. There are many remnants of earlier ages to be seen here including the Great Tudor Hall, exceptional tapestries, period

Cotehele House, Calstock

furniture and, outside, a medieval stewpond (a fish pond) and a domed dovecote. The house also incorporates some charming individual features such as a secret spy-hole to the Great Hall, a private chapel, and a tower clock with a bell but no face or hands, that is believed to be the oldest working example of its kind in the country. Near the house, a great medieval barn contains a gift and plant shop and a restaurant with dishes that reflect the special character and history of Cotehele. In the grounds, at the foot of a combe stands a tiny chapel situated on a promontory 70 feet above the river's edge. This was built in the 15th century by Sir Richard Edgcumbe, a Lancastrian, to show thanks for his escape from the Yorkist forces of Richard III who had been pursuing him through Cotehele Woods. Edgcumbe avoided capture by placing a stone in his cap and throwing it into the fast-flowing River Tamar, a clever ploy which made his pursuers think that he had jumped into the torrent and

drowned. Also along the river, and close to the estate's old cider house and restored corn mill, lies **Cotehele Quay**, a busy river port in Victorian times. The quay buildings now house an outstation of the National Maritime Museum, an art and craft gallery and a licensed tea room. The restored Tamar sailing barge *Shamrock* is moored alongside the museum. Cotehele House and the surrounding estate are owned by the National Trust.

Upstream, beyond Calstock, **Morwellham Quay** was another important 19th century river port, from which the ore and minerals extracted from the local mines was transported to the coast.In 1844 the largest copper lode in Europe was discovered four miles from the quay, and a company called the Devon Great Consols was formed to exploit it. A railway was built in 1856 to bring the ore to the quay, and another "inclined plane" railway was built as well, passing beneath the cottages in a specially dug tunnel. In its day, Morwellham Quay was the greatest copper exporting port in Britain, and supported a population of 300 people. Today, staff in Victorian garb help to bring history alive. Visitors can take a riverside tram ride and explore the George & Carlotte copper mine; watch blacksmiths, potters and carpenters at work in the old cottages; say hello to the shire horses; take a carriage ride around the village; and make the most of the countryside in the nature reserve, a mixture of marshland, woodland, meadows and fields that is designated both an Area of Outstanding Natural Beauty and a Site of Special Scientific Interest. Besides the permanent attractions, there's a long list of special events at the Quay: Victorian market days, river trips, Punch & Judy shows, Morris dancers, excavation weeks, jazz festivals, ploughing with heavy horses and a Christmas pantomime.

Torpoint

3 miles SE of Saltash on the A374

This small town grew up around the ferry service that began running across the **Hamoaze** (as the Tamar estuary is called at this point) between here and Devonport in the 18th century. From its position on the northern arm of the Rame Peninsula, Torpoint offers some excellent views across the river to the Royal Navy Dockyards. Close by lies HMS *Raleigh*, the naval training centre for ratings and artificer apprentices. Commissioned in 1940, *HMS Raleigh* is also the home of the Royal Marine Band (Plymouth).

The **Torpoint Ferry** runs betwen the town and Plymouth, of which it is now practically a suburb. It was established in 1791 by an Act of Parliament, and in 1832, when the Liskeard road was greatly improved, a steam ferry was introduced. However, such were the unusual tidal conditions, that was eventually replaced by a chain ferry. Much of its trade declined with the opening of the Tamar Bridge further up river in the early 1960s, but the ferry still operates today. South of Torpoint is **St John's Lake**, an inlet of the sea, and one of the few salt water lakes in England.

Lying a mile north of Torpoint is **Antony House**, a superb example of an early 18th century country mansion, now in the care of the National Trust. The estate has been the home of the influential Cornish Carew Pole family for nearly 600 years, and this superb pale silver-grey stone building was

QUEENS ARMS

King Street, Torpoint, Cornwall PL11 2AS
Tel/Fax: 01752 813158

The charming **Queens Arms** is housed in an early 19th century building on a corner site in this popular town opposite Plymouth. It is popular with both tourists and locals alike, and has an open plan bar/lounge that is spacious and attractive, with new carpeting and furniture that gives it that extra something. There is, of course, a wide range of drinks available and the food is simple, unpretentious pub food · but always beautifully cooked and presented. Big

portions, small prices · that's the motto here, and it is served all day, every day, with the Sunday roast being particularly popular.

constructed between 1718 and 1729 in a neo-classical style that consists of a forecourt enclosed by brick colonnades with both the east and west wings fashioned in red brick. Inside there is a wealth of paintings (many by Sir Joshua Reynolds), tapestries and furniture to be seen while, outside, the house is surrounded by glorious grounds. Landscaped with the assistance of Humphry Repton in the late-18th century, the superb **Antony Woodland Gardens**, which overlook the River Lynher, are at their best in the spring when the rhododendrons, magnolias, camellias and azaleas are in full bloom, and in autumn when the exotic and indigenous species of trees provide a vivid and colourful display. Also worth seeing are the 18th century dovecote and the Bath Pond House. The Gardens are not National Trust, but entrance is free to NT members on days when the house is open (Tel: 01752 812191).

Cremyll

4 miles SE of Saltash on the B3247

This village, which is linked to Plymouth by a foot ferry first started in about 1204, is an excellent place from which to explore **Mount Edgcumbe House**, the 16th century home of the Earls of Edgcumbe who moved here from Cotehele House, near Calstock. After marrying Jean Durnford, the heiress to considerable estates on both sides of the Tamar estuary as well as the Cremyll ferry, Piers Edgcumbe received a royal

licence in 1539 to enclose the wooded grounds of the estate on the Rame peninsula and cerate a deer park. Following his death, his son, Richard, had the splendid Tudor mansion built between 1547 and 1553. The house survived a direct hit by bombs in 1941 during an air raid on Plymouth, and was restored between 1958 and 1964. The contents include paintings by Sir Joshua Reynolds, Irish Bronze Age horns, 16th century tapestries and 18th century Chinese and Plymouth porcelain. In the adjacent Earl's Garden are several ancient and rare trees, notably a 400-year-old lime and a Mexican pine. The extensive, magnificent grounds, which incorporate land from Cremyll westwards along the peninsula to Tregonhawke, include the historic 18th century gardens that contain an orangery, and Italian, French, English, American and New Zealand gardens. Since 1976, Mount Edgcumbe has housed the National Camellia Collection. The Country Park, which takes in a stretch of heritage coast line, has freely roaming fallow deer and numerous buildings sited to create views and atmosphere.

Maker

5 miles S of Saltash off the B3247

Dating from the 15th century and retaining much of its original charm, Maker church, whose name is derived from a Cornish word meaning 'ruin', was comprehensively restored in the 19th century. It is the family church of the

FRIARY MANOR

Maker, Nr Kingsand, Cornwall PL10 1JB
Tel: 01752 822112 Fax: 01752 829187
website: www.friarymanor.co.uk

The elegant and extremely comfortable **Friary Manor** is an upmarket hotel and restaurant sitting on the Rame Peninsula in South Cornwall. The building dates from 1724, and is a country house set in a secluded location. Extensive refurbishment has turned it into one of the best establishments of its kind in the area, with seven elegant bedrooms (five en suite) and a restaurant that is renowned for

its excellent lunches, dinners and traditional cream teas. It makes an excellent base from which to explore both Cornwall and Devon.

Edgcumbes, and inside the church is a copy of a portrait of the early 18th century vicar here, Thomas Smart. It is not the subject but the artist which makes this work particularly special: at the age of 12, Joshua Reynolds made drawings of the vicar on the back of his hymn book during a service and then, back at a Cremyll boatyard, painted the original portrait on to canvas.

Just north of the church, surrounded by woodland and hidden within an oratory, lies **St Julian's Well**, which is dedicated to the 5th century saint who

is, aptly for this area, the patron saint of ferrymen. Also known as "the poor man", he was a popular saint in Western Europe, which has also made him the patron saint of innkeepers and - curiously enough - circus performers.

Cawsand and Kingsand
5½ miles S of Saltash off the B3247

It is hard to believe that these two small and attractive neighbouring villages once operated one of the largest smuggling fleets in Cornwall. The

THE HALFWAY HOUSE INN

Fore Street, Kingsand, Cawsand Bay,
Nr Torpoint, Cornwall PL10 1NA
Tel: 01752 822279 Fax: 01752 823146
e-mail: info@halfwayinn.biz
website: www.halfwayinn.biz

The Rame Peninsula is Cornwall's forgotten corner, and it is here, only yards from the sea, that you will find **The Halfway House Inn**. It is an old, attractive inn with a distinctly Victorian feel that speaks of hospitality and value for money, and has six fully en suite rooms that are comfortable and cosy. It is popular with both locals and visitors, and sells a selection of real ales, spirits and wines. The small, informal restaurant leads off the bar,

and specialises in sea food, all locally supplied. This is the ideal place for a quiet, relaxing holiday, so you can't go wrong if you make this your base when exploring both Cornwall and Devon!

CAWSAND BAY HOTEL & GALLEON RESTAURANT

The Bound, Cawsand, Cornwall PL10 1PG
Tel: 01752 822425 Fax: 01752 823527
e-mail: bookings@cawsandbay.co.uk
website: www.cawsandbay.co.uk

Cawsand is an unspoilt fishing village near Penlee Point, south of Torpoint. It was reputed to be the haunt of smugglers in days gone by, but now is more famous for the **Cawsand Bay Hotel & Galleon Restaurant**, one of the finest hotels in the whole area. It has one of the best locations of any hotel in England - right on its own private sandy beach on Cawsand Bay, with stunning views out over the ocean from many of the windows. Across Plymouth Sound you can get also wonderful glimpses of Dartmoor, or

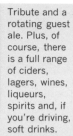

you can just relax and watch the boats large and small sail up and down the Sound.

The hotel has ten superb rooms available for discerning guests, all fully en suite and all spacious, comfortable and well furnished and decorated. Two twin rooms are on the ground floor, and just a step away from the clean, warm sand of the beach, and there are a number of family units that can accommodate up to six people. Special reductions are available for children sharing the family units, and all rooms have a colour TV, showers, central heating and tea and coffee making facilities.

Special out of season deals of three nights for the price of two are also available (not including Christmas or New Year), and there are also deals for weekend or long weekend breaks.

The hotel is fully licensed, and sells three real ales - Sharpe's Doom Bar, St Austell's

Tribute and a rotating guest ale. Plus, of course, there is a full range of ciders, lagers, wines, liqueurs, spirits and, if you're driving, soft drinks.

Excellent food is served from 12 noon until 2 pm and from 7 pm until 9 pm daily. The Galleon restaurant is justifiably renowned throughout Southeast Cornwall, and seats 60 in absolute comfort. No stay at the Cawsand Hotel is complete without dining here! There is a wide and varied choice of menu, from full à la carte to tasty bistro meals or even just a light snack or lunch.

The head chef, David Trethewey, takes a great pride in using only the finest and freshest of local produce, all locally sourced if possible. Lasagnes, local fish, succulent, sizzling steaks with all the trimmings, curries, vegetarian dishes and traditional English cuisine can all be found here, cooked to perfection and presented with flair and imagination. Plus, of course, there is a good choice of fine wines to accompany your meal.

All the amenities of Plymouth, such as the shops, restaurants and leisure facilities, are within easy reach using the Torpoint Ferry or the Tamar Bridge, and the famous South West Coast Path runs right behind the hotel. The Eden Project is an hour's drive away and there are many picturesque fishing villages to be explored.

landing place of the future Henry VII after the battle of Bosworth, it was not long afterwards that **Cawsand Bay** and the narrow streets of the two villages began to see the illegal night-time activities that were to peak in the late 18th and early 19th centuries. Thousands of barrels of brandy, silk and other contraband were landed here in secret and transported through the sleeping villages to avoid the attentions of the revenue men. For centuries an administrative quirk put the twin villages in different counties (Cawsand in Cornwall and Kingsand in Devon). Before the **Plymouth Breakwater** was completed in 1841, the Royal Navy fleet used to shelter from the frequent southwesterly gales at anchor in the sheltered Cawsand Bay, which led to the opening of a surprising number of inns that are welcomed to this day by locals and holidaymakers alike. Taking some 30 years to construct, from several tons of local limestone, the breakwater was designed and engineered by John Rennie. At either end, some 5,000 feet apart, are beacon lights, and at the eastern end lies a large lobster-pot on top of a 24 feet pole which acts as a refuge to shipwrecked mariners. Please note that dogs are banned from Cawsand Bay from Easter until October.

Rame
6 miles S of Saltash off the B3247

Positioned at the southeastern end of Whitsand Bay and the southernmost

---

HALFWAY HOUSE

Polbathic, Near Torpoint, Cornwall PL11 3EY
Tel: 01503 230202
website: www.halfwayatpolbathic.co.uk

Halfway House is a picturesque old inn dating from the 15th century that once was part of the estate of the Eliots, local lords of the manor. It is a whitewashed building that was a former coaching inn, and during its lifetime it has had three name changes. But it is as the Halfway House (so called because it lay half way between the Torpoint Ferry and Liskeard) that it has gained a reputation as being one of the finest inns in this part of Cornwall.

It has four fully en suite rooms on offer to discerning guests, all en suite and all having TVs and hospitality trays. They are comfortable, cosy and immaculately clean, making Halfway House the idea base from which to explore this part of Cornwall. It serves two real ales, Sharpe's Doom bar and a rotating guest ale, and has a great reputation for its fine food.

The food is served from 12 noon to 2 pm and from 6 pm until 9 pm Monday to Saturday, with the evening hours being 7 pm to 9 pm on Sunday. There is a separate, no smoking restaurant that is smart yet traditional, with dark wood and comfortable carpeting. A separate function room doubles up as an overspill for the restaurant, so there is always plenty of room to eat! You can choose from an imaginative menu or a daily specials board and all the food is cooked on the premises from fresh local produce wherever possible. Children are very welcome and the inn accepts all major credit cards.

To the back of the inn is an unusual feature - a pétanque court where the French game of "boules" can be played in the summer.

point of Mount Edgcumbe Country Park, spectacular **Rame Head** guards the entrance to Plymouth Sound. There are, naturally, superb views from the 400 feet cliffs but this beautiful headland has its own special feature - the ruined 14th century **St Michael's Chapel**, from which a blazing beacon told of the coming of the Armada. In the little hamlet of Rame itself is the older, 13th century **Church of St Germanus**, which is still lit by candles; for centuries its west tower and spire acted as a landmark for sailors. The **Eddystone Lighthouse**, which can be seen on a clear day, lies 10 miles offshore from Rame Head; it was from this point in July 1588 that the English fleet had their first encounter with the Spanish Armada.

Whitsand Bay
5 miles S of Saltash off the B3247

Running between the hamlet of Portwrinkle and Rame Head, this impressive stretch of beach is more a series of coves than one continuous expanse of sand. There are various paths leading down the slate cliffs - some of which are over 250 feet high - to the gently curving bay which though peaceful has notoriously strong cross currents of which bathers should be wary.

Portwrinkle
5 miles SW of Saltash on the B3247

This small seaside village on Whitsand Bay developed around its medieval harbour and once had a thriving fishing industry. Now a tiny holiday resort, it boasts a large Victorian hotel that was moved here from Torpoint at the turn of the 20th century. Portwrinkle has two sand-and-shingle beaches with rock pools. If you walk east out of the village towards Crafthole, a signpost points you towards **Tregantle Fort**, built between 1858 and 1868 as part of the Plymouth defences.

St Germans
4 miles W of Saltash on the B3249

Situated on a tributary of the River Lynher, this rural village was, for half a century before the Anglo-Saxon diocese of Cornwall was incorporated with Exeter in 1043, a cathedral city. The present **St Germans Parish Church** is named after St Germanus, bishop of Auxerre in France in the 4th and 5th centuries. It stands on the site of a Saxon cathedral and was the largest church in the county until the construction of Truro Cathedral in 1910. In 1877, when Cornwall became a diocese in its own right, St Germans was one of the places that put its name forward as the site of the cathedral (see also Bodmin, St Columb Major and Truro)

The original cathedral was said to have been built by King Athelstan in AD 926, and there was certainly a cathedral here in 1027, when the bishop was a man called Leofric. In 1043 the cathedral was moved to Crediton, and then Exeter, and Leofric founded a priory in its place. Then, in 1180, a priory of Augustinian canons was founded, which survived until 1539, when Herny VIII dissolved it. For a short while afterwards it was used as a brewhouse. In 1358 it acquired some sacred relics of St Germanus - a piece of arm bone and part of his shroud - and it became a place of pilrimage for a while. The present church dates from Norman times, and as well as having a particularly fine west front, it has two curiously dissimilar towers dating from the 13th and the 15th centuries, one octagonal, the other square. Inside the church are several striking features, the most impressive being the Burne-Jones east window and the monument to Edward Eliot. The Eliot family acquired the priory shortly after Henry VIII's Dissolution of the Monasteries and renamed their new estate Port Eliot. The present house, with its Gothic style turrets, is largely 19th century, although it does include fragments of the ancient monastic buildings. The grounds date from the late 18th century when they were laid out by Humphry Repton. Port Eliot is not open to the public.

Back in the church is an old chair that has a series of carvings depicting the story of Dando, a 14th century priest from the priory. According to local stories, Dando enjoyed the pleasures of life too much, and had a fat face and a pot belly. He also enjoyed strong drink and the company of women. One Sunday morning he left his devotions to go out hunting with a wild group of friends. At the end of the chase, Dando called for a drink, but there was none - he had finished it all earlier. A stranger riding a black horse, who had joined them earlier, presented him with a richly decorated drinking horn. Dando quenched his thirst and saw that the horseman was stealing his game. Despite the priest's curses, the stranger refused to return the game and, in a drunken frenzy, Dando swore that he would follow the stranger to Hell in order to retrieve his prizes. The horseman then pulled Dando up on to his horse and rode off in the direction of the River Lynher where both the horse and the two riders were seen to disappear under the water with a hiss of steam. Years later, the priest is said to have returned to the parish in the form of a demon, and even today he can sometimes be glimpsed as he rides the countryside, looking for last souls to take back to his Dark Master.

Another of St Germans' exceptional buildings, the **Sir William Moyle's Almshouses**, were built in 1583 to an unusual design - the row has prominent gables and a long first-floor balcony which is reached by a sturdy external staircase. Surrounded by neatly kept stone cottages set in flower filled gardens, the almshouses were restored in 1967.

Looe

The two Looe rivers, the East Looe and the West Looe, create a tidal harbour which has been a fishing and seafaring port from at least the beginning of the 13th century through to the 19th century when stone and copper from the

CAPERS RESTAURANT

Higher Market Street, East Looe,
Cornwall PL13 1BS
Tel:01503 265437

Situated in one of Looe's narrow, picturesque streets, **Caper's Restaurant** is *the* place for good food and drink while in this part of Cornwall! Housed in a 17th century listed building, it seats up to 40 in absolute comfort, with room for another 16 out of doors in the warmer months. It is spacious and comfortable, and you can order everything from a simple snack to beautifully cooked, freshly caught sole. An à la carte menu is available in the evenings, and during the daytime it serves a full range of meals, with seafood being a speciality. Why not pay it a visit?

quarries and mines in the north were shipped for export. Even today, it still has Cornwall's second largest fishing fleet. Originally two separate towns called East Looe and West Looe which faced each other across the narrow estuary, they were first connected by a bridge of 14 arches in about 1411, the first estuary bridge in Cornwall. They were finally, officially incorporated in 1883. For many years, these two small communities each dutifully elected their own MP; a practice that eventually ceased in 1832. Unlike its neighbour, East Looe was originally a planned town, built to a grid plan on a large spit of sand.

The present day seven-arched bridge dates from 1853 and carries the main road linking the two towns. In common with many other Cornish coastal settlements which have had to scratch a living by whatever means available, Looe has always been something of a jack-of-all-trades. As well as having a long established pilchard fishing fleet, it has also served the mineral extractors of

Bodmin Moor and been a place popular with smugglers. Looe is still Cornwall's second most important port, with fish auctions taking place at East Looe's bustling quayside market. Nearby is the famous stone-built **Banjo Pier**, which takes its name from its shape. It is more of a protective breakwater for the harbour than a pier, however.

Of the two distinct parts of the town, East Looe is the more famous and also the older with its narrow cobbled streets and twisting alleyways. Housed in one of the town's several old buildings is the **Old Guildhall Museum** in Higher Market Street, East Looe. It dates from 1500, and details much of Looe's history along with that of the surrounding area. The building's old magistrates' bench can still be seen here as well as three log books of Looe's lifeboats, the official town regalia and a collection of minerals and ores. As early as 1800, a bathing machine was constructed overlooking East Looe's sandy beach and, after the opening in 1879 of the Looe Valley Line (a railway branch line to replace the Liskeard and Looe Canal - see under Liskeard) the development of the two towns as a holiday resort began in earnest. Fortunately, the character, particularly of the older East Looe, has been retained and West Looe remains essentially a residential area with many Victorian and Edwardian buildings.

More recently, Looe has regularly hosted an International Sea Angling Festival. In November 2002 a shark caught by accident was measured at almost 14 feet in length and weighed nearly a quarter of a tonne. The shark was sold for £400 to Ray Lindsey, manager of the Oxford fishmonger Haymans, who put it on display in his shop window before cutting it up into hundreds of fillets, all of which he sold in a day! All profits went to the Royal National Mission to Deep Sea Fishermen charity. This imposing beast was a thresher shark, alarming but not dangerous to humans, and was the second largest of its kind to be caught in British waters in recent years.

Looe is also an important venue for sailing events and is the traditional home of the Redwing. It was a style of boat designed in the 1930s by Uffa Fox specifically for Looe Bay, and was reasonably cheap to build while still seaworthy enough to cope with the Cornwall coast. Half a mile offshore lies **Looe Island** (variously known as St George's Island and St Nicholas' Island), which is now a haven for birds, notably

BARCLAY HOUSE HOTEL & RESTAURANT

St Martins Road, East Looe,
Cornwall PL13 1LP
Tel: 01503 262929 Fax: 01503 262632
e-mail: info@barclayhouse.co.uk
website: www.barclayhouse.co.uk

Built in 1890 for a prosperous merchant trader, **Barclay House** nestles in the hillside above the town and the sea. The six acres of grounds provide a tranquil, scenic setting and spectacular views, and the resident owners Nick and Kelli Barclay lead a team that offers friendly service and modern comforts in spacious, elegant surroundings. The hotel, which is in the 2005 Good Hotel Guide and has a 4 Diamond Silver Award, has 11 refurbished, well-appointed bedrooms with bath and/or shower en-suite, telephone, tv, tea/coffee makers and thermostatically controlled radiators. In the award winning restaurant (Taste of the West) Best Restaurant in Cornwall 2003 and 2004, top chef Nick Barclay masterminds a dinner menu of Modern British Coastal Cuisine

featuring locally sourced ingredients, and the fine food is complemented by an expertly chosen wine list that tours the globe and also features the local Camel Valley wines from Bodmin. This really is a food led establishment now.

Steps and paths lead up from the hotel to eight superbly equipped 5 Star cottages built of Cornish stone in the 1990s, with one, two or three bedrooms sleeping up to six guests. All rooms are en suite, most with jacuzzi-style tubs, and the cottages are provided with every modern amenity to guarantee a very luxurious self-catering holiday. The owners have compiled a special information folder with details of the many local activities and places of interest.

BEACH HOUSE

Marine Drive, West Looe, Cornwall PL13 2DH
Tel: 01503 262598 Fax: 01503 262298
e-mail: enquiries@thebeachhouselooe.com
website: www.thebeachhouselooe.com

With a view out over the sea, the **Beach House** is undoubtedly Looe's top guest house. The six rooms are luxurious and individually decorated, with four being fully en suite and two having private facilities. They come with a TV/video (with a wide selection of videos), hospitality tray and hair dryer. The spacious dining room has superb sea views, and during the winter months evening meals can be served by prior arrangement. The Beach House has a private car park. This is the place to stay when enjoyng this lovely part of Cornwall!

shags and cormorants. It is one mile in circumference and rises to a height of 150 feet.

The island comprises 22 acres of woodland and was made famous by the Atkins sisters, Babs and Evelyn, in their books *We Bought an Island* and *Tales from our Cornish Island*. Since their deaths, it has been handed over to the Cornwall Wildlife Trust. Looe Island can be reached, throughout the summer, by boarding one of the many pleasure boats offering trips to the island and along the coast. Looe Island has also been the refuge for one of the Cornish coast's many notorious pirates and smugglers, Black Joan, who, along with her brother Fyn, terrorised the population of this lonely stretch of coast. Babs Atkins, the last surviving sister, died aged 86 ion 2004, having left the island three years earlier to the Cornwall Wildlife Trust.

For an all round view of the area's fauna and flora, the **South East Cornwall Discovery Centre** is ideal. Situated in West Looe, through high-tech displays and video presentations, visitors to the centre are introduced to the wealth of wildlife, plant life and the splendid scenery of southeast

TALLAND BARTON FARM

Talland Bay, Nr Looe, CornwallPL13 2JA
Tel: 01503 272429
website: www.tallandbartonfarm.co.uk

For over 40 years, Rose-Marie Brown has been offering superb B&B accommodation to discerning holidaymakers and tourists at **Talland Barton Farm**, one and a half miles west of Looe. This elegant and substantial farmhouse boasts three fully en suite rooms, and makes the ideal base from which to explore this lovely area of Cornwall.

The breakfasts are hearty and filling, and there is a choice of dishes, from full English to

Continental. So if you're in South East Cornwall, then Talland Barton Farm is the place for you!

Cornwall. In the West Looe Valley, **Kilminorth Woods** are a Local Nature Reserve rich in woodland plants and wildlife. The area has been wooded since at least 1600, and also here is the Ancient Monument known as the Giant's Hedge, a 6th century bank about 15 miles long between Looe and Lerryn, probably built to defend the territory of a local chieftain.

Two miles west of Looe, at Murrayton, is the famous **Monkey Sanctuary** - the world's first protected colony of Amazonian woolly monkeys. The sanctuary was set up to provide a safe environment for monkeys rescued from lives of isolation in zoos and as pets, and the monkeys roam freely in the gardens of the outdoor enclosures. Talks and indoor displays explain more about the monkeys' life and their natural habitat in the Amazonian rainforest, and the gardens around the sanctuary are home to many native plants and insects. Plants for the monkeys to eat are grown in a forest garden, and the Tree Top Café takes care of hungry humans.

Around Looe

Seaton

3 miles E of Looe on the B3247

Once a favourite place with smugglers, who would land their contraband on the sandy beach, this village at the mouth of the River Seaton offer some excellent clifftop walking. There is also the **Seaton Valley Countryside Park**, a woodland walk along a river valley. It is now a local nature reserve with a level path which is suitable for wheelchairs.

Duloe

3½ miles N of Looe on the B3254

This charming Cornish village of stone cottages surrounding the **St Cuby's Parish Church** is also the location of a **Stone Circle**. Some 38 feet in diameter and with eight standing quartz stones, this circle is said to be older than

THE SMUGGLERS INN

Seaton, Cornwall PL11 3JD
Tel: 01503 250646

Close to the fishing port of Looe on the B3247, this friendly inn has an enviable location almost at the waters edge. All five bedrooms are en-suite, very well appointed and are rated 4 Diamonds by the AA.

Dine in the restaurant and sample the excellent food which is cooked by the Michelin award-winning chef. Bar meals and childrens meals are also available. The Smugglers Inn has entertainment nights as well as pool, darts, bar billiards and Sky Sports.

Stonehenge. Duloe is said to mean "two loos", the "loos" being the East and West Looe Rivers. The **Duloe Torque**, a gold bracelet from the Bronze Age, was discovered in a field near the village, and is now in Truro Museum.

Pelynt

4 miles W of Looe on the B3359

The **Parish Church of St Nonna** in this large and rather exposed village not only has an unusual classical aisle (dated 1680) but it is also associated with Bishop Trelawny (1650-1721). Hawker's famous song *Song of the Western Men*, which is almost a Cornish 'national' anthem, recounts the story of Bishop Sir Jonathan

Trelawny's incarceration in the Tower of London. As well as seeing the chair put inside this 14th century church in his memory there is also a fragment of the bishop's coffin and his pastoral staff. The Trelawney family lived at Trelawne, one and a half miles south east of the village.

Lanreath

5 miles NW of Looe on the B3359

This pretty village, with traditional cob cottages at its centre, is home to the **Lanreath Folk and Farm Museum**, which can be found in Lanreath's old tithe barn. What started as a personal collection of agricultural implements by John and Lily Facey has grown into a

PENKELLY

Pelynt, Looe, Cornwall PL13 2QH
Tel: 01503 220348
website: www.penkellyfarm.co.uk

Owned and personally run by Elizabeth and John Trewin, **Penkelly** is an old, extremely comfortable, stone-built farmhouse about six miles west of Looe. It has three excellent rooms (1twin ensuite, 1 double & 1 twin with private bathroom) that are comfortable and cosy. The whole place is spotlessly clean, and represents great value for money. There is a guest lounge where tea and coffee are always

on tap - just the place for relaxing after exploring this picturesque part of Cornwall. It is open between mid April and Mid October each year.

PORFELL ANIMAL LAND WILDLIFE PARK

Trecangate, Nr Lanreath, Liskeard, Cornwall PL14 4RE
Tel: 01503 220211

The peace and tranquillity of the Cornish countryside combine with the exotic world of wild animals at **Porfell Animal Land Wildlife Park**. In 15 acres of fields bounded by streams and woodland, visitors can meet wallabies, marmosets, lemurs, zebra,

meerkats and porcupines, and feed the deer, goats, ducks and chickens. After a stroll through the woods, visitors can relax and

enjoy some refreshments in the cosy Peacock Tea Room, housed in an attractive old barn. The Park is signposted on the B3359 south of the A390 St Austell-Liskeard road.

massive collection. There are numerous vintage exhibits here, many of which can be touched, including old implements, mill workings, engines, tractors, a traditional farmhouse kitchen and a bric-a-brac shop. Craft workshops and a pets' corner complete the museum. At nearby Trecangate is **Porfell Animal Land** (see panel opposite), whose residents include zebras, wallabies, meerkats, lemurs and snakes.

St Keyne
5 miles N of Looe on the B3254

This small village is named after Keyne or Cain, one of the 24 daughters of King Brychan Brycheiniog, a Welsh king. Being very beautiful, many noblemen sought her hand in marriage, but she decided to devote herself to God and remain a virgin. So she crossed the Severn and settled here during the 5th century, and her famous holy well, **St Keyne's Well**, lies a mile southeast of the village. According to local legend, the first member of a newly married couple to drink from the well will be the one to wear the trousers in the marriage. This notion captured the imagination of the Victorians and brought newly-weds here in their thousands. It is still customary for a newly married couple to rush here from the church to see who drinks the waters first. Robert Southey (1774-1843) the poet even wrote a famous poem about it.

One of the more curious episodes in St Keyne's history took place during the reign of Catholic Mary Tudor, when the local rector and his wife (who had married during the reign of Protestant Edward VI) were dragged from their bed in the middle of the night and placed in the village stocks.

The attraction at St Keyne which brings most visitors here today is **Paul Corin's Magnificent Music Machines**, first opened in 1967. It is a fantastic display of mechanical instruments that use paper rolls, metal discs and punched cards to produce the music. Paul Corin was the last miller in the village and in the lovely old mill close to the bridge over the East Looe River, his son, also

THE WELL HOUSE

St Keyne, Liskeard, Cornwall PL14 4RN
Tel: 01579 342001 Fax: 01579 343891
e-mail: enquiries@wellhouse.co.uk
website: www.wellhouse.co.uk

Tucked away down a country lane deep in Cornwall's exquisite Looe Valley, this enchanting nine-bedroomed country house with its award-winning restaurant is set in three acres of tranquil gardens, complete with all-weather tennis court, swimming pool and croquet lawn. Near to the picturesque fishing villages of Polperro, Looe and Fowey, and with the famous Eden Project and Lost Gardens of Heligan within easy reach, this is the ideal

spot from which to discover the charms of romantic Cornwall.

Paul, now looks after this amazing collection. There are continuous tours throughout the day and visitors can view and listen to a wide range of sounds and music from the AMPICO Player Pianos with rolls of great pianists such as Rachmaninov to a 1908 piano-playing machine that was owned by the real life 'Model of a Modern Major-General' in Gilbert and Sullivan's opera *The Pirates of Penzance*. Here, too, are an 1895 Polyphon musical box and a 1929 Wurlitzer theatre pipe organ from the Regent Cinema, Brighton. This collection has featured in numerous television and radio programmes though the family is no stranger to media fame as Paul's grandfather, Bransby Williams (1870-1961), was the only great Music Hall star to have had his own BBC television show in the early 1950s.

Dobwalls
8 miles N of Looe on the A38

Just to the north of this large modern village lies **Dobwalls Adventure Park**, a

popular theme park which offers something for all the family. There is a charming Edwardian countryside museum, with a permanent exhibition on the life and work of English wildlife artists Steven Townsend and Carl Brenders; a miniature steam railway, based on an old North American railroad, that runs for two miles around the park's grounds; woodland play areas; indoor attractions and a restaurant and café.

Liskeard
7 miles N of Looe on the B3254

A picturesque and lively market town, situated on undulating ground between the valleys of the East Looe and Seaton Rivers, Liskeard was one of Cornwall's five medieval stannary towns - the others being Bodmin, Lostwithiel, Truro and Helston.

The name stannary comes from the Latin word for tin, 'stannum', and these five towns were the only places licensed to weigh and stamp the metal.

However, the town is an ancient one, and was mentioned in the *Domesday Book* in 1086. In 1240 it was granted its first Royal Charter by Robert, Earl of Cornwall, brother of Henry III, giving it the right to hold a market. In 1294 the town sent two members to parliament and continued to do so until the Reform Act of 1832. Notable among the MPs were Edward Gibbon, author of *The Decline and Fall of the Roman Empire*, and Isaac Foot, father of the famous Foot family.

The town has a long history as a centre for mineral extraction and, for centuries, the medieval Cornish tinners brought their smelted tin down from Bodmin Moor for weighing, stamping and taxing. The construction of the **Liskeard and Looe Union Canal**, linking the town with Looe, saw, by the 19th century, great quantities of both copper ore and granite also passing through Liskeard bound for the coast and beyond. In the 1850s, the canal was replaced by the Looe Valley branch of the Great Western Railway and a scenic stretch of the line is still open today, though the industrial cargoes have long since been replaced by passenger carriages. There are still remnants of the canal, which was finally drained and abandoned in 1910, to be seen. An annual walking festival using the railway takes place each September. The **Looe Valley Line** starts from its own station in Liskeard and drops under the main line to the quiet junction at Coombe. Here the

driver and guard change ends and the train reverses along the East Looe Valley for the seven-mile trip to Looe.

Though a small town, Liskeard boasts two sets of public buildings which are a reminder of its past importance and prosperity. The **Guildhall** was constructed in 1859 while the Public Hall opened in 1890 and is still used as the office of the town council. The local Museum is housed in Foresters Hall. Adjacent to the Passmore-Edwards Public Library stands **Stuart House**, a handsome Jacobean residence where Charles I stayed in 1644 while engaged in a campaign against the Parliamentarian forces at nearby Lostwithiel. **St Martin's Parish Church** is also worthy of a mention as, not only is it the second largest parish church in Cornwall, but this mainly 15th century building stands on Norman foundations, and has an early 20th century tower that blends in perfectly with the medieval architecture. In June 2002 HRH Prince Charles formally opened the **Liskeard and District Museum**, housed in the former Foresters Hall. It has a lively display of artefacts connected with the town. Finally, one of Liskeard's most curious features can be found in Well Lane, where an arched grotto marks the site of **Pipe Well**, also known as the "Well of St Martin's" and the "Well of Lyskerit", a medieval spring that is reputed to have curative powers, especially afflictions of the eyes. The well has never been known to run dry.

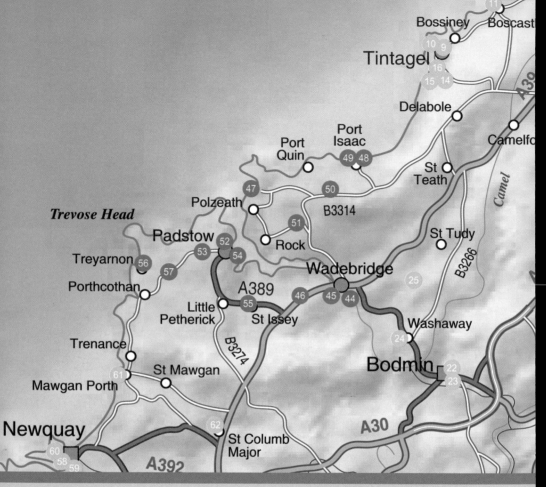

PLACES TO STAY, EAT AND DRINK

Denotes entries in other chapters

3 Padstow, Wadebridge and the Camel Estuary

The area around the River Camel and its estuary centres on the two towns of Wadebridge and Padstow. The former, located inland, was once a busy river port and, following the building of the 'Bridge on Wool', the historic lowest crossing place. An ancient and now quiet town, from which the Camel Trail heads off towards the foothills of Bodmin Moor, Wadebridge not only clings on to its trading past by being the home of the Royal Cornwall Agricultural Show but is also home to the John Betjeman Centre.

The Poet Laureate was introduced to the villages around the Camel estuary during boyhood holidays and thus began a life-long romance with the area. He died in 1984, at his second home, Trebetherick, and he is buried, along with his parents, in the graveyard of the ancient Church of St Enodoc, which stands among the sand dunes overlooking Padstow Bay. Those familiar with the great poet's verse will discover on a visit to this region many of the places of which he wrote, many of which remain little changed today.

Closer to the mouth of the River Camel, which is guarded now by Doom Bar, lies Padstow, a small fishing town that is now synonymous with the restaurateur Rick Stein and his seafood restaurant. Another old port, which is named after St Petroc, who landed here at the beginning of his missionary work in the West Country, Padstow has seen many distinguished visitors down the

Padstow Harbour

years, including Sir Walter Raleigh, who lived here for a time as Warden of Cornwall.

Nearby Prideaux Place, which also dates from the first Elizabethan age, is a marvellous mansion house that was built on the site of St Petroc's monastery. This family residence - the ancient Prideaux-Brune family have lived here for over 400 years - not only contains many treasures but it is also surrounded by beautiful parkland and gardens.

Wadebridge

Standing at the historic lowest bridging point on the River Camel, this ancient port and busy market town is now a popular holiday resort that is not only attractive but also is renowned for its craftware. Linking the moorland with the sea, Wadebridge has always been a bustling place and its establishment as a trading centre began in earnest in the 15th century. The first recorded mention of the town of Wadebridge was in 1313, when a market and two fairs were granted. In those days it was simply known as Wade. A major development occurred in the next century. The Reverend Lovibond, the vicar of St Petroc's, was seeking to convey his flock of sheep across the river in safety and in the 1460s he built the 320 foot long and now 14-arched bridge which can still be seen today. One of the longest bridges in Cornwall today, it originally had 17 arches and it is said that it was constructed on bridge piers that were sunk on to a foundation of woolsacks - hence its nickname of the **Bridge on Wool**. However, it seems more likely that the name refers, not to the building material, but to the source of the money to build it. So important was it that Oliver Cromwell himself came with 1500 troops to take it.

The bridge still carries the main road which links the town's two ancient parishes. The churches of these two parishes can still be seen today: 13th century **St Breock's Parish Church** stands in a picturesque wooded valley that is known as Nancient (from the Cornish for 'holy well') while across the

WEST PARK HOUSE

106 Egloshayle Road, Wadebridge, Cornwall PL27 6AG
Tel/Fax: 01208 813279

West Park House was built in 1820 as a gentleman's residence on the outskirts of Wadebridge and is set in well-kept, mature gardens with private off-street parking. The property enjoys views over the River Camel, while the surrounding countryside is an Area of Outstanding Natural Beauty and is ideal for a wide range of activities. The house itself is the beautiful home of Caroline Bishop, and

she is able to offer three guest rooms within the main house together with a self-catering cottage for two people.

BRIDGE ON WOOL

The Platt, Wadebridge, Cornwall PL27 7AQ
Tel: 01208 812750

The delightful **Bridge on Wool** is a pub that is packed with olde worlde charm. Its name comes from an old tradition that a 15th century bridge across the River Camel was built on sacks of wool. Sitting in the centre of town, it today combines tradition with modern standards of service, and is a friendly hostelry that is popular with visitors and locals alike. The décor is spotless and there is plenty of seating. Its choice of real ales is renowned, and it serves a good range of simple but tasty food in the summer months. There's a beer garden, and live music at weekends. Truly a pub to be proud of!

river from the main town, stands **St Petroc's Parish Church**, in Egloshayle, the church at the centre of Reverend Lovibond's ministry and to which he donated the money to build the imposing 80 feet tower.

To the southwest of St Breock lies **St Breock Downs**. In the heart of this exposed land stands the ancient **St Breock Downs Monolith** (English Heritage), a striking Bronze Age — standing stone that was originally 16 feet high and now weighs at least 16.75 tonnes, making it the heaviest in the county. It is also known as the Men Gurta (the Stone of Waiting). Other prehistoric remains, such as the **Nine Maidens,** a row of nine stones dating from the Bronze Age, can also be found on the downs.

This Bridge on Wool saw a steady growth in trade through Wadebridge and, with the advent of the railway in the 19th century, the port and town thrived. As a result the town's architecture is chiefly Victorian and, though now a quieter place, this busy shopping centre also draws to it local artists and craftsmen as well as holidaymakers and, each June, just to the west of the town centre, the **Royal Cornwall Show** is held. Another popular annual event is the **Wadebridge Folk Festival**, a feast of dance, music and fun that takes place on August Bank Holiday. The town's former railway station is now home to the **John Betjeman Centre** that is dedicated to the life and work of the Poet Laureate. Among the many tributes and intimate artefacts to be seen here are the poet's desk and chair and drafts of his books.

Another reminder that this is an ancient town can be found just to the south of the centre of Wadebridge, at Trevannion Culverhouse. This medieval **Dovecote** is one of only a few such structures in the county that have survived; it was used to provide both fresh eggs and fresh meat for the local manor house.

Although the railway line, which opened in 1899, closed in the 1960s, a stretch of the trackbed has been used to

THE ROYAL CORNWALL SHOW

Wadebridge, Cornwall PL27 7JE
e-mail: info@royalcornwall.co.uk
website: www.royalcornwall.co.uk

Over three days each June, an event that involves and reflects all aspects of life in Cornwall takes place at a permanent site just outside Wadebridge. It's the **Royal Cornwall Show**.

Besides being a truly Cornish event from the roots up, the show is a fantastic, multi-faceted spectacular which no visitor can afford to miss. Entertainment happens big-time at the Royal Cornwall Show.

The main ring programme changes each year and features the sort of acts you rarely get a chance to see altogether. Military bands, parachute teams, acts of daring, speed and skill combine to provide a truly enthralling display.

Then there's the shopping. Hundreds of trade stands offering massive choices on thousands of products. Garden machinery, garden furniture, wonderful craft works, books, art, Wellington boots ... the list is endless.

Food and drink is a feature of the show that every visitor must sample. Cornwall prides itself on the quality of its home-grown produce and the variety of eatables and drinkables on sale at the show is immense.

Tempting aromas abound. See if you can resist!

There's a massive motor fair, extravagant steam fair, a flower show full of wonder and colour; in the NatWest Countryside Area, conservation and country life provide a mix of fascination and tranquility.

Above all, the Royal Cornwall is an agricultural show. It is one of country's very best and for many people, the chance to wander round the cattle sheds, horse lines and sheep and pig pens is the highlight of their visit.

The Royal Cornwall Show takes place over the 9th, 10th & 11th June 2005 and 8th, 10th & 11th June 2006.

create the superb **Camel Trail**. Either walking or cycling, the trail leads up into the foothills of Bodmin Moor, to the east of Wadebridge, whilst to the west the path follows the River Camel to Padstow through an area that is rich in wildlife and, particularly, in wading birds such as herons. Wadebridge is more or less in the middle of the Camel Trail, which is part of the Cornish Way, a network of cycle routes covering Cornwall.

Around Wadebridge

Rock

4 miles NW of Wadebridge off the B3314

This former fishing village lies in a small estuary inlet opposite Padstow, and though fishing has all but ceased from here, Rock has retained its strong nautical links. With a sailing club and sailing and waterskiing schools, this is an ideal spot for those interested in watersports and, during the summer, is a bustling and popular place. The sandy beach, just north of the cove, is the departure point for the *Black Tor*, a passenger ferry to Padstow which runs a regular service throughout the summer. Anyone wishing to make the journey out of season has to summon the ferry from Padstow by waving the flag that is left at the ferry point for this very purpose. Open-air readings of the poetry of Sir John Betjeman are held during the summer on **Brea Hill** at Rock.

Trebetherick

5 miles NW of Wadebridge off the B3314

The simple yet delightful **St Enodoc Parish Church**, a Norman building with a squat 13th century stone spire, overlooks Padstow Bay and lies in the shadow of Brea Hill. On a number of occasions throughout its history this church has been all but submerged by windblown sand and, at these times, the congregation and the vicar would enter the building by way of an opening in the roof, though some say that this is no more than a fanciful tale. The sand was finally cleared away in the 1860s, when the church was restored, and the bell in the tower, which came from an Italian ship that was wrecked nearby, was added in 1875. The beautiful churchyard contains many graves of shipwrecked mariners who came to grief on the local sandbank known as Doom Bar or at other treacherous places along this stretch of coast. But what draws many people to this quiet place is **Sir John Betjeman's Grave**, who is buried just inside the gate. His mother lies buried by the north wall, and there is a memorial tablet to his father inside the buidling. The fondly remembered Poet Laureate spent many of his childhood holidays in the villages and coves around the Camel Estuary and his affection for the local people and the surrounding countryside was the inspiration for many of his works. One of his most famous poems, simply called *Trebetherick*, recalls his boyhood days spent here.

The church is reached across St Enodoc's Golf Course, which is regarded as one of the most scenic links courses in the country. The beach at Trebetherick is well known for its fine bathing and excellent surfing.

Polzeath and New Polzeath
5 miles NW of Wadebridge off the B3314

Surfers and holidaymakers flock to these two small resorts as the broad west-facing beach is not only ideal for surfing but the fine sands, caves and tidal rock pools make it a fascinating place for children. To the north of the villages, and much loved by Sir John Betjeman, is a beautiful coastal path that takes in the cliffs and farmland of **Pentire Point** and **Rumps Point**. Much of the coastline here is owned by the National Trust and, on the delightful Rumps Point promontory, stands **Rumps Cliff Castle**, an Iron Age fortification where the remains of its three defensive ramparts, two of which only were in use at any one time, can still be seen. One of three hill forts that once existed on the headland, this area is also known for its wild tamarisk, an elegant flowering shrub that is more commonly found around the shores of the Mediterranean.

In the 1930s, Pentire Head was saved from commercial development thanks to local fund raisers who bought the land and donated it to the National Trust. This lovely stretch of coastline is completely traffic free and offers some excellent walking country with views over the spectacular Camel Estuary.

Port Quin
5 miles N of Wadebridge off the B3314

This tiny hamlet, along with its small shingle cove, suffered greatly in the 19th century when the railways took away the slate trade from its once busy quay. The demise of the port was so swift that, at one time, outsiders thought that the entire population of Port Quin had been washed away in a great storm. The village remained more or less deserted for decades but, fortunately, it has now been restored with help of the National Trust and today it has a seasonal community who come here to holiday in the restored cottages that make up this pleasant and peaceful little village.

Situated to the west on Doyden Point, and overlooking Port Quin, stands **Doyden Castle**, a squat 19th century castellated folly which is now a holiday home owned by the National Trust.

Port Isaac

Port Isaac

5 miles N of Wadebridge on the B3267

Surrounded, like its neighbour Port Gaverne, by open countryside, Heritage Coast land and an Area of Outstanding Natural Beauty, Port Isaac is a

PORT GAVERNE HOTEL

Port Isaac, North Cornwall PL29 3SQ
Tel: 01208 880244 Fax: 01208 880151

Situated near a secluded cove close to the ancient fishing port of Port Isaac, the **Port Gaverne Hotel** reflects all that is best in Cornish hospitality and tradition. Step outside the door and you can swim in crystal clear waters or sunbathe on a warm beach with one or two small boats pulled up beyond the waterline. Truly idyllic!

The hotel was once an old inn frequented by the crews of the slate vessels that called in at Port Gaverne and is full of history and charm. It now offers all the amenities you would expect from a first class hotel with its 14 comfortable en-suite rooms, equipped with all the modern comforts.

A well stocked bar carries a wide range of good local ales, wines and spirits, whilst the restaurant is famous throughout the area for the quality of its food, prepared by one of the best chefs in Cornwall. The food is fresh and locally sourced wherever possible, ensuring a culinary experience you will remember.

The Port Gaverne Hotel makes an ideal base from which to explore an area steeped in history and rich in scenery and there are numerous outdoor activities, including golf, sailing and fishing, to indulge in within the vicinity. If that sounds too active, why not just laze away the days in the warm Cornish climate!

THE CROW'S NEST

4 The Terrace, Port Isaac, Cornwall PL29 3SG
Tel/Fax: 01208 880305
e-mail: sharonandtony@crowsnestweb.co.uk
website: www.crowsnestweb.co.uk

The Crow's Nest is a friendly, family-run pub located high up above the bay at Port Isaac, and worth visiting for the superb views if nothing else! The bar is simply furnished, with the large windows looking out to sea providing all the spectacle you could possibly need. The bar stocks a variety of local ales and tasty home-made food is served all day every day, with breakfasts from 9.30am. Three comfortable en-suite guest rooms are also available.

wonderful old-world fishing village that has retained much of its ancient character and charm. At one time it exported corn, which is how it got its name, "Porth Izic", meaning the "port of corn". A busy port since the Middle Ages, fishing is still an important industry here, though the heyday of Port Isaac was in the 19th century when not only fish, but cargoes of stone, coal, timber and pottery were loaded and unloaded on the quayside.

At one time, huge quantities of pilchard were landed and processed here and, after the arrival of the railway, these were gutted and packed in the village's many fish cellars before being despatched by train to London and beyond. One of these old cellars is now an inshore lifeboat station, while others have found a wide variety of other uses. At the harbour, known locally as the Platt, fishermen still land their catches, and for visitors sea fishing is available either from off the rocks or from chartered boats. The centre of this conservation village is concentrated around the protected harbour where 18th and 19th century cottages line the narrow alleys and 'opes' that wend their way down to the coast. One lane is particularly narrow and goes by the name of 'Squeeze-'ee-belly Alley', which provides a warning to visitors of the dangers of indulging in too many Cornish cream teas. In fact, some people have claimed that it is the narrowest street in the world.

Just inland from the village can be found the double ramparts of Tregeare Rounds, a Celtic hill fort that was excavated in 1904. Among the finds uncovered here were pottery fragments thought to be around 2000 years old. Some think it is the "Dimilioc" where, Geoffrey of Monmouth tells us, King Arthur was born. King Uther Pendragon lay siege to and killed the Earl of Cornwall because he (Pendragon) had fallen in love with the earl's beautiful wife, Igerna. After the earl's death, Igerna fled to Tintagel where, with the help of Merlin, Uther seduced Igerna, who later gave birth to the future King Arthur.

Port Gaverne

5 miles N of Wadebridge off the B3267

A busy fishing port in the 19th century where, in one season, over 1,000 tons of pilchards were landed and processed in the village's fish cellars or 'pilchard palaces', Port Gaverne also saw over 100 ships a year docking to pick up slate from the Delabole quarry. Today, most of the large stone buildings, including some of the old fish cellars, have been converted into holiday accommodation and tourism has taken over as the mainstay of the local economy. One of the safest beaches along the North Cornwall coast, Port Gaverne beach is pebbled and, at low tide, an expanse of sand dotted with rock pools is revealed. Sixteen acres of land and some property is owned here by the National Trust, including some of the cellars.

Trelights

4½ miles N of Wadebridge off the B3314

Close to the village lies the only public garden on the North Cornwall coast - **Long Cross Victorian Gardens** (see panel below) which now belong to a hotel. A real garden lover's delight, it has a fascinating Victorian maze and a secret garden as well as some superb panoramic views. Granite and water have been used to create imaginative features amongst the 19th century plants and plantings and children will delight in visiting the Pets Corner and using up some energy in the adventure playground in the beer garden. Cream teas and meals are served in the garden, and weekly folk nights are held in the summer.

LONG CROSS VICTORIAN GARDENS

Trelights, Port Isaac, Cornwall PL29 3TF
Tel: 01208 880243
e-mail: info@longcrosshotel.co.uk
website: www.longcrosshotel.co.uk

On Cornwalls North coast, near Port Isaac, is the Long Cross Victorian Garden, owned by the Long Cross Hotel and now beautifully restored after many years of neglect.

The garden was laid out to overcome the difficulties of the local climate with its strong winds laden with salt. Many of the plants have shiny or leathery leaves to afford protection from the salt and those most tolerant are planted in hedge form to protect the rest.

In the centre of the garden is the Prospect, from where there are panoramic views over the coastline. An ornamental pond can be found in the centre of the garden, close to

which is the tea garden. An aviary is in one corner and children are well catered for with a playground and pets corner.

The Hotel itself offers well-appointed accommodation and excellent food, while the Tregenna Tavern also serves morning coffee, lunches, cream teas and dinner.

THE FOURWAYS INN

St Minver, Wadebridge, Cornwall PL27 6QH
Tel: 01208 862384
website: www.fourwaysinn.co.uk

The Fourways Inn is a traditional 17th-century inn which has been owned by the Mercer family for over three quarters of a century. With an immaculate, freshly painted white frontage and prominent corner site, the pub attracts locals as well as many tourists. Venturing inside you will find a traditional bar boasting an open log fire, slate floors and low beamed ceilings. The pub is open daily for real ales and tasty home-made food.

Accommodation is available with 9 en-suite rooms all recently refurbished to a very high standard.

St Minver

4 miles NW of Wadebridge off the B3314

The village is visited mainly because of **St Menefreda's Parish Church**. A church certainly stood here in Saxon times, though the present one dates at least from the mid 13th century, when William of Saint Menefreda paid homage to the Prior of Bodmin. The slate pillars in the north aisle are Norman, and the granite pillars of the south aisle are 15th century. The bench ends date from the 15th century, and are the church's greatest glory. One represents Adam and Eve, while another represents Henry II. The church also owns three "Vinegar Bibles" printed in 1717, which, instead of having "The Parable of the Vineyard" in Chapter 20 of St Luke's Gospel has instead "The Parable of the Vinegar". the Vinegar Bibles have other misprints as well, and can be viewed by arrangement.

St Endellion

4 miles N of Wadebridge on the B3314

This charming village has the particularly interesting **Parish Church of St Endelienta**, built of Lundy Island granite, which houses a major work of the sculptor known as the Master of St Endellion. An anonymous artist in every respect of his life, the Master of St Endellion has, however, been immortalised by his superb tomb, which is beautifully carved in black Catacleuse stone. The church itself is dedicated to St Endelienta, a Celtic saint who lived solely, so it is said, on cow's milk. When a local lord killed her cow in a dispute with a local farmer, he was himself killed by King Arthur, who was St Endelienta's godfather. She was able to bring both the cow and the lord back to life. When she died a cart pulled by an ox carried her body, as she had decreed, and when it stopped, that was to be the place of her shrine. The church has a long tradition of bell-ringing and is also the venue of an annual music festival, where a string quartet named in honour of the church performs. It was at St Endelienta's that Sir John Betjeman worshipped.

St Kew

3½ miles NE of Wadebridge off the A39

There are only a few buildings neighbouring the light and airy 15th century **St Kew and St Doghow Parish Church**, which can be found in a wooded hollow, and they include the large late Georgian rectory and an Elizabethan inn. The village is also home to an **Ogham Stone**, an unusual feature in Cornwall and one that is more commonly associated with southwest Ireland. Given its name because it is inscribed with the Ines of Ogham script, the stone also bears a Latin inscription. The ancient name for the village was Landochou, meaning the Church of Doghow. Kew and Doghow were said to be brother and sister.

Padstow

For many centuries, Padstow's sheltered position in a narrow gulley on the western side of the Camel estuary has made it a welcome haven for vessels seeking respite from the perils of the sea. The only safe harbour along this stretch of the North Cornwall coast, after the

---

THE METROPOLE

Station Road, Padstow, Cornwall PL28 8DB
Tel: 01841 532486 Fax: 01841 532867
e-mail: info@the-metropole.co.uk
website: www.the-metropole.com

Part of the new Richardson Group of hotels, **The Metropole** enjoys a prime location overlooking the Camel estuary and only moments from the town centre and harbour. An imposing and substantial building, it opened its doors as a hotel in 1904 (at that time it was called the South Western).

It has 50 bedrooms, some with sea views, all en suite, with tv, direct-dial telephone and tea/coffee making facilities; the range comprises standard rooms, feature rooms, mini-suites and four-posters. An excellent menu changes daily in the restaurant, where the chefs use high-quality produce, including fish fresh from the sea, in imaginative, well-conceived dishes.

The Met Café Bar is a pleasant spot for a light lunch, afternoon tea, cream teas or a less formal evening meal: fish cakes, chicken Caesar salad, sausages and mash, sautéed king prawns, to name but a few. All these dishes can be ordered in small or large portions, and to accompany the food are wines from their extensive selection by the bottle or two sizes of glass.

Amenities at the Metropole (General Manager Andrew Jenkins) include an outdoor pool open in high summer.

rocks, currents and winds of the river mouth have been negotiated, the town has been settled by many different people over the years including the prehistoric Beaker folk, Romans, Celtic saints and marauding Vikings. However, the silting up of the River Camel in the 19th century created a new hazard for shipping coming in and going out of Padstow harbour and the evocatively named **Doom Bar**, which restricts entry into the estuary mouth, effectively put an end to this ancient settlement continuing as a major port. The silting up also necessitated moving the Padstow lifeboat on to the open sea, at Trevose Head, five miles away. A van is on constant standby to take the crew from the town to the boathouse as soon as the maroon goes off.

Padstow was originally called Petrocstow, after the missionary St Petroc landed here in the 6th century. The son of a Welsh chieftain, St Petroc, like St Francis of Assisi, had a special empathy with animals and according to legend drew the splinter from the eye of a dragon, saved a deer from a hunt and, most spectacularly, rescued a sea monster trapped in a lake. Before moving on to Bodmin Moor to continue his missionary work, St Petroc founded a Celtic monastery here and **St Petroc Major Parish Church** still bears his name. On his death, St Petroc was buried in Padstow; then, in the 12th century, his bones were transferred to St Petroc's Church in Bodmin, where they were placed in an ivory casket, which can

WOODLANDS COUNTRY HOUSE

Treator, Nr Padstow, Cornwall PL28 8RU
Tel: 01841 532426
e-mail: info@woodlands-padstow.co.uk
website: www.woodlands-padstow.co.uk

Pippa and Hugo Woolley and their family greet guests with a friendly smile and a cup of tea at **Woodlands Country House**. Their fine Victorian house, its redbrick façade adorned with white detailing, enjoys a tranquil rural setting with views that stretch over farmland to Trevose Bay.

The house has nine letting bedrooms for Bed & Breakfast, all with bath or shower en suite, tv/video, telephone with modem access, beverage tray and top-quality linen, towels and toiletries; the Bay Room boasts a handsome four-poster, and two of the rooms are suitable for disabled and wheelchair users. They are on the ground floor and have a ramped entrance.

Cornish clotted cream fudge and fresh milk are typical thoughtful touches that make a stay here even more special. The Blue Room is a good spot to relax with a drink and a book, and the garden (with croquet lawn) is a pleasant place for a summer stroll.

Days at Woodland start in splendid style with a superb breakfast with options including home-made muesli, fruit compote, prime Padstow bacon and sausages, devilled kidneys, kedgeree, kippers, eggs benedict and a fine selection of teas.

Padstow Harbour

Today, Padstow's harbour and nearby shopping streets throng with visitors throughout the summer who come here to see the narrow alleyways and tightly packed slate hung buildings of the old quarter, which has managed to retain much of its medieval character. The influence of the sea is never far away in Padstow and, more recently, it has become linked with seafood and the famous chef and restaurateur Rick Stein.

still be seen. Today's building dates from the 13th and 14th centuries and, as well as the octagonal font of Catacleuse stone carved by the Master of St Endellion, there is a striking Elizabethan pulpit and some rather amusing bench ends. Beginning at the door of the church is the **Saints Way**, a middle distance footpath that follows the route that was taken by travellers and pilgrims crossing Cornwall on their way from Brittany to Ireland.

The monastery that St Petroc founded here was destroyed, along with most of the town, during a Viking raid in the 10th century. Later, in the 10th century, King Athelstan granted the town the Right of Sanctuary, enabling criminals to seek refuge from the law here, that was only repealed by Henry VIII at the time of the Dissolution.

Any exploration of Padstow should begin at the town's focal point, its **Harbour,** which is now home to a fishing fleet and which resists the rise and fall of the tide by means of a sluice gate. Here can be found many of Padstow's older buildings including, on the South Quay, **Raleigh's Cottage** where Sir Walter Raleigh lived when he was Warden of Cornwall, and the minute **Harbour Cottage**. **Raleigh's Court House**, where he collected the taxes, stands close by beside the river. A popular attraction here is the **National Lobster Hatchery** (see panel on page 84), a centre filled with information about lobsters; visitors can see lobsters developing from an egg, still attached to a female, into a juvenile ready to be released into the wild.

On North Quay is the 15th century **Abbey House** that is now a private residence but was, once, a meeting place for local merchants. Padstow also continues to celebrate May Day in a traditional way that has its origins back in pagan times. Beginning at midnight on the eve of May Day and lasting throughout May 1, the townsfolk sing in the new morning and then follow the **Obby Oss** - a man in a black frame-hung cape and wearing a grotesque mask - around the narrow streets of Padstow until late evening on May 1 when the Obby Oss retires. The suggested origins of the Obby Oss are many and diverse: rain-maker, fertility symbol, a deterrent to a feared landing by the French, or simply a welcome to summer.

On the northern outskirts of Padstow (follow the brown signs off the B3276) stands **Prideaux Place**, a magnificent Elizabethan mansion that for over 400 years has been the home of the Prideaux-Brune family. The origins of this ancient Cornish family go back to the 11th century, and William, one of the present owner's sons, is named after his 26 times great grandfather William the Conqueror. Built on the site of St

THE NATIONAL LOBSTER HATCHERY

South Quay, Padstow, Cornwall PL28 8BL
Tel:01841 533877
e-mail:
hatchery@NationalLobsterHatchery.co.uk
website: www.hatchery.freeserve.co.uk

The National Lobster Hatchery is dedicated to promoting and contributing to the responsible management of coastal marine resources, whilst also acting as a resource for education, conservation and research.

At the forefront of the work carried out here is the lobster restocking project, where fishermen bring egg laden female lobsters in to enable them to release their offspring where there are no predators. The young lobsters are then raised to a size where they can look after themselves and are released back into the sea. This work is on view for anyone coming into the visitor centre, along with a wealth of information and activities.

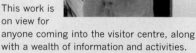

One of the main aims of the hatchery is education and groups from schools and colleges can be provided with activities and workshops to further their knowledge of aquaculture. Research is another very important aspect, from analysing lobster behaviour to investigating the dietary composition for larval lobsters.

The National Lobster Hatchery is open all year 7 days a week and there is a gift shop selling marine related items and a range of books.

'Obby 'Oss, Padstow

Prideaux-Brune, when he was a boy playing in the house.

The Elizabethan oak front door still has its original lock, and throughout the house there are reminders of the history of this area of Cornwall, and of events in Britain, and of the American Army. In the dining room is a carving of Queen Elizabeth I standing on a pig - this apparently represents her stamping out vice. The treasures in the Drawing Room include a very diplomatic miniature showing Charles I on one side and Oliver Cromwell on the other. A wonderful and interesting house, Prideaux Place is surrounded by fantastic gardens and parklands, including one of the oldest deer parks in England, which were laid out in Capability Brown-style in the 18th century. Also in the grounds are a temple, Roman antiquities, a 9th century Cornish cross and the newly restored stables with their plaster coat of arms and two exhibitions - one of old farm equipment, the other of past film location work at the house. Peter O'Toole, Joanna Lumley, Ralph Fiennes, Helena Bonham Carter, Mel Smith, Ben Kingsley and Richard E Grant have all recently acted at Prideaux Place.

Petroc's monastery, this E-shaped house was completed in 1592, with later additions and alterations in a variety of architectural styles. In the 18th century Edmund Prideaux added the formal Italian gardens, and in 1810 Edmund's grandson Charles extended and altered the house in the Gothic style, which was fashionable at the time due to the building of Strawberry Hill at Richmond near London. The house has 81 rooms, of which 44 are bedrooms, and of these just six are habitable. The place is also reputed to be haunted. Some of the other rooms are as the American Army left them at the end of the Second World War. Visitors to the house can see a wealth of family and royal portraits, paintings by John Opie, an 18th century artist from St Agnes, fine furniture, exquisite porcelain and also a splendid 16th century plaster ceiling in the Great Chamber which was rediscovered by present owner, Peter

Around Padstow

Tredinnick

3 miles S of Padstow off the A389

To the south of this small stone-built village lies **Shires Family Adventure Park** - one of the county's best kept family parks. Along with the shire horses and new born foals on show here, which include a World Champion, there are numerous other farmyard friends as well as a wealth of other activities to keep the whole family happy for hours. There are woodland trails through the Enchanted Forest to Greengate Meadow, where there is the chance to sight moles, badgers and other shy woodland creatures, whilst the adventure playground, with aerial bridges and slides, provides another source of entertainment. Inside, the fun does not stop as there is a complete indoor play area and, for those needing refreshment, the Camelot Café.

St Issey

2 miles S of Padstow on the A389

St Issey was either yet another of King Brychan Brycheiniog of Wales's 24 daughters, or, more likely, an Irish saint (also called Itha or Ida) who was born about AD 480 and was descended from one of the Irish High Kings. On 1st February 1869, the medieval tower of **St Issey's Parish Church** collapsed and, remarkably, its destruction was captured by an early photographer, the resulting photograph of the tower's demise also showing a top-hatted policeman looking on helplessly. The present St Issey Parish Church dates from 1871, though there are remnants of some 14th and 15th century work still to be seen. Not only did the church have to be rebuilt, the Catacleuse stone altar piece by the Master of St Endellion had to be meticulously rebuilt piece by piece. There are references to a church at this

THE WHITE HOUSE

St Issey, Nr Padstow, Cornwall PL27 7QE
Tel: 01841 540884
website: www.whitehousebandb.co.uk

The **White House** is an extremely comfortable B&B that appeals to people who enjoy peace and quiet, great standards of service and outstanding value for money. It sits on the A389 between Padstow and Wadebridge, and makes a great base from which to explore this beautiful part of Cornwall. It has three en suite rooms that are both spacious and comfortable, with designer-

inspired décor. Beautifully cooked breakfasts are served in the cosy dining room, and though there are no evening meals, there is a friendly pub just yards away that serves wonderful food.

spot going back to 1190, when the bishop of Exeter gave its patronage to the dean and chapter of Exeter cathedral.

Whilst visiting Padstow in October 1842, the novelist Charles Dickens, inspired by his time in the ancient port, wrote his much-loved story, *A Christmas Carol*, in which he mentions both Tinnens Cottages and a lighthouse - the one at Trevose Head. His friend, Dr Miles Marley, whose son, Dr Henry Frederick Marley, practised in Padstow for 51 years, provided the surname for Scrooge's partner, Jacob Marley. In this heartwarming seasonal story, Dickens actually reworks an idea that first began as an interlude in *Pickwick Papers* and it is plain that the Gabriel Grub character was a prototype for the grasping and miserly Ebenezer Scrooge. Dr Henry Marley died in January 1908, at the age of 76, at his home in Mellingey, St Issey, and his funeral took place in the parish church.

Little Petherick
2 miles S of Padstow on the A389

This village sits close to St Issey, on the opposite bank of a little creek. By 1858 **St Petroc's Parish Church** (originally built in the 13th and 14th centuries) was in such a ruinous state that it was rebuilt, using as much of the old material as possible, and also incorporating some material from other local

medieval churches that had been demolished. The footpath that follows Little Petherick Creek to its confluence with the River Camel also leads to a splendid viewpoint at which there can be seen an **Obelisk** that was built in 1887 to celebrate Queen Victoria's Golden Jubilee.

Bedruthan Steps
5½ miles SW of Padstow off the B3276

By far the best view of this beach, with its curious rock formations, can be found from the grassy clifftops 300 feet above. A steep flight of steps, cut into the cliff by the National Trust, leads the way

Bedruthan Steps

Looking out to Sea, Bedruthan Steps

down to the rock strewn beach which, at low tide, also incorporates a long sweep of sand. The giant slate rocks scattered here have been eroded by the waves and their uniform shape has helped to account for them being, according to local legend, thought of as the stepping stones used by the Cornish giant Bedruthan.

One of the most interesting and dramatic sights to be found along this stretch of the North Cornish coast, some of the larger of these massive flat-topped slabs have been given names of their own. **Samaritan Island** is named after a ship wrecked on the beach in 1846 - with the locals 'rescuing' the cargo of luxurious silks and satins for themselves. Another rock, whose curious formation

has been likened to the profile of Queen Elizabeth I, is referred to as **Queen Bess Rock**. However, any resemblance there ever was to the Virgin Queen has long since been wiped away by the wind and the waves. The National Trust has built a small visitor's centre. Bathing at Bedruthan Steps is not recommended.

Porthcothan
4½ miles SW of Padstow on the B3276

This tiny village overlooks a deep, square cove, with a sandy beach, that is protected by two headlands, at each side of the cove. Today, much of the land around the cove is owned by the National Trust, and there is a car park and toilets operated by the local council.

TREGLOS HOTEL

Constantine Bay, nr Padstow,
Cornwall PL28 8JH
Tel: 01841 520727 Fax: 01841 521163
e-mail: stay@tregloshotel.com
website: www.tregloshotel.com

Overlooking Constantine Bay and at the heart of what has become known as Betjeman Country, **Treglos Hotel** is a delightful place that provides superb accommodation for the discerning holiday-maker. The hotel has been in the same family for more than 30 years and today is owned and personally run by Jim Barlow with the aid of his professional and friendly staff.

Carefully manicured lawns lead up to the hotel where the atmosphere is more that of a country house than a seaside hotel. The values of a bygone age have not been forgotten here – afternoon tea is served to guests resting in a shady part of the well-established gardens, or before a roaring fire in the cosy lounge.

The sea air here is sure to give guests an appetite and the restaurant at the Treglos Hotel provides an evening meal that will satisfy the hungriest guest. Local seafood is the speciality of the house and, along with vegetables from the hotel's own gardens and a well-stocked wine cellar, dining here is a treat to savour. Fine dining, glorious views and gracious living certainly draw many guests to this luxurious hotel and, for the more energetic, there are magnificent coastal walks, golf at several courses close by, special bridge holidays, sea fishing and the hotel's own heated indoor swimming pool.

In days gone by, this cove was the haunt of smugglers, who were able to land their contraband here safely and in secret. The footpath over the southern headland leads to **Porth Mear**, another secluded cove beyond which, on a low plateau, is a prehistoric earthwork of banks and ditches.

Treyarnon

3½ miles W of Padstow off the B3276

This small hamlet lies at the southern end of **Constantine Bay** and has one of a succession of fine sandy beaches that can be found on either side of Trevose Head. Though conditions here are ideal for surfing, the strong currents around the beach make swimming hazardous. The sand dunes backing the beaches along Constantine Bay are covered with marram grass and tamarisk shrubs and through here runs the **South West Coast Path** on its way northwards to Trevose Head.

Trevose Head

4 miles NW of Padstow off the B3276

This remote headland is reached via a toll road, but it is a trip well worth making as, from the headland, there are wonderful views down the coast that take in bay after bay. Two and a half miles of coast here has been designated as the Tevose Head Heritage Coast. At the tip of the headland stands **Trevose Lighthouse**, which was built in 1847 and has a beam that reaches 20 miles out to sea. Built on the sheer granite cliffs, the light of the house stands some 204 feet above sea level and from here, at night, lights from four other lighthouses can be seen. Still very much a working lighthouse today, a tour can be taken of the building (on week days only).

After Padstow had lost three lifeboats on the sand bars of the silting up Camel estuary, the lifeboat station was moved to **Mother Ivey's Bay**, on the eastern side of the headland, in the 1960s. Also on the eastern side of Trevose Head lies **Harlyn Bay** where the site of an Iron Age cemetery was excavated. The remains that were unearthed here can be seen in the Royal Cornwall Museum in Truro.

St Merryn
2 miles W of Padstow on the B3276

St Merryn was a Welsh saint born around AD 496 who went to live in Brttany. On his way, he founded a small church, where the present **St Merryn's Parish Church** now stands. Dating originally from the 13th and 14th centuries, it was partially restored in the 20th century, when the windows, floor, pews and roof were replaced, but there is still much to be admired. The font came from the ruins of the nearby St

SEVEN BAYS

1 Crossroads, St Merryn, Near Padstow, Cornwall PL28 8NF
Tel: 01841521560

The picturesque hamlet of St Merryn is home to one of the best bistros in Cornwall - the **Seven Bays**. It is owned and managed by Sue Pennington and Tim Ellsmore. Tim dedicates his life to the cooking and serving of good food, and once cooked alongside Rick Stein at Padstow. Step inside this restaurant and you're in a food lover's paradise.

As you would imagine, classic fish dishes are served here, but Tim also likes to use fresh, local beef and vegetables in his cuisine, which is fast establishing a fine reputation in the area. Pay it a visit and be prepared to be amazed at the imaginative menus!

Constantine's Church.

In the garden of a private house in this small village is a modern day Celtic monument that is as impressive as any of the many prehistoric sites found in Cornwall. **The Angel's Runway**, three large granite standing stones with a huge, flat capstone, was built in 1987, and is a direct copy of a Neolithic chamber tomb. There are other copies of famous Cornish stone circles and rocking stones to be seen here. The parish of St Merryn has no fewer than seven unspoilt beaches on its seaward boundary.

Trevone

1½ miles NW of Padstow off the B3276

Sheltered by Trevose Head and Rumps Point, the seemingly gentle and quiet sandy cove at Trevone is guarded by vicious offshore rocks. A quiet place that can be reached by way of the coastal path from Padstow, the rock pools that are formed on the beach at low tide, particularly one that is around six feet deep, provide the safest bathing. An 80-feet deep blowhole jut above the beach is a great attraction.

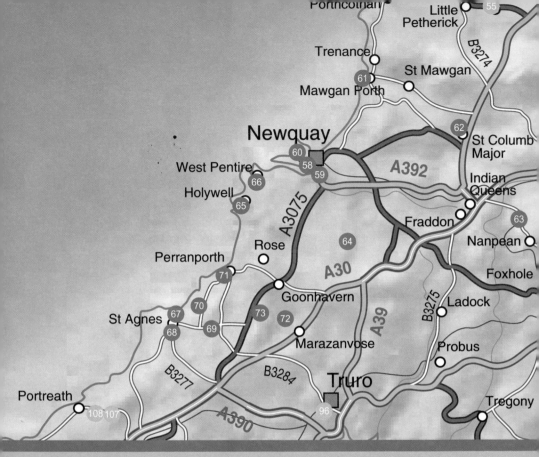

PLACES TO STAY, EAT AND DRINK

● Denotes entries in other chapters

4 Mid Cornwall North

With some of the most spectacular coastal scenery certainly in Cornwall if not the whole of England, the rugged coastline in and around Newquay is well worth exploring. Synonymous with surfing, it is undoubtedly Cornwall's most popular holiday resort, with all the traditional trappings. Though not as picturesque as St Ives or some of the other seaside towns in the county, it has managed to retain some of its past, particularly around the harbour. In earlier days it was a fishing village that was very dependent on pilchards, and on Towan Headland still stands the Huer's Hut from which the shoals of fish were spotted and their whereabouts passed on to the fishermen.

Further down the coast lies St Agnes, a place that is littered with the reminders of Cornwall's mining tradition and, standing on a clifftop, are the stark yet atmospheric remains of Wheal Coates. Other remains to be seen include, near St Newlyn East, East

Wheal Rose, Cornwall's richest lead producing mine and also the scene of the industry's greatest disaster. The *Poldark* novels of Winston Graham, who wrote from his base in Perranporth, brought the beauty, romance and harsh realities of life of this mining area of Cornwall to thousands.

However, the history of this northern coastal area of Cornwall dates back well beyond mining. As well as the Iron Age remains of Castle-an-Dinas, near St Columb Major, a site associated with St Piran, the patron saint of Cornwall, who journeyed here from Ireland on a millstone in the 6th century, there stands a splendid Celtic cross and a

Newquay Beach

plaque marking the place of St Piran's Oratory. St Columb Major, though denied the honour of playing host to Cornwall's cathedral in the late 19th century, does still carry on the tradition of hurling the silver ball each year. A cross between hurling and football, this boisterous game, which involves two large teams, has its roots in the ancient kingship contests.

Tucked away in a maze of narrow, leafy lanes, close to Kestle Mill, lies Trerice, a magnificent Elizabethan manor house that is considered a particularly fine architectural gem. Built by Sir John Arundell in 1571, and now in the care of the National Trust, this charming house with a Dutch-style gabled façade retains many of its fine original features, and highlights include fine oak and walnut furniture, collections of clocks and drinking glasses, English and Oriental porcelain, portraits by the celebrated Cornish painter John Opie and a magnificent window in the hall, made up of 576 panes. The Cornish game called 'kayles', a form of skittles, can be played on the parade ground, and in part of the great barn is an unusual attraction in the form of a lawnmower museum, with more than 100 machines spanning 150 years.

Newquay

Despite first appearances this is an ancient settlement, and there is evidence of an Iron Age coastal fort among the cliffs and caves of **Porth**

TREWYTH TEA GARDENS & RESTAURANT

76 Edgcumbe Avenue, Newquay,
Cornwall TR7 2NN
Tel: 01637 874417

If you visit the **Trewyth Tea Gardens and Restaurant** in Newquay, you'll never forget the experience. It is reckoned to be the finest tearoom and restaurant, not just in Newquay, but for many miles around. It is a trim, well-maintained building with plenty of character high up on Edgcumbe Avenue.

A former private house, it has been owned and run by Havina and David Emery for over 20 years. Inside is just as trim and smart as its exterior, with plenty of space and light to enjoy the good food that is always on offer.

People return again and again to the Trewyth, and it is no wonder. One look at the menus tells you that the food is special. From simple snacks such as jacket potatoes, sandwiches and cakes and pastries during the day to a comprehensive evening menu, there is something for everyone. Plus, of course, you could always indulge in a gorgeous Cornish cream tea! Main courses in the evening range from prime steaks with all the trimmings, to breast of Barbary duck, local fish and shellfish and Thai green curry. The place seats 30 inside, plus 30 more in the newly added conservatory. In the summer months, up to 80 people can be seated on the decked terraced area.

Trewyth is closed for two weeks in November, Christmas Day and from January 6 to St Valentine's Day. On all other days it is open from 9.30 am to 9.30 pm. It is licensed for diners only, and all major credit and debit cards are accepted. Sunday roasts are available between 12 noon and 2 pm on Sundays. Booking in advance is advisable.

Newquay Harbour

Island - a detached outcrop which is connected to the mainland by a sturdy wooden bridge supported by girders. The old part of Newquay is centred around the **Harbour**, which was, for centuries, the heart of this once small fishing community. An important pilchard fishing village right up until the industry's decline at the beginning of the 20th century, the town also became a port for both the china clay and the mineral extraction industries, particularly with the coming of the railway. However, the harbour was too shallow to take the larger boats that were increasingly being used, and the trains brought tourists instead, turning it into Cornwall's major holiday resort. Now, with its beautiful rocky coastline and acres of golden sands, Newquay is famous throughout the world for its surfing.

The town takes its name from the 'New Kaye' that was built in the mid 15th century by the villagers who wanted to protect this inlet. As with many other villages along the coast, the main catch of Newquay's fishermen were pilchards and, on Towan Headland, the **Huer's Hut** (see also St Ives) can still be seen. Here, the Huer would scan the sea looking for shoals of pilchards, which caused the water to turn red, and, once spotted, he would alert the fishing crews by calling 'hevva, hevva', meaning 'found, found', through a long loud-hailer. He would then guide the boats towards the shoal with semaphore-style signals using a pair of bats known as bushes. The term 'hue and cry' comes from the same source.

Pilchards are still caught off many Cornish ports and are the chief ingredient of one of the county's most famous dishes. For **Stargazy Pie** (see also Mousehole), pilchards stuffed with onion and parsley are put into a pie with bacon, chopped hard-boiled egg, onion and seasoning. The heads of the fish are pushed through holes in the pastry to 'gaze' up at the stars as they cook, while allowing the oils in the head to soak down into the dish and flavour it. This dish is just one of several Cornish

THE LANHERNE

32 Ulalia Road, Newquay, Cornwall TR7 2PZ
Tel: 01637 872308

The **Lanherne,** a freehouse and restaurant, is by far the best family-run public house in Newquay, a holiday resort famous for its pubs and eating places. It sits in Ulalia Road, just a short walk from the centre of the town, the sea front and Newquay Zoo.

It has been owned and managed by Anne and Mark Lacayo for over five years, and together they have over 25 years experience in the licensing and catering trade, so know how to run a first class establishment. Originally built over 100 years ago as a private house, it has had many uses over the years, including a hospital during World War II and later a small maritime museum. Since the 1960s it has become a public house, and

is famous, among locals and visitors alike, for its hospitality, its friendliness, its great standards of service and its value for money.

Anne and Mark are constantly updating and renovating the place to make sure that it retains its great reputation, something that is greatly appreciated by the people who return again and again to experience its warm, friendly atmosphere and cosy ambience.

The Lanherne is open all day, every day, and sells three real ales, Sharp's Doom Bar, and two rotating ales that are always brewed in Cornwall. Plus there is a fine selection of beers, lagers, cider, wines and spirits.

The pub serves first class food between 12 noon and 2 pm and between 6 pm and 9 pm daily, and has a no smoking restaurant that seats 40 in absolute comfort. However, you can eat throughout the premises, or even

outside on the patio on summer days. All the food is freshly cooked on the premises using fresh local produce wherever possible, with Steve the head chef overseeing everything to make your meal a memorable one. You can choose from either a comprehensive printed menu or a daily changing specials board.

Specialities include homemade lasagne and steak and ale pie, which are both delicious! There are also homemade curries, fillet of salmon, a range of excellent sweets, as well as soup, burgers and sizzling steaks with all the trimmings.

On Sundays there is a special carvery, and you are well advised to book in advance for this. Children are more than welcome at this friendly establishment, and all credit and debit cards, with the exception of Diners and American Express, are accepted.

Newquay is one of Cornwall's most favourite resorts, the oldest part grouped round its harbour. It is an excellent place to have a family holiday, and so much of all that the county has to offer is within an easy drive.

specialities. Among others are **Cornish Pasties**, an all-in-one savoury pie of meat and vegetables for which there are almost as many recipes as cooks; Hevva Cake, now usually called Heavy Cake, a sweet loaf traditionally decorated with a criss-cross pattern resembling a fishing net (hevva - see above - was a term associated with the hauling in of the catch); Saffron Cake, somewhere between a fruit loaf and a fruit cake; Cornish Fairings, scrumptious ginger biscuits; and Cornish Splits, brioche-style sweetened rolls. The most famous ingredient is without a doubt **Cornish Clotted Cream**, still made by hand in small quantities on many farms as well as in bulk in dairies, and the essential highlight of a Cornish cream tea.

Though there is some Regency architecture to be found in Newquay, the rise of the town's fortunes, in the late 19th century, saw a rapid expansion and many of the large Victorian hotels and small residential houses still remain. It is the sea and beach which draw many here and, along with the more traditional English seaside pursuits, there is also a wide variety of attractions in and around the town to entertain the whole family.

Situated in Towan Bay, the **Blue Reef Aquarium** (previously called Sea Life Aquarium, but now one of a series of attractions around Britain with the same name - see panel below) is home to a wide variety of creatures that live beneath the waves. From the shallowest

BLUE REEF AQUARIUM

Towan Promenade, Newquay, Cornwall TR7 1DU
Tel: 01637 878134 Fax: 01637 872578
website: www.bluereefaquarium.co.uk

Blue Reef Aquarium takes visitors on an undersea voyage that explores the amazing range of marine life from around the world, from the beaches and cliffs of the local Cornish coastline to the spectacular 'underwater gardens' of the Mediterranean and the dazzling beauty of exotic tropical reefs.

The centrepiece of the museum is a stunning coral reef display housed in a giant 250,000 litre ocean tank that is home to hundreds of brightly coloured reef fish, puffer fish and black tip reef sharks.

This amazing spectacle can be seen from a boardwalk overlooking the atoll, from inside a glass cave or from inside an underwater walk-through tunnel. Open daily from 10 o'clock, the Aquarium has more than 30 living displays · the sea horses and the friendly rays are great favourites · and holds regular talks and feeding demonstrations.

Watergate Bay, Newquay

rock pool to the mysterious depths of the world's oceans, visitors here can see amazing fish and other creatures in their natural habitat and, by walking through an underwater tunnel, come face to face with the sharks.

Anyone looking to discover the characters and events that have shaped the history of this part of Cornwall will find that **Tunnels Through Time** holds many attractions. Through more than 70 realistic life-size figures dressed in authentic costumes and set in carefully constructed tableaux, the days of smugglers and highwaymen, plague victims and miners, King Arthur and Merlin are brought excitingly to life. The scariest part is the Dungeon of Despair, where visitors can hear the screams of victims suffering pain and torture in the name of old-time 'justice'. Children can enter only if accompanied by an adult.

Towan Beach is one of a succession of fine beaches overlooked by the town, and is the closest to the town centre. It is also ideal for children as it has a tidal paddling pool. **Great Western** and **Tolcarne** are also popular with families, though usually less crowded. In recent years, Newquay has acquired a reputation as one of the finest surfing centres in Britain and, throughout the year, thousands of surfers arrive here to catch the waves of the mile-long **Fistral Beach** or to watch the increasing number of national and international competitions held along this part of the

North Cornwall coast.

Along with the cafés and gift shops, the streets of Newquay are lined with a refreshing variety of shops offering everything for the surfer, both to buy and to hire. Another colourful summer attraction involves Newquay's fleet of traditional pilot gigs (30 feet rowing boats) which race each other over a six mile course set out in the bay. The biggest and most spectacular of Newquay's beaches is **Watergate Bay**, 3 miles out of town on the Padstow road. Here and at Crantock, Fistral, Towan, Great Western, Porth and Mawgan Porth beaches a lifeguard service operates in the summer. The first full-time lifeguards were hired by Newquay Town Council in 1959, and during the 1960s lifeguards were recruited from as far afield as Australia, South Africa and Hawaii. Since that time the local lifesaving clubs have been producing 'home-grown' lifeguards. During the 2001 season, Newquay was part of a pilot scheme run by the RNLI, who have made a commitment for 5 years to roll out Beach Rescue in the southwest in partnership with the local authorities, thus providing a better standard of training for lifeguards and consequently an improved service for visitors.

As well as boasting some of the finest beaches in Britain, Newquay has a green jewel in the shape of the 26-acre **Trenance Gardens**, formal gardens with streams and a boating lake next to the Gannel estuary, a haven for wildlife. Here the mild climate caused by the Gulf Stream ensures that palm trees flourish. The historic Heritage Cottages celebrated their 300th year in 2002 with a major restoration programme. Within Trenance Leisure Park, **Waterworld** offers two indoor swiimming pools, a 60 metre flume and other entertainment; there's also crazy golf and a mini train ride.

The park is also home to **Newquay Zoo**, where conservation, education and entertainment go hand in hand. With zebra, antelope and lions from the African plains to the nocturnal world of the Rodrigues bats, zoo trails and talks by the keepers, there is always plenty here to see and do for visitors of all ages. Two Siberian lynx are the latest additions to the animal collection.

Easter 2002 saw the launch of the Newquay Discovery Trail, with two trails starting at Killacourt and marked throughout their length by numbered slate discs. There are also hourly site-seeing tours of Newquay by bus during the summer season, leaving from Bank Street, though you can board or leave the bus at any point on the tour.

Around Newquay

Porth
1 mile E of Newquay on the A3059

Originally a separate village, with its own shipbuilding yards and pilchard cellars, Porth has now been engulfed by its larger neighbour Newquay. However, the fine wide sandy beach here still

Merrymoor Inn

Mawgan Porth, Cornwall TR8 4BA
Tel/Fax: 01637 860258
e-mail: info@merrymoorinn.com
website: www.merrymoorinn.com

All are welcome at the **Merrymoor Inn**, close to all the beaches in the wonderful resort of Mawgan Porth. Built in the 1930s, it has constantly been upgraded and improved over the years, making it one of the best inns in the area. With seven en suite rooms, as well as bar, lounge and restaurant facilities, it has something that is sure to appeal to everyone.

The service is immaculate, the prices are always reasonable, and the place has a fresh, efficient yet friendly feel to it that is sure to draw you back again and again.

brings visitors and **Trevelgue Head** becomes an island at high tide. An Iron Age fort once stood here.

Mawgan Porth
4 miles NE of Newquay on the B3276

On the coast at Mawgan Porth, which is a thriving community of 30 houses and several hotels, the remains of a Saxon settlement can be made out. Various 9th to 11th century dwellings that formed part of this fishing and herding community can be seen near the beach as well as the foundations of a larger courtyard house and a cemetery.

The coastline between here and Padstow, to the north, is rugged and among the most impressive to be found in Cornwall.

St Mawgan
4½ miles NE of Newquay off the B3276

This village, found inland from Mawgan Porth and in the beautiful, deep and

wooded Vale of Lanherne, provides a real oasis of calm. The restored 13th century **St Mawgan and St Nicholas Parish Church** has one of the finest collections of monumental brasses in the country and most are of the Arundell family (see also St Columb Major) whose 13th century former manor house, **Lanherne**, was taken over by a closed Carmelite order of nuns in 1794 who had fled the French Revolution. There is also a fine pulpit dating from 1553 and a 15th century rood screen.

Outside, in the churchyard, stands a beautifully carved lantern cross dating to around 1420, while here too can be seen an extraordinary timber memorial in the shape of the stern of a boat that is dedicated to ten unfortunate souls who froze to death in their lifeboat after being shipwrecked off the coast in 1846.

The village inn, **The Falcon**, is reputed to have been named during the Reformation when it was the practice to release a bird into the air to signal that a secret Catholic mass was about to take place.

Roche

10½ miles E of Newquay on the B3274

This old mining village, whose name is pronounced Roach, has the restored **St Gomonda Parish Church**, with a medieval granite tower from the 15th century and a pillared Norman font of Pentewan blue stone. However, what chiefly brings people to this unassuming place lies not in Roche but to the southwest on the granite outcrop of **Roche Rock**. A feat of medieval engineering, the 14th century two-storey **Hermitage** dedicated to St Michael perched here has, remarkably, stood the test of time and various legends have grown up around this refuge. It is thought that this cell and chapel were the final retreat of a leper, who survived with the help of his daughter Gundred, who brought food and water from a holy well up the hill each day to sustain him. Roche Rock is also associated with the legendary Cornish scoundrel, Jan Tregeagle, who attempted to seek sanctuary in the chapel while being pursued across the moors by a pack of headless hounds.

The rock itself is supposed to be connected to the Arthurian legend of Tristan and Iseult. It was here, in Ogrin's Chapel, that the lovers found refuge from King Mark of Cornwall.

St Columb Major

6 miles E of Newquay on the A39

Now thankfully bypassed by the main road, this small town was once considered as the site of Cornwall's cathedral, along with Bodmin, St Germans and Truro. However, the town's claims for this prestigious prize were not unfounded as the 12th to 15th century **St Columba's Parish Church** is unusually large and is also home to some of the finest 16th and 17th century monumental brasses in the county - those dedicated to the influential Arundell family (see also St Mawgan). It was several centuries earlier that Sir John Arundell, having supported Edward III in his wars against the Scots, was rewarded by the granting of a Royal

Charter, in 1333, which gave St Columb Major market town status.

There has been much conjectrure about who St Columba was. Some say he is the same Irish saint who crossed to Iona in Scotland, though why his influence should have stretched so far south is unclear. Others say that the St Columba commemorated here was in fact St Columba the Virgin, who was either French or Irish. According to legend, she scorned the advances of an unbeliever who wanted her to marry his son. When she resisted, he killed her at Ruthvoes, a couple of miles to the south of the town.

During the 19th century, this now quiet town enjoyed a period of great prosperity and, so sure were the town's officials of having Cornwall's cathedral sited here, that in the 1850s, a moated medieval tower house was rebuilt as a possible bishop's palace. Now called the **Old Rectory** it retains much of its grandeur. Another interesting building here is **The Red Lion Inn** which is renowned for its former landlord, James Polkinghorne, a famous Cornish wrestler who is depicted in action on a plaque on one of the inn's external walls.

St Columb Major has also managed to continue the tradition of playing, 'hurling the silver ball', a once common pastime throughout the county that is thought to have derived from the ancient kingship contests. Each Shrove Tuesday, and again eleven days later, two teams of several hundred people - the countrymen and the townsmen -

endeavour to carry a ball made of apple wood and encased in sterling silver through goals set two miles apart. A cross between hurling and football, the game is played here with great passion and enthusiasm, so much so in fact that the windows of houses and shops in the area have to be boarded up for the occasion. A similar game is played in St Ives in February each year.

A couple of miles southeast of St Columb Major, on Castle Downs, lie the remains of a massive Iron Age hill fort. Called **Castle-an-Dinas**, this was the major fort of the Dumnonia tribe who were in the area in around the 2nd century BC and, from here, they ruled the whole of Devon and Cornwall. The three earthwork ramparts enclose an area of over six acres and those climbing to the gorse-covered remains, some 700 feet above sea level, will be rewarded with panoramic views over the leafy Vale of Lanherne to the northwest and the unearthly landscape created by the china clay industry to the south.

Kestle Mill
2½ miles SE of Newquay on the A3058

Found hidden in the lanes two miles west of Kestle Mill is the exceptionally attractive small Elizabethan manor house, **Trerice**, which is now owned by the National Trust. A real architectural gem, this pretty limestone E-shaped house was built in the 1570s, on the site of its medieval predecessor, for the influential Arundell family. Sir John

Arundell served Elizabeth I in the Low Countries, and was greatly influenced by the architecture there, so there is a hint of Dutch styling to the house. The beautiful window in the great hall contains 576 small panes of 16th century glass, and it also has huge ornate fireplaces, elaborate plasterwork and fine English oak and walnut furniture. Several rooms contain fine Oriental and English porcelain, and among the more esoteric collections are clocks and drinking glasses.

There are portraits by the renowned Cornish painter John Opie. The grounds in which the house stands are equally charming and, as well as the unusual summer flowering garden, there is an orchard planted with old and, in many cases, forgotten fruit trees. The Parade Ground was used as a training ground by the Home Guard in the 1940s, and here you can play the Cornish game of 'kayles', an early form of skittles. The **Lawnmower Museum** traces the history of the lawnmower and contains more than 100 machines, and tea rooms, gift

shop and plant sales can also be found in the house's various outbuildings. All parts of the garden may be used for picnicking. Trerice was the 'Trenwith' of Winston Graham's *Poldark* novels.

To the southeast of Kestle Mill is another place well worth visiting that is rather different from Trerice - **DairyLand Farm World**. This is a real, working dairy farm and, amongst the other attractions here, visitors can see the 140 cows being milked to music.

Indian Queens
6 miles E of Newquay off the A30

Close to an area dominated by china clay quarries, this chiefly Victorian village is home to **Screech Owl Sanctuary** which lies just to the northeast. A rehabilitation, conservation and education centre, the sanctuary has the largest collection of owls and birds of prey in the southwest of England (over 140) and, as well as offering visitors the chance to see hand tame owls at close quarters, the centre runs a number of courses on owl welfare.

St Newlyn East

3 miles S of Newquay off the A3075

St Newlyn East, also known simply as Newlyn East, was a flourishing mining village in the 19th century, the imposing old engine house and chimney stack of **East Wheal Rose** mine can still be seen to the east and can be reached by taking a short journey on the **Lappa Valley Steam Railway** (see panel below). Cornwall's richest lead producing mine, East Wheal Rose was the scene, in July 1846, of Cornwall's worst mining disaster when 39 miners were drowned in a flash flood caused by an unexpected cloudburst.

The village's cockpit (where cockfighting had been held for centuries) was restored as a memorial to the dead and, although the mine reopened a year after the accident, it closed for good in 1885.

The village itself is grouped around the handsome **St Newlina Parish Church**, named after St Newlina the Virgin, and the fig growing from the walls of the building is said to be her staff.

Holywell

3½ miles SW of Newquay off the A3075

This pretty hamlet, with its attractive beach and towering sand dunes, was obviously named after a holy well but the exact location of that well is unknown; it may have been inside a cave on the north side that can be visited at low tide - take a torch if you plan a visit, and watch out for the slippery rocks! Its waters were supposed to cure skin diseases in children. **Holywell Bay** is sheltered, at either end, by two headlands, Kelsey Head and Penhale Point and provides superb swimming and surfing which have helped to make this a popular summer seaside resort. An additional attraction here, apart from the dolphins that can sometimes be seen out in the bay, is the **Holywell Bay Fun Park** that offers a

LAPPA VALLEY STEAM RAILWAY

St Newlyn East, Nr Newquay,
Cornwall TR8 5HZ
Tel: 01872 510317
website: www.lappavalley.co.uk

Lappa Valley Steam Railway is one of the most popular attractions in the whole county, offering a great day out for families. The centrepiece is the 15" gauge steam railway that runs through beautiful countryside from Benny Halt to East Wheal Rose, but there are two other, tinier railways, one of them featuring a miniature Intercity 125. The site provides a good habitat for wildlife, and other attractions include nature trails, woodland walks, a nine-hole golf course, a boating lake, a brick path maze, play areas, coffee and gift shops and an old mine engine house.

TREGUTH INN

Holywell Bay, Near Newquay,
Cornwall TR8 5PP
Tel: 01637 830245

Imagine a traditional, whitewashed Cornish pub with a thatched roof and full of real, olde worlde character. That's the **Treguth Inn**, parts of which date back as far as 1284, though the service and the value for money are as modern as you can get! It serves wonderful food, and people come from miles around to eat here. It also serves a splendid range of beers, wines and spirits in its bar and lounge, which are full of genuine character. Coach parties are more than welcome to sample the traditional atmosphere of one of the best pubs in the county.

whole range of activities for young and old. Ideal for families, there is pitch and putt golf, various rides and a maze among the amusements.

Crantock

2 miles SW of Newquay off the A392

This pretty little village lies across the Gannel estuary from Newquay and had, from the 12th century until it closed in 1545, a famous college which was a great seat of learning. But the village's history goes back even further than that, as a Celtic monastery was founded here long before the Norman Conquest. After the Conqest it was given to a Norman nobleman, who in turn gave it to Montacute Priory in Dorset. **St Carantoc Parish Church,** which was once collegiate, contains a particularly beautiful rood screen. In 1412 the tower of the Norman church collapsed, destroying the nave.

Although the beach at Crantock looks inviting, with the high dunes backing a

CRANTOCK BAY HOTEL

Crantock, Cornwall TR8 5SE
Tel: 01637 830299
e-mail: stay@crantockbayhotel.co.uk
website: www.crantockbayhotel.co.uk

The **Crantock Bay Hotel** must have one of the most spectacular settings in Cornwall. This part of the county has rocky headlands, lovely countryside, picturesque villages, safe surfing beaches and wooded creeks aplenty · everything, in fact, that makes Cornwall so special. Most of the hotel rooms have spectacular sea views, and families are more than welcome. There are great amenities, such as the indoor swimming pool, the spa bath, the gardens and the tennis courts. Only the highest quality West Country produce is used in the kitchens, making the menus attractive and innovative. In fact, the hotel has earned a reputation for its cuisine. So make the Crantock Bay hotel your first port of call!

large expanse of sand, the currents around the mouth of the River Gannel, which runs into the sea at the northern end of the beach, make swimming dangerous. At low tide, two bridges become exposed which cross the river but, at all other times during the summer, a small rowing boat ferries passengers over the river. Not surprisingly, a few centuries ago, Crantock attracted smugglers and the village's old thatched inn, **The Old Albion**, was a well known hideaway.

St Agnes

This charming village, which lies at the head of a steep valley, has since the early 20th century been a popular seaside resort but its sleepy and peaceful appearance today is very far removed from the days when it was the centre of a great tin mining area. Once known as the source of the finest tin in Cornwall, the community still retains reminders of those days and, especially around the

narrow-spired Victorian **St Agnes Parish Church,** there can be found old miners cottages and mine owners houses. In particular, at the bottom of the village, there is a steeply terraced row of 18th century miners cottages known as **Stippy Stappy**. Many visitors to St Agnes follow the Craft Trail, which passes Stippy Stappy and runs down to Trevaunance Cove (see below). The Trail takes in several galleries and workshops displaying paintings, pottery, designer clothing, furniture, ceramics, jewellery, metalwork, cards, prints and many more examples of local crafts.

Surrounding the village are the remains of many mine workings including the picturesque group of clifftop buildings that were once part of one of the county's best known mines - **Wheal Coates**. The word 'wheal' (originally 'whel') is the Cornish for 'work', though it has gradually come to mean a mine working in particular. Now in the hands of the National Trust,

the mine was in operation for 30 years between 1860 and 1890 and the derelict Engine House is an exceptionally atmospheric local landmark. It stands close to a high cliff edge, and the workings used to go out under the sea. Many other abandoned pump houses and mine shafts still litter the area (walkers should always keep to the footpaths) and from the remains of **Wheal Kitty** there are views across the landscape to other disused workings. In the steep valley north of Wheal Kitty the Wills family run the **Blue Hills Tin Stream Visitor Centre**, perpetuating the skills of the tinner in processing ore into high grade concentrate, which they smelt and refine by a process of liquation and

Wheal Coates Tin Mine, St Agnes Head

poling. Tin has been produced hereabouts for many centuries, first from the beaches and valley floor, later from tunnels in the hillsides that followed the rich veins of ore. The Blue Hills mines were worked until 1780, when they had reached a depth beyond the capabilities of a water-driven pump system; they opened again in 1810 when steam power was introduced, but closed again in 1897 in the face of opposition from the new tin mining fields discovered in Australia and Malaysia.

Those skills have been revived at Blue Hills, where the refined tin is cast into ingots which are melted down as required to produce a unique range of jewellery and gifts that can be purchased in the workshop. **St Agnes Museum**, which is run by volunteers, aims to promote the heritage of the village and the series of displays here not only cover the mining and seafaring history of St Agnes but also the natural history of the surrounding area. An important recent acquisition is the figurehead of the *Lady*

RAILWAY INN

10 Vicarage Road, St Agnes,
Cornwall TR5 0TJ
Tel: 01872 552310

The **Railway Inn** in St Agnes, near the north Cornish coast, dates back to the early 17th century, and is a solid, stone built building which is full of character and charm. Old prints adorn the walls, and there are real open fires during the winter months. It became a public house in the 18th century, and has remained popular ever since.

The inn is managed by Tim Doolan and his fiancée Gemma, who bring a wealth of experience to the job. It is open all day and every day for real ales, with three or four always on tap, including a rotating guest ale. Plus, of course, it has a wide range of wines, ciders, lagers, spirits and soft drinks.

The resident chef Matthew is responsible for the food, which only uses the finest local produce wherever possible. In winter, no food is served on Sunday evenings or all day on Monday, but the rest of the time you can eat between 12 noon - 2.30 pm and 6 pm - 9.30 pm through the week, and until 10 pm on Friday and Saturday. Sunday lunch, which is roast only, is cooked by Tim and served between 12 noon and 3 pm. They are always popular, so you are well advised to book. There is a printed menu or a daily specials board, and dinner dishes include such things as char grilled chicken, halibut steak, rib eye steak or grilled sole.

On Saturday night, there is always an international food themed evening, and you should ring for details. The inn accepts all credit and debit cards, except American Express and Diners Club. The inn is said to be haunted - ask about it if you dare!

Agnes, a two-masted schooner of 91 tons that was launched at Trevaunance Cove in 1877. Four schooners were built on the beach between 1873 and 1877, all for harbour owner Martin Hitchins, and it was John Hitchins, a descendant of Martin, who unveiled the figurehead in March 2002. The figurehead had been bought by an American at a Christie's auction in 1989 and taken across the Atlantic; it was tracked down and after some serious fundraising was returned, restored and put on display next to the Museum's mining displays - particularly apt, as the schooner's main job was shipping copper ore to Wales for smelting, returning with coal for the mines.

Among the many other interesting items in the Museum are a self-portrait of the locally born Georgian society painter, John Opie; an 80-year-old leatherback turtle washed up on Porthtowan beach in 1988; and a US Army issue Louisville Slugger Soft Ball Baseball Bat given to a local boy by an American GI camped at St Agnes in the run-up to D-Day in 1944.

St Agnes was introduced to thousands through the *Poldark* novels of Winston Graham - in which St Agnes became St Ann. Overlooked by the buildings of Wheal Coates, Wheal Charlott (a copper mine) and Charlott United, **Chapel Porth** is a sandy shingle-backed beach where both swimmers and surfers should be aware of the strong currents and undertows. The remains of the 11th

ROSE-IN-VALE COUNTRY HOUSE HOTEL

Mithian, St Agnes, Cornwall TR5 0QD
Tel: 01872 552202 Fax: 01872 552700
e-mail: reception@rose-in-vale-hotel.co.uk
website: www.rose-in-vale-hotel.co.uk

The **Rose-In-Vale Country House Hotel** is an elegant yet comfortable food-lovers' paradise. Once the residence of a country gentleman, it dates from 1785 and has been transformed into a place where good taste melds with a warm, friendly welcome while still retaining many traditional features. Food is king here - the cuisine is simple yet inventive and uses only the finest and freshest of West Country produce. The secret of their success is attention to detail, creating a reputation that goes far beyond Cornwall. There are 18 fully en suite rooms, all cosy yet spacious, and all reflecting the history of the house in their furnishings and decoration.

century chapel can still be seen. A cave behind the beach is linked with the legendary giant called **Bolster**, who fell in love with Agnes, a local young maiden. As proof of his devotion to her, Agnes asked the giant to fill a hole above the cliffs at Chapel Porth with his blood - a task he willingly undertook as the hole seemed tiny. However, unknown to Bolster, the hole was bottomless and opened into a cave which in turn opened into the sea; as his blood drained away, he became so weak that he eventually died. The story is enacted at Chapel Porth in early May, using giant puppets in a colourful pageant and procession. Bolster also presides over the St Agnes Carnival in August and the Christmas Lights and Lantern Procession in December. The local beaches are all patrolled throughout the summer by professional lifeguards. St Agnes and Porthtowan also have popular Surf Life Saving Clubs, with courses run throughout the year by qualified instructors.

LITTLE TREVELLAS FARM

Trevellas, St Agnes, Cornwall TR5 0XX
Tel: 01872 552945
e-mail: velvetcrystal@ukonline.co.uk
website: www.stagnes.co.uk

A 250-year-old house on a working farm on the B3285 provides a peaceful, comfortable base for a holiday that will appeal to lovers of both coast and countryside. Mary Andrew welcomes visitors to **Little Trevellas Farm**, where a double room and two singles, offer en suite Bed & Breakfast accommodation with tv and tea-making facilities. An excellent breakfast with farm eggs and home-baked bread starts the day, and Mary can cater for vegetarian or special dietary needs if previously advised. Dogs are welcome - as long as they can mix with Mary's sheepdogs!

A footpath from the beach leads northwards, along the coast, to St Agnes Head and **St Agnes Beacon**. A local landmark now in the hands of the National Trust, it is from the beacon that St Agnes derives its Cornish name, Bryanick, meaning pointed or prominent hill. At 629 feet above sea level the beacon is well worth climbing as, from the summit, both coasts of Cornwall and, at night, some 12 lighthouses can be seen. It was from this summit that, in the 16th century, a fire was lit to warn of the coming of the Spanish Armada though, more recently, in 1977, another fire was lit as part of the Queen's Silver Jubilee celebrations.

The beach to the north of the village is now popular with surfers and fishermen although, up until 1915, **Trevaunance Cove** was the main harbour for the mines in and around St Agnes. Outgoing cargoes were delivered to the harbour by means of a chute while incoming goods were hoisted up the hillside using a horse. In 1915 a great storm washed away the poorly maintained harbour and only a few granite blocks can be seen today.

Around St Agnes

Porthtowan
4 miles S of St Agnes off the B3300

This small holiday resort has a gently sloping sandy beach backed by 'towans' (the Cornish name for sand dunes) It is sheltered by a cove, and is an excellent family beach. The sea also provides good surfing, while the seaside cafés and shops cater for holidaymakers' needs. At the foot of the East Cliff is a natural rock pool where swimming is allowed. Evidence of copper mining is never far away in this part of Cornwall and, in the village, a 19th century mining engine house has been converted into a private residence. Above the beach are the remains of **Wheal Towan**, once one of the most prosperous copper mines in Cornwall. It is said that its owner, Ralph Allen Daniell of Trelissick, earned a 'guinea an minute' from it in the 18th century. Inland, at **Tywarnhale**, more evidence can be seen in the remains of various copper mine buildings.

Perranporth
3 miles NE of St Agnes on the B3285

From a one time pilchard fishing and mining village that had also played host to smuggling gangs in the past, the arrival of the railway, at the beginning of the 20th century, ensured that Perranporth would survive, this time as a pleasant and popular holiday resort. The three mile long stretch of golden sand lies at the heart of Perranporth's success and it is a place that draws both surfers and bathers though because of the strong currents care has to be taken.

Though there is little left to see around Perranporth of its mining past, this small town's Celtic heritage is still remembered on an annual basis, during

Perranporth Beach

the **Lowender Peran Festival**, which brings all the Celtic nations together through music and dance.

About a mile from the town, high up in the sand dunes overlooking Penhale Sands, lies **St Piran's Oratory**. Built on the site of St Piran's grave, the remains of this 6th or 7th century building lay under the shifting sands until, in 1835,

they were revealed. Legend has it that when the remains were uncovered, three headless skeletons were also discovered. Reburied today, a simple plaque marks the site of the burial place of the saint who is said to have travelled from Ireland to Cornwall on a millstone. The saint's landing place is marked by a tall granite cross, **St Piran's Cross**, which is

TIDE'S REACH HOTEL

Ponsmere Road, Perranporth,
Cornwall TR6 0BW
Tel/Fax: 01872 572188
e-mail: jandf.boyle@virgin.net
website: www.tidesreachhotel.com

The whitewashed **Tide's Reach Hotel** will appeal to those people who appreciate the finer things in life. Just off the high street and only a short walk from the beach; having eight fully en suite rooms recently upgraded to a high standard, earning four coveted diamonds. All have TV, radio alarm, hair dryer and hospitality tray. The hotel offers an ideal place for either relaxing in the hot tub and garden; enjoying a quiet drink in the lounge after a day out, or a delicious meal in the restaurant. Full Cornish breakfasts are served, or something lighter if you prefer. For a quiet and enjoyable holiday, choose the Tide's Reach Hotel!

one of only a very few three-holed Celtic crosses in the county.

The name of the parish in which Perranporth is located is called Perranzabuloe, meaning 'Piran in the sand', and it gives its name to the local museum, the **Perranzabuloe Folk Museum**, located in the town's Ponsmere Road. It has local collections on archaeology, science and social history For most people, however, Perranporth will forever be linked with Winston Graham, the author of the *Poldark* novels. Born in Manchester, Graham settled in Perranporth in the 1930s and, while staying here, wrote the first volumes in the series which were published between 1945 and 1953. Local beauty spots, towns, villages and various old mine workings all appear either as themselves or in disguise in the books and, in some cases, his characters take their names from local villages.

Penhale Camp
6 miles NE of St Agnes off the A3075

Penhale Camp is the site of a 940-acre armed forces training base, so great care should be taken when visiting the area, and restriction notices should be observed. According to local legend, the old town of **Langarroc**, a supposedly beautiful place with seven fine churches, lies buried beneath the dunes of Penhale Sands. The town gained its wealth from mining and it also proved to be the cause of the town's undoing as, during a great storm that lasted three days,

Langarroc and its inhabitants were engulfed - some said as retribution for their ungodly ways. On stormy nights it is said that ghostly cries for help can still be heard above the sound of the wind and the waves. Before the planting of marram grass, sandstorms did much damage in this part of Cornwall, so the legend may be based on a real sandstorm which obliterated a late Iron Age settlement. Over the years some bones have occasionally been dug up on the site.

Rose
4½ miles NE of St Agnes off the B3285

Close to this tiny village lies **St Piran's Round**, an Iron Age enclosure that was used for miracle plays performed in the Cornish language in the Middle Ages, and later for Cornish games such as wrestling. Possibly the oldest theatre site in Europe, it is still used from time to time.

Goonhavern
5 miles NE of St Agnes on the A3075

The main attraction in this village is the **World in Miniature**, a wonderful model village that is set in glorious gardens. Here, visitors can see such world famous sights as Mount Rushmore, the Leaning Tower of Pisa, the Parthenon, Buckingham Palace, the Taj Mahal and the Pyramids all perfectly reproduced and set in beautiful gardens. Also in this superb family attraction are a wraparound cinema, an animated Wild West town, a ball pool, Super X simulator ride, Jurassic adventure world and a maze. The latest 'miniature' to be added here is that of the Eden Project.

St Allen

6½ miles E of St Agnes off the A30

Like many parts of Britain that have a Celtic tradition, Cornwall has its own 'little people' - the piskies. One legend surrounding these mischievous people tells of a boy, living in St Allen who was out picking wild woodland flowers near his home. When he failed to return home for supper, his mother and other villagers began a frantic search. After three days, the boy was found, sleeping peacefully in exactly the same spot where he was last seen; he had no idea what had happened to him in the intervening days. However, what he

CHYVERTON GARDEN

Zelah, Nr Truro, Cornwall TR4 9HD
Tel: 01872 540324 Fax: 01872 540648

The core of the house at Chyverton was built in 1730 and in 1770 two wings were added by John Thomas, a wealthy mine owner. Over the next 55 years he created a Georgian landscape garden on the property: he dammed a small stream to form a lake, built a bridge and a walled garden and planted 94 acres of woodland.

The first rhododendrons, for which **Chyverton Garden** is renowned, were planted in 1890; most of them are the old hybrid Cornish Red and many are of an immense

size, perhaps the largest in cultivation in Europe. The garden also has notable magnolias and camellias and a fine collection of conifers. In 1924 the estate changed hands for the first time and became the home of Treve and Muriel Holman, keen gardeners who added many exotic plants brought back from plant hunting trips to the Far East and who created a woodland garden.

The whole garden is now looked after by their son Nigel, who has encouraged the wild and natural appearance that is such a feature. Some of the plants are named after Treve Holman and Nigel's late wife Elisabeth, and in the memorial garden is a wooden bridge designed by Nigel that commemorates the death of Treve in 1959.

could remember was that while picking the flowers he had heard a bird singing so beautifully that he had followed the sound of the bird deep into the woods. As day turned into night and the stars came out, the boy had realised that the stars were, in fact, piskies and they had led him to a fantastic cave with crystal pillars studded with jewels where he had been fed on the purest honey. When he awoke from this incredible adventure he found himself back in the woodland close to his home.

A little way north of St Allen, a mile west of the village of Zelah, lies **Chyverton Garden** (see panel on page 113), in the grounds of a grand Georgian house built for a wealthy mine owner. The landscaping was added by John Thomas over a 55 year period. He created a small lake by damming a stream, built a bridge and planted 94 acers of woodland. The place is renowned for its rhododendrons and magnolias.

Penhallow
3 miles E of St Agnes on the A3075

Cornwall is traditionally a cider-making area, and at one time over 50 varieties of apple were grown for the purpose, with names like Whimple Honeydrop and Sweet Hoary Morning. Just south of Penhallow lies the **Callestock Cider Farm**, a commercial farm that is also open to visitors. There are tours of the fruit orchards from which over 40 varieties of delicious fruit products are made, including jams, country wines, honey, mead, apple brandy and, of course, cider and traditional farmhouse scrumpy. Whatever the season there is always something to see here of the cider making process, from harvesting and pressing to bottling and labelling, and after the tour, there is the opportunity to sample the product. Here, too, is the **Cider Museum** where the fascinating history of cider making is charted,

VENTONGIMPS MILL BARN

Ventongimps, Callestick, Truro,
Cornwall TR4 9LH
Tel: 01872 573275

A mill has existed at Ventongimps since 1313, and the present one stands within 7 ½ acres of garden and mature woodland. Situated some two miles from Perranporth beach it is here that you will find the **Ventongimps Mill Barn,** two self catering units that are comfortable, spacious and full of character. The historic city of Truro is some 5 miles away. Both self catering units come fully equipped for an enjoyable holiday and sleep six. This stunning development will surely become more and more popular with tourists.

through displays of old equipment and artefacts, that include a horse-drawn mill and a cooper's workshop.

Towan Cross
2 miles S of St Agnes off the B3277

The countryside around this village was one of the richest tin and copper mining areas in the country and the minerals were extracted here until the 1920s. To satisfy the thirst of the miners, there were once many inns here and in the surrounding area and the village's name comes from the horizontal stone cross that lay outside Towan Cross's 16th century inn, on which coffins were rested while the bearers called in for refreshment in the days of walking funerals.

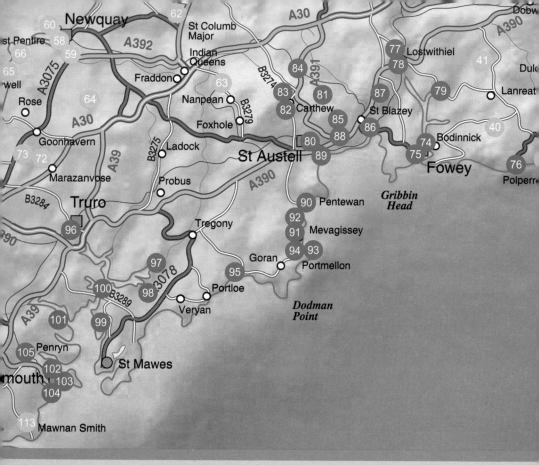

PLACES TO STAY, EAT AND DRINK

● Denotes entries in other chapters

5 Mid Cornwall South

It was a Quaker called William Cookworthy who transformed this part of Cornwall. In 1746 he discovered huge reserves of high quality china clay in the area, at a time when Britain was having to import clay of a lesser quality from Europe. The discovery saw a dramatic change to the small town of St Austell and the surrounding landscape. Mines opened, villages grew, and the ports along the coast expanded. Still one of the world's largest producers of the surprisingly versatile china clay, St Austell has fortunately managed to keep its market town appearance and is still an interesting place to visit. However, the countryside around St Austell has suffered from the industry and the great conical spoil heaps, the industries waste product, have led to the area being dubbed the Cornish Alps. Landscaping of the heaps is changing the horizon again and of particular note is the hugely successful Eden Project, built on the site of an old china clay pit, which aims to explain and provide understanding of the vital relationship between plants, people and resources.

PLACES TO STAY, EAT AND DRINK

East of St Austell is the historic fishing port of Fowey, while to the southwest lies Truro, another town built on the proceeds of the mineral extraction industry, which became a city when an Act of Parliament of August 1876 created a new diocese for the county of Cornwall. The magnificent Truro Cathedral, with its splendid triple spire front, was completed in 1910 and has some of the finest Victorian stained glass in the country. At the entrance to Carrick Roads, at the top of which Truro lies, is Falmouth, a key deep-water anchorage that is also the world's third largest natural harbour. A busy port, Falmouth and the other ports in the shelter of Carrick Roads have been protected for centuries by Henry VIII's two fine fortresses, Pendennis and St Mawes Castles.

Surrounding these delightful Cornish towns are numerous pretty villages and coastal ports that are certainly well worth exploring. The countryside of the beautiful Roseland Peninsula offers visitors the chance to investigate the area's wealth of flora and fauna, while those interested in gardens will find that there is plenty of choice. The famous Lost Gardens of Heligan have been restored to their original 19th century splendour, while other gardens in the region also show the benefits of the Gulf Stream in creating this mild and pleasant climate.

Fowey

A lovely old port and historic seafaring town, Fowey (pronounced Foy) guards the entrance to the river from which it takes its name. An attractive place, with steep, narrow streets and alleyways that lead down to one of the best natural harbours along the south coast, Fowey exhibits a pleasant mixture of architectural styles that range from Elizabethan to Edwardian. An important port in the Middle Ages, though it is known to have been previously used by the Romans, the town lay on the trade route between Ireland and continental Europe which crossed Cornwall via the Camel Estuary. It is now a long distance footpath called the Saints Way.

As a busy trading port, Fowey also attracted pirates and was home to the

Alley in Fowey

SHIP INN

Trafalgar Square, Fowey, Cornwall PL23 1AZ
Tel: 01726 832230 Fax: 01726 834935
e-mail: aldwd@msn.com

Dating to the 16th century, the whitewashed and gabled **Ship Inn** sits on a corner site in Fowey's main thoroughfare, and is a traditional-style pub with a wonderful restaurant that specialises in locally caught, fresh fish and shellfish. The menu also serves a wide range of other dishes and snacks. The whole place has a traditional feel, with wooden floors, a beamed ceiling and a cosy, atmospheric bar where St Austell real ales are served. It has a reputation that is second to none among locals and visitors alike.

Fowey Gallants, who not only preyed on ships in the Channel but also raided the French coast. Recruited during the Hundred Years War, these local mariners were brought together to fight the French but, after the hostilities were over, they did not disband but continued to terrorise shipping along this stretch of coast and beyond. The maritime tradition continued into the 19th century, only more peacefully, when Fowey became a china clay port and its harbour was filled with sailing ships of all kinds; today it is still a busy place, but the barques and brigantines and tall East Indiamen have been replaced by big ships calling at this deep water harbour along with both fishing boats and pleasure craft.

For the last 700 years, Fowey has been connected to Bodinnick by a car ferry which has, for many years, been known locally as **The Passage**. Around the town's main square, bordering the Town Quay, are several interesting old buildings, including the **Toll Bar**, which dates from the 14th, 15th and 16th centuries, and the Ship Inn, which stands on the opposite side of the street. The inn was originally a town house,

POLSCOE GUEST HOUSE

Fowey, Cornwall PL23 1HG
Tel: 01726 832407
e-mail: polscoe@yahoo.co.uk
website: www.polscoe.co.uk

Everyone is welcome at the **Polscoe Guest House** in Fowey! It is only ten minutes from the centre of this small resort, and sits on a spacious site with parking for six cars. The gardens are picturesque, and the six comfortable rooms are all fully en suite, and come with TV and hospitality tray. The house has recently been renovated to turn it into one of the best establishments of its kind in the town, with a choice of beautifully cooked and presented breakfasts, served in the light, airy breakfast room overlooking the gardens. When in Fowey, the Polscoe Guest House is the place for you!

built by the influential Rashleigh family in the 15th century, and inside can still be seen the carved ceilings and, above a fireplace, the inscription: 'John Rashleigh - Ales Rashleigh 1570', which remembers a family wedding.

Seen rising above trees is the tower of **St Fimbarrus Parish**

Boats in the Bay, Fowey

Church. St Finbarrus, or Finbar, was an Irish monk who passed through the town on his way to Rome. The church was built on the site of a 7th century chapel to St Goran. A Norman church took its place in about 1150, which was rebuilt in the early 14th century after a raid by pirates. In reprisal for the many raids made by the Gallants, the French, during their devastating raid on Fowey in 1456, partially destroyed this church once more, with restoration work starting soon after 1460 by the Earl of Warwick. The church's font is a legacy of the deeds of the Gallants as it was made from panelling seized by them from a Spanish galleon in 1601.

Fowey and the area around the town have many literary connections, and next to the church is the **Daphne du Maurier Literary Centre**, where the rich literary heritage includes features on du Maurier, Kenneth Grahame (1855-1932, and who was married in the parish church in 1899), Leo Walmsley (1892-

1966), and Sir Arthur Quiller Couch (1863-1944). The town's **Museum** is an excellent place to discover Fowey's colourful history, from the days of piracy and smuggling to the rise of the town's harbour and the china clay industry. Fowey has two main literary connections: with Daphne du Maurier (1907-1989) , who lived at Bodinnick; and with Sir Arthur Quiller Couch, who lived for over 50 years at **The Haven**, on the Esplanade just above the Polruan ferry. Sir Arthur, who wrote as 'Q', was a Cambridge professor, sometime Mayor of Fowey, editor of the *Oxford Book of English Verse* and author of several books connected with Fowey (he called it Troy Town). He died after being hit by a car and is buried in St Fimbarrus churchyard.

To the south of Fowey lies **Readymoney Cove**, whose expanse of sand acts as the town's beach, and further along the coast lies **St Catherine's Castle**. Part of a chain of fortifications along the south coast, this small fort was built by Henry VIII to protect the harbour and, now in the hands of English Heritage, it enjoys fine views over the river estuary and the surrounding coastline.

To the west of Fowey lies the seven-feet tall **Tristan Stone**, which, although not thought to be in its original location, is a 6th century monument bearing a Latin inscription which translates as: 'Drustanus lies here, son of Conomorus'. Drustanus is an alternative version of Tristan and it is believed that this is the same Tristan who was a knight of King Arthur. The son of King Mark, Tristan fell in love with Iseult (Isolde), his father's young bride, after they had both drunk the love potion prepared for Mark's wedding night.

wrote her first novel, *The Loving Spirit*. Another writer, Leo Walmsey lived further along the river in a hut and here he wrote his romantic story, *Love in the Sun*. Sir Arthur Quiller Couch is remembered at Bodinnick by a monolithic memorial which stands at Penleath Point on the coast facing Fowey. The three-mile **Hall Walk** takes you from Bodinnick, past Pont Creek and on to Polruan.

Lanteglos-by-Fowey
2 miles NE of Fowey off the A3082

Here can be found a lonely church whose isolated position can be attributed to it being built to serve Polruan as well as several other scattered hamlets in this area. Though some remnants of the

Around Fowey

Bodinnick
½ mile E of Fowey off the A3082

This pretty hamlet runs up hill away from the ferry slipway which provides a car and passenger service across the river to Fowey. Close to the slipway stands the house in which Daphne du Maurier lived before her marriage and where she

Bodinnick

Polperro

Cornish fishing village. It stands at the point where a steep-sided wooded combe converges with a narrow tidal inlet from the sea and the village's steep narrow streets and alleyways, some only six feet wide, are piled high with white-painted fisherman's cottages.

All routes in Polperro seem to lead down to its beautiful **Harbour** which is still a bustling port, with an assortment of colourful boats usually to be seen.

original Norman building exist, the **St Wyllow's Parish Church** is chiefly 14th century and was fortunate enough not to be over zealously restored in the 19th century. It's tower is over 70 feet high. St Wyllow was a Christian hermit who lived in the area and died a martyr well before St Augustine landed in Kent in the 6th century.

Polperro
5½ miles E of Fowey off the A387

This lovely old fishing community is many people's ideal of the typical

While for centuries the village was dependent on pilchard fishing for its survival, Polperro also has a long association with smuggling and the practice here was so rife in the 18th century that many of the village's inhabitants were involved in shipping, storing or transporting contraband goods. To combat what was such a widespread problem, HM Customs and

THE TEA CLIPPER

Fore Street, Polperro, Cornwall PL13 2QR
Tel: 01503 272198
e-mail: the.teaclipper@tiscali.co.uk

The Tea Clipper is an eating place you can't afford to miss. It sits in the heart of this well-known and picturesque fishing village, and has a reputation that has spread far beyond it. It seats 28 people inside and 12 outside, and during the day and in the evenings has a menu plus a daily specials board. The place has opening hours according to the season, and is closed in December and January. One of its strong points is its range of special dietary needs dishes, such as gluten free and dairy free. There is no children's menu, and all major credit cards are accepted. Try their cream teas - scrumptious!

Excise established the first 'preventive station' in Cornwall at Polperro in the 1800s. At the **Polperro Heritage Museum of Smuggling and Fishing** near the harbour a whole range of artefacts and memorabilia from around the 18th century are used to illustrate the myths, legends and larger-than-life characters who dodged the government taxes on luxury goods. A model of *Lady Beatrice*, a traditional large, gaff-rigged fishing boat that is typical of Polperro, can also be seen. Also on display is a model of *HMS Recruit*, onto which local lad **Robert Jeffrey** was press-ganged in 1807. He was subsequently cast ashore on a desert island in the West Indies for drinking the captains's beer. He was eventually rescued and brought back to London in 1810 to a hero's welcome. Questions were asked in Parliament about the incident, and the *Recruit's* captain was dismissed from the service. Robert eventually married and settled in Polperro.

The Guernsey sweaters knitted for the local fishermen by their wives were called **Polperro Knitfrocks**, and they are similar to the ones used by Guensey fishermen, showing the strong links between this part of Cornwall and the Channel Islands.

Around the rest of the village there are numerous interesting buildings to be seen, including the **House on Props** and **Couch's House**, the 16th century house where Dr Jonathan Couch, the naturalist and grandfather of author Sir Arthur Quiller Couch, lived. Set within beautiful formal gardens, the **Model Village** is a perfect miniature replica of old Polperro that is well worth visiting.

Just west of Polperro harbour lies **Chapel Hill**, from which there are superb panoramic views both inland and out to sea. At the bottom of the hills lies a cavern that is known as **Willy Willcock's Hole**. Willy was a fisherman who, walking here one day, decided to explore the cave. Unfortunately he lost his way in the maze of underground tunnels and was never seen again and, so the story goes, his lost soul can still be heard crying out for help. A two-mile clifftop walk eastwards from Polperro leads to **Talland Bay**, a sheltered shingle cove that is overlooked by the 13th century **St Tallan Parish Church**.

Bertween 1812 and 1813 a new curate called the 'Rev'd Whitmore' served in the parish church, and carried out several wedding ceremonies, baptisms and funerals. It was later discovered that he was an impostor, and many couples had to go through a second wedding ceremony and have their children baptised a second time, as the original ones were illegal. That is why some marriages and baptisms from that time are recorded twice in the parish registers.

Lansallos
3 miles E of Fowey off the A387

From the 14th century **St Ildierna's Parish Church**, in the centre of this small village, there is a path which follows a tree-lined stream down to the coast and sheltered Lantivet Bay. Here also lies the small shingle beach of Lansallos Cove. The name Lansallos in Cornish means the 'church of unknown name', as no one could originally agree on who St Ildierna was. Some records say he was a bishop of the Celtic Church, while others claim that he was a she, and a virgin.

Polruan
1 mile S of Fowey off the A3082

Facing St Catherine's Castle across the mouth of the River Fowey, Polruan is a pretty village of cottages climbing high above the waterfront; it can be reached by ferry from Fowey. Beside the harbour, which is still busy with pleasure craft and china clay vessels, lies the late 15th century **Polruan Blockhouse**. One of a pair of artillery buildings that was constructed to control the entrance to Fowey, it was from here that, during the Hundred Years War, heavy linked chains were stretched between the two to prevent a sea invasion by the French. The grooves made by the chains can still be seen carved into the rock.

On top of Polruan Hill are the ruins of **St Saviour's Chapel**, dating originally from the 8th century, though it was considerably enlarged in 1488. It was from here that people kept a look out for French vessels intent on plundering Fowey during the 100 Year's War. To the southwest of St Saviour's Point is **Punche's Cross**, said to have aasociations with Pontius Pilate. It is claimed that Joseph of Arimathaea

passed by the spot with the young Jesus when he brought him to Britain.

Gribbin Head
2 miles SW of Fowey off the A3082

The beacon on Gribbin Head, **Daymark Tower**, was built in 1832 to help seafarers find the approaches to Fowey harbour. This craggy headland is best known for being close to the home of Daphne du Maurier, who lived at **Menabilly**. Originally the country retreat of the wealthy local Rashleigh family, it was her home for many years and featured as 'Manderley' in her most famous novel, *Rebecca*: 'Last night I dreamt I went to Manderley again' is among the best known opening lines in the language. After her death in 1989, her children scattered her ashes on the cliffs near the house.

Golant
2 miles N of Fowey off the B3269

A delightful waterside village where St Sampson built his monastic cell in the 6th century. On the site of the cell stands **St Sampson's Parish Church**, and, by the porch, another of Cornwall's many holy wells. Close to the village can also be found the **Castle Dore Earthworks**, the remains of an Iron Age fort. Castle Dore was the place where 6,000 Roundheads surrendered to King Charles in 1644.

It is also where, it is said, King Mark of Cornwall's palace stood, and yet another of the places where the story of

Tristan and Iseult was played out. Iseult is supposed to have worshipped at the church, then part of a Celtic monastery, and given her wedding dress to a priest to be made into a chasuble, a sleeveless cloak worn over the alb by priests during the saying of Mass.

Of all the Cornish saints, St Sampson is perhaps the one we know most about, thanks to a biography written about him in the early 7th century. He was the son of a Welsk king who eventually became abbot of Caldey Island off the Pembokeshire coast. One day, near Easter, he saw an angel who told him to leave Wales and travel across the sea. He did so, and reached Padstow, where he began a walk across Cornwall on what is now the Saint's Way. He eventually reached Golant, and converted the people there to Christianity after seeing them worshipping an idol. He set up a small monastery before continuing on his way to Brittany, where he founded the Bishopric of Dol. It is said that he was particularly good at curing lepers.

Lostwithiel

This attractive small market town's name means, literally, 'lost in the hills', which perfectly describes its location - nestling in the valley of the River Fowey and surrounded by wooded hills. The capital of Cornwall in the 13th century and one of the stannary towns, Lostwithiel's history is very much governed by its riverside position, as the Fowey was still navigable here to large vessels at one time. It was founded by the Normans, who named it 'the Port of Fawi'. It was the second busiest port on the south coast of England, and for centuries, tin and other raw materials were brought here for assaying and onward transportation until the upstream mining activity caused the quay to silt up and force the port further down river.

Lostwithiel was a major crossing place on the River Fowey and the original medieval timber bridge was replaced and then gradually altered until Tudor times when the bridge seen today was

EARL OF CHATHAM

Grenville Road, Lostwithiel,
Cornwall PL22 0EP
Tel: 01208 872269

The Earl of Chatham dates back to the 16th century, and the traditional stone-built inn, which has ample parking, can be found on a small side street just half a mile from the centre of Lostwithiel.

The stone walls continue inside where they are combined with a large log fire and a cosy atmosphere. Open daily at lunchtime and in the evening, there is a tempting range of home-cooked food on offer. Children and well behaved dogs are welcome and a beer garden can be found at the rear.

Three comfortable guest rooms are available for overnight accommodation.

completed. Alongside the banks of the River Fowey and downstream from the bridge lies the tranquil **Coulson Park**. Opened in 1907, the park was named after the American millionaire, Nathaniel Coulson, who grew up in the town and who put up the money for the park's construction.

Across the river from the town lies the **Boconnoc Estate**, the home of the Pitt family who gave Britain two great Prime Ministers. Throughout Lostwithiel there are reminders, in the buildings, of the former importance of this pleasant and picturesque place. The remains of the 13th century **Great Hall**, which served as the treasury and stannary offices, can still be seen, and in Fore Street there is a fine example of an early 18th century arcaded Guildhall. Built in 1740 by Richard, Lord Edgcumbe, the ground floor was originally an open Corn Market with the town lock-up behind and the guildhall on the first floor. Today, the building is home to the **Lostwithiel Museum** and provides the

perfect atmosphere in which to tell the story of this interesting town and to display photographs documenting everyday life in Lostwithiel from the late 19th century to the present day. 16th century **Taprell House** in North Street (now partly occupied by the Methodist Church) is worth finding for an unusual plaque which declares that 'Walter Kendal founded this house and hath a lease for 3,000 years beginning 29 September 1652'. It also hosts occasional art exhibitions.

The striking **St Bartholomew Parish Church** has a distinctive octagonal spire and its Breton-style design is a reminder of the close links between the Celts of Cornwall and those of northern France. Dedicated to the patron saint of the sick and of tanners (tanning was another industry of medieval Lostwithiel), the church, like other parts of the town, still bears some scars from the Civil War when the area became a battleground between the opposing forces. **Braddock Down**, to the east, was the site of a

Royalist victory in 1643. During that war, Cornwall was strongly Royalist, and in 1644 the Parliamentarians tried to take the town once more, this time succeeding. A curious tale is told of how the Parliamentarian

Restormel Castle

troops led a horse into St Bartholomew's Church and baptised it 'Charles', using water from the church's font. By September of the same year they had been forced to abandon the town to the Royalists.

Polscoe

On a minor road 1 mile N of Lostwithiel

Lostwithiel's strategic position, as a riverside port and important crossing point, led to the building of **Restormel Castle**, which stands perched on a high moated mound overlooking the wooded valley of the River Fowey. The magnificent Norman keep of local slate shale rock was built in the early 12th century by Edmund, Earl of Cornwall, and with walls that are over 300 feet thick in places and a deep moat surrounding the whole fortress, this was certainly a stronghold worthy of the powerful Earls. The bailey (a fortified

courtyard in front of the castle) has disappeared, as has the deer park, where the earl kept 300 deer. The Black Prince held court here in 1354.

Lerryn

2 miles S of Lostwithiel on a minor road

A quiet and peaceful village found by a sleepy creek, it is hard to imagine that Lerryn was once a busy riverside port. Those familiar with Kenneth Grahame's novel *The Wind in the Willows* may find the thickly wooded slopes of Lerryn Creek familiar, as they are thought to have been the inspiration for the setting of this ever popular children's story. The bridge was built in 1573 on the orders of Queen Elizabeth.

St Cyrus's and Juleietta's Parish Church is in the curiously named village of St Veep, a mile south of Lerryn. St Veep, or Vepa, or Vepus, may have been yet another daughter of the

SHIP INN

Lerryn, near Lostwithiel, Cornwall PL22 0PT
Tel: 01208 872374
e-mail: shiplerryn@aol.com
website: www.cornwall-online.co.uk/shipinn-
lerryn/welcome.html

Cornwall is a land of creeks, and none is more beautiful than the one on which sits the picturesque village of Lerryn, just of the River Fowey. And here you'll find the **Ship Inn,** a fine old hostelry that dates back to the 16th century at least. This is the ideal spot for a Cornish holiday, with the Ship Inn itself boasting five en suite rooms that are both comfortable and spacious. The inn's "olde-worlde" feel comes from its authenticity, and not from the drawing board of some designer, so tradition is all important. The bar is cosy, the lounge is comfortable and quaint and the conservatory-style restaurant is light and welcoming.

prolific King Brychan Brycheiniog of Wales. The church was once dedicated to her, but was rededicated to its present saints in 1336.

St Austell

This old market town, which for many centuries had been at the centre of the local tin and copper quarrying and mining industries, was transformed in the second half of the 18th century when William Cookworthy discovered large deposits of kaolin, or china clay. A Quaker chemist from Plymouth, Cookworthy saw the importance of the find as china clay was, and still is, a constituent of many products other than just porcelain, including paper, textiles and pharmaceuticals. Over the years, the waste material from the clay pits to the north and west of the town has been piled into great conical spoil heaps which dominate the landscape around St Austell and these bare, bleached uplands have caused this area to be dubbed the **Cornish Alps**. More recently, steps have been taken to soften the countryside and the heaps and disused pits have been landscaped to recreate Cornish heathland. They now have gently undulating footpaths and nature trails.

Although the china clay industry has dominated St Austell since it was first discovered, the town is also the home of another important local business - the St Austell Brewery. Founded by Walter Hicks, a farmer from the parish of Luxulyan, in 1851, the brewery began as a malting house before, having moved into premises in the Market Square, Hicks built a steam brewery in 1867. Boosted by the town's expansion on the proceeds of the china clay industry the brewery continued to flourish and, still a family-run business today, it continues to go from strength to strength. The history of the company and an insight into the brewing process can be found at the informative **St Austell Brewery**

CARLYON ARMS

Sandy Hill, St Austell, Cornwall PL25 3AS

Tel/Fax: 01726 72120

Situated in an area of St Austell that was formerly called "Sandy Bottoms" (the locals still refer to it as "The Sandy"), the **Carlyon Arms** is a 19th century inn with plenty of period character and up to date facilities. It's a St Austell Brewery pub, and in 2003 the licensees, Julie and Glyn Price, won the tenant of the year award for the way they ran the pub, keeping it friendly, clean, well run and smart. The interior especially looks exactly as a good pub should - lots of dark wood, cosy corners and old plates and prints adorning the walls

It is open all day for the sale of St Austell ales, including Tinners, Tribute and HSD (Hick's Special Draught), or as the locals call it, "high speed diesel"! Good food is available from 11.30 am until 2.30 pm and from 6 pm until 9 pm daily, with Julie preparing all the food. You can choose from a printed menu and roasts are added on Sunday lunchtime, when you are advised to book in advance.

Choose from such dishes as steak and kidney pie, ham and mozzarella melt panini, beef stew and dumplings of crispy coated garlic mushrooms. All represent great value for money, and all are beautifully cooked and presented. There is also a selection of baked potatoes with fillings, baguettes and salads.

There is an excellent games area, making the place popular with both locals and visitors alike, and there is live entertainment on Wednesday and Saturday evenings, as well as a disco on Friday evenings. All major credit and debit cards are welcome, and the place is child friendly.

Visitor Centre, from where visitors are also taken on a guided tour of the brewery that includes a sample of the traditional cask-conditioned ales.

The narrow streets of old St Austell create an atmosphere more befitting a market town than a busy mining and industrial community. The main thoroughfares all radiate from **Holy Trinity Parish Church**, an imposing building with a tall 15th century tower that has, inside, a curious Norman font that is carved with an assortment of grotesque human heads and mythical creatures. It was orginally dedicated to St Austolus, from whom the town takes its name. He was the godson and great friend of St Mewan, and it is said they

died within weeks of each other. Elsewhere in the town there are some other notable older buildings including the 17th century Market House, a Quaker Meeting House built in 1829, and the White Hart, a town house.

Meanwhile, just to the east of the town centre, lies, among rhododendrons and beech trees, **Menacuddle Well**. Another of Cornwall's many holy wells, this particular source of curative water is housed in a small granite shrine. It was originally built in the 15th century, but restored by Sir Charles Graves Sawle in 1922. As well as curing a number of ailments, good luck could be had by throwing a crooked pin into its waters.

INNIS INN & FLY FISHERY

Innis Moor, Penwithick, St Austell,
Cornwall PL26 8YH
Tel: 01726 851162 Fax: 01726 852825
e-mail: innis@tiscali.co.uk

The **Innis Inn** was created in 1990 with fishermen in mind. It was formerly the Innis Trout Farm, but in that year Pam together with David hit upon the idea of a place that appealed to fishermen who wanted an all-in fishing experience that offered excellent B&B accommodation as well.

It now also offers all the comforts you expect in a modern, custom built guest house that blends in perfectly with the older buildings in the area. There are five guest rooms of varying sizes, each one having a shower, TV and tea coffee making facilities. All are located upstairs.

perfect place to stay if you want to explore all it has to offer. There are many other attractions in the area such as the Wheal Martyn Heritage Centre, which explains the china clay industry.

The friendly, family run guest house offers breakfasts which are filling and hearty, with lighter options available if required. If you prefer, you can also choose the touring caravan and camping site which allows access to all the facilities.

The clear waters of the lakes at Innis are full of plump rainbow trout, and they have a good reputation for fine sport and a great flavour. Started in 1983 with just a single lake, the fishery now boasts three lakes covering 15 acres, presenting each fly fisher with a range of challenging conditions to satisfy all levels of skill. The lakes are freshly stocked each week with well grown trout, and fishing is allowed from 8 am to dusk every day.

You don't have to be a fisherman to stay here of course. The place is open at lunchtime and in the evenings for food and drink, and there is a good selection of beers available, as well as wines, spirits and soft drinks. Food is available from 11.30 am to 2.30 pm and from 6.30 pm until 8.30 pm from Monday to Saturday, and from 11.30 am to 2.30 pm on Sunday. You can choose from a printed menu, which contains a good range of beautifully cooked and presented dishes. There is a carvery every Sunday lunchtime and this is so popular that you're advised to book well in advance.

The Innis Inn lies only a couple of miles from Cornwall's most famous attraction - the Eden Project, so it's the

SAWLES ARMS

Carthew, St Austell, Cornwall PL26 8XH
Tel: 01726 850317

Situated off the A391 north west of St Austell, the **Sawles Arms** is a traditional old Cornish pub that is a favourite with visitors and locals alike. It's whitewashed, picturesque exterior gives a hint of what to expect inside · that "olde worlde" charm that makes a place so inviting and friendly. It serves good, honest ales, as well as wines and spirits and, of course, soft drinks if you're driving. The food is delicious, and can best be described as simple, tasty pub grub at sensible prices. It is

set back from the road, with plenty of parking spaces, and is the idea stopping off point for a meal or quiet drink.

Around St Austell

Carthew

2 miles N of St Austell on the B3274

Situated in the heart of the Cornish Alps, this tiny village, which lies in a small valley, is surrounded by the spoils of the china clay industry. Just to the south lies Wheal Martyn, an old clay works that is now home to the **Wheal Martyn China Clay Museum** (see panel below). At this open-air museum, the 200-year story of the industry is explored

WHEAL MARTYN CHINA CLAY MUSEUM

Carthew, St Austell, Cornwall PL26 8XG
Tel/Fax: 01726 850362
website: www.wheal-martyn.com

Production of china clay in Cornwall has been a 250-year saga, and a visit to the **Wheal Martyn China Clay Museum** by the St Austell river will provide a fascinating and memorable insight into this historic and still important industry. Following an audio-visual introduction in the theatre, the Historic Trail takes visitors through the old clay works, where the largest working waterwheel in Cornwall is an impressive sight, and other equipment includes sand and mica drags, settling pits and tanks and a linhay (clay store).

Undercover exhibitions include the great Fal Valley engine, while in the transport yard are examples of the various forms of transport used in the clay industry. Of special interest are two steam locomotives, a clay

wagon and the American Peerless lorry dating from 1916. The Nature Trail covers hilly and sometimes uneven terrain through a wide range of natural and man-made habitats and leads to a viewing platform above the working modern clay pit. Children can use up a little surplus energy on the exciting commando-style Adventure Trail. Back in the reception area, housed in the settling tanks of the old Gomm Clayworks, visitors can relax over some refreshments in the tea shop and browse through the souvenirs for sale in the gift shop.

and, through a wide variety of displays including a stimulating audio-visual show, visitors can take a journey back through time (see panel opposite). The museum is closed until March 2005 for refurbishment.

Bugle
4 miles N of St Austell on the A391

This relatively modern village was built in the 19th century to house miners and their families, who were brought into the area to work at the numerous china clay pits. In common with other mining communities throughout the country, Cornwall's mining villages also have a musical tradition and, in Cornwall, it was common for villages to have their own brass band. Each year, the musicians came together to show off their skills and compete in competition. As a music festival was held here, Bugle has a particularly apt name, though in fact the name comes from a pub which still stands here.

Luxulyan
4 miles NE of St Austell off the A390

Found lying between the moorland above and the steep, wooded Luxulyan Valley below, this old village of granite cottages has a very scenic location. Across this boulder strewn valley stands the remarkable **Treffry Viaduct**, which was built between 1839 and 1842 by Joseph Thomas Treffry as part of the railway line between Par and Newquay. Over 90 feet high and 670 feet long, the viaduct was important in the establishment of the newly-created port of Par and mineral ores, quarried stone and fresh water were all transported along the line to the port.

St Blazey
3½ miles E of St Austell on the A390

To the west of the village, in the heart of the china clay area, lies a disused pit that has become the centre of the

THE BUGLE INN

Fore Street, Bugle, Cornwall
Tel: 01726 850307 Fax: 01726 850181
e-mail: bugleinn@aol.com
website: www.bugleinn.co.uk

The village of Bugle may not be one of Cornwall's liveliest, but **The Bugle Inn** has much to recommend it. Run by Simon and Pam Rodger, the couple have been here for ten years and have established a well-liked, friendly pub. The interior is cluttered and cosy, with a warm atmosphere and friendly staff. The chef keeps the kitchen open from 8am to 9pm each day, with a wide choice of

freshly prepared un-fussy dishes, together with daily big value specials, on offer. Also five good-sized guest rooms available for bed and breakfast.

THE EDEN PROJECT

Bodelva, St Austell, Cornwall PL24 2SG
Tel: 01726 811911
website: www.edenproject.com

Since its opening in May 2001, the **Eden Project** has been a huge international success, bringing many thousands of visitors and much needed revenue to Cornwall. It began with the simple idea of telling the story of how the whole world relies heavily on plants, and from that has sprung what has been called one of the wonders of the modern world.

The Project is the brainchild of a former record producer Tim Smit, who started to formulate the idea when driving around the china clay district in 1994. An abandoned

china clay pit just outside St Austell has become home to the largest conservatories ('biomes') in the world where, in the space of a day, visitors can walk from steamy rain forests to the warmth of the Mediterranean in a project that aims to "promote the understanding and responsible management of the vital relationship between plants, people and resources". In the huge Humid Tropic Biome, 787 feet in length and 180 feet high, orchids, sugar cane, rubber trees, tea and coffee plants, bananas and pineapples flourish, fed by water from a waterfall that drops from the top of the biome into pools below.

The second covered biome, the Warm Temperate Biome, is filled with plants from temperate zones, including olive trees and fruits and flowers from the Mediterranean, California and South Africa. The Roofless Biome contains plants from our own temperate climate. A third covered biome, already at the planning stage, will be dedicated to plants from arid zones and will show how plants and humans manage to survive in areas where there is almost no

water. Keeping this biome dry for the desert plants will be a major drainage operation, and when it opens it will, says Tim Smit, further enhance Eden's progress towards the status of one of the world's 'must see' tourist destinations. Outside the biomes, the gardens at the Eden Project are planted with many plants that are native to Cornwall. In each area, visitors will learn about the intimate connection between the plants and the human population. There are many other attractions, too, including some fine sculptures. The aim of this most exciting and ambitious project has always been both to entertain and to educate.

Regular talks, workshops and demonstrations take place in the Living Theatre of Plants and People, with different themes for each month, and in the Eden Arena some of the world's most famous and talented musicians and performers help to raise funds for the Eden Trust, supporting artists from developing countries. Three restaurants offer a wide range of dishes that reflect the enormous variety of the ingredients grown on site, and there are juice bars and small refreshment outlets around the site.

ambitious and already world-famous **Eden Project** (see panel on page 133), named after The garden of Eden. The aim of this on-going project is to promote the understanding and responsible management of the vital relationship between plants, people and resources. At the bottom of a giant crater over 160 feer deep are the largest conservatories in the world where, in the space of a day, visitors can walk from steamy rainforests to the warmth of the Mediterranean. Throughout, the long and sometimes fragile relationship between man and plants is explored with a view to informing and educating visitors as well as looking ahead towards the future.

The Project was officially opened on March 17 2001, and since then over £100m has been invested. The very first £25,000 came from the local council, and Lottery funding amounted to £37.5m, while the NatWest Bank put up £12m. The rest came from various sources. It is unbdoubtedly Great Britain's most successful Millennium Project, and draws thosuands of vsiitors each year.

St Blazey's Parish Church, at the south end of the village, dates from around 1440, and is dedicated to St Blaise, a fourth century bishop from Armenia who was tortured by having his flesh torn from his bones, then being beheaded.

Par

3 miles E of St Austell on the A3082

The harbour was built here in the 1840s as part of the expansion of the china

---

THE ROYAL INN

66 Eastcliffe Road, Par, Cornwall PL24 2AJ
Tel: 01726 815601 Fax: 01726 816415
website: www.royal-inn.co.uk

The Royal Inn at Par is only four miles from the world-famous Eden Project and is the perfect base from which to explore the exciting new development as well as the rest of this part of Cornwall. A newly built extension means that the inn now offers superb Bed & Breakfast accommodation which includes double and twin rooms, a family room and a room specifically designed for people with disabilities. All are fully en suite and have full size baths with shower over, two seater sofas or twin easy chairs, plus a TV and tea/coffee making facilities.

The restaurant is located in the spacious and airy conservatory, a beautiful, sunlit area with traditional Cornish slate flooring and attractive French oak dining tables and chairs. As only the finest and freshest local produce is used, the menu changes to reflect the seasons, and the chefs try to cater for all tastes, including vegetarian and children's meals.

The bar area has an open fire and slate floors, making it cosy and inviting. The inn is included in the CAMRA Good Beer Guide, and serves a good range of real ales, such as Sharp's Doom Bar and Skinner's Betty Stoggs, as well as two guest ales. There is also a good range of draft beer, cider, lager, spirits and wines. The inn is very popular and you'll be made more than welcome if you drop in for a drink, have a meal, or stay a few days.

CARMINOWE BARN RESTAURANT

Strickstenton, Par, Cornwall PL24 2TU
Tel: 01708 873073

Owned and personally managed by Sue Hawkey, the **Carminowe Barn Restaurant** has rightly been described as a "food lover's place". It is a stone-built former barn with original oak beams, which now has an air of elegance and spaciousness. The menu is full of tempting, beautifully cooked dishes, and the wine list compliments them perfectly. Why not try the huge mixed grill, which has become a legend among the many patrons? Booking is essential for the popular Sunday lunches. Functions and coach parties can also be catered for.

clay industry and, today, the terminals, erected in the 1960s, still handle the clay. The tall and slender chimneys of the clay processing plants can be seen from **Par Sands**, where at low tide the flat beach can extend over half a mile out to sea. The dunes and brackish lagoons behind the beach are noted for their wildlife. Contrastingly, to the east of the beach lies a low rocky cliff where, at low tide, **Little Hell Cove** can be reached.

Tregrehan Mills
2 miles E of St Austell off the A391

Lying just southeast of the village is the 19th century **Tregrehan Gardens**, where visitors can not only see many mature trees from places such as North America and Japan, but there are also rhododendrons and a range of Carlyon Hybrid Camellias. The glasshouses date from 1846, and the house and estate has been the home of the Carlyon family from 1565.

Carlyon Bay
2 miles SE of St Austell off the A390

This modern seaside resort lies almost at the centre of the long and sweeping **St Austell Bay**. Sheltered by Gribben Head and Dodman Point, this bay is

BRITANNIA INN

St Austell Road, Tregrehan, Par,
Cornwall PL24 2SL
Tel: 01726 812889 Fax: 01776812089
e-mail: info@britanniainn.net
website: www.thebritanniainn.net

The elegant, stone-built **Britannia Inn** is a former coaching inn that now offers superb hospitality in a modern and customer-friendly ambience. It is famous for its range of six real ales (two of which are rotating) and its cosy atmosphere in the bright public bar and the lounge. The 40 seat restaurant serves a wide range of tempting dishes that show a real flair for traditional cooking,

with only the freshest of local produce being used wherever possible. The whole place is spotlessly clean, and is popular with locals and visitors alike. Plus there is a beer garden and children's play area, making it the perfect stopping place for families.

THE SHIPWRECK & HERITAGE CENTRE

Charlestown, St Austell, Cornwall PL25 3NJ
Tel: 01726 69897
e-mail: admin@shipwreckcharlestown.com
website: www.shipwreckcharlestown.com

The Centre is housed in an old clay dry built on top of the tunnel formerly used to transport clay to the harbour and through which you can still walk. The tunnel leads to a viewing gallery where one of the best views of Charlestown harbour can be enjoyed. It is estimated that there are 3000 wrecks around the coast of Cornwall and the centre has an amazing collection of artefacts and memorabilia from some of them.

One of the most famous shipwrecks of all time was the Titanic and the displays include letters from Frederick James Banfield, born in Helston in 1884, who perished in the disaster, along with various Titanic artefacts.

The Diving Display portrays underwater scenes of salvage and rescue and has an array of diving suits and apparatus. Treasure and artefacts from around 200 wrecks can be seen such as muskets, coins, telescopes, candlesticks, pieces of eight and even a large consignment of Chinese porcelain.

The shop sells a wide selection of maritime souvenirs, coins and 'treasure' for the children, as well as fudge, cards, books and Titanic memorabilia. Above the Centre, with splendid views of the harbour, is the Bosun's Diner where refreshments are available.

home to numerous beaches, including, at Carlyon Bay, Crinnis and neighbouring Polgaver.

Charlestown
1 mile SE of St Austell off the A390

This was originally a small fishing village called West Polmear. In the 1790s a local mine owner Charles Rashleigh built a harbour here to support the growing china clay industry and also for the importing of coal. He is remembered in the name of the town and in the name of one of its inns, the Rashleigh Arms. Other ports with better facilities, such as Fowey and Plymouth, contributed to the decline of trade through Charlestown's harbour in the 19th century, and though some china clay is still exported from here, today this harbour and village remains a Georgian time capsule. As well as providing a permanent berth for square-rigged boats it is a popular destination with holidaymakers and was also used as the location for both the *Poldark* and *The Onedin Line* television series.

Close to the docks, and housed in a historic clay building, is the **Charlestown Shipwreck, Rescue & Heritage Centre** (see panel above), with, underneath, the tunnels which took the clay too and from the harbour. The centre offers an insight into the town's history, local shipwrecks and the various devices that have been developed over the years for rescuing and recovering those in peril at sea. As well as the typical scenes from village life in

The Lost Gardens of Heligan

place to site such a centre. It also has one of the largest underwater equipment collections, including John Lethbridge's famous wooden barrel of 1740. You can try the life raft and breeches buoy that form part of the Life Savers display. The latest display tells the story of Frederick James Banfield, who was born in Heltson in 1884. He perished in the sinking of the Titanic, and though his body was never recovered, many of the original letters he sent to his family are on display, along with other Titanic artefacts.

This interesting, informative and fun centre covers many other aspects of Cornish life, including mining, the skills of the blacksmith and the cooper, and a feature on gas (the first domestic gas available was in Cornwall).

Charlestown, visitors can see a large collection of artefacts that have been recovered from over 150 shipwrecks. It is estimated that there have been over 3,000 recorded shipwrecks round the coast of Cornwall, so this is the ideal

Pentewan
3 miles S of St Austell off the B3273

The east-facing shoreline, to the south of St Austell, shelters some pretty

THE COVE

3 The Square, Pentewan, St Austell, Cornwall PL26 6DA
Tel: 01726 843781
e-mail: the.cove@virgin.net

Pentewan is a delightful coastal village and **The Cove** can be found on the village square, offering spacious en-suite bed and breakfast rooms all year round.

Between Easter and November they are open daily serving an excellent range of coffees, teas and light snacks to suit all tastes. Also served are fantastic cream teas made with fresh home made scones and Boddingtons strawberry jam grown and made

in the next village. Seating inside and out, pets welcome in restricted areas.

villages, including Pentewan, which is pronounced Pen-tuan. It is famous for its stone, which was quarried nearby, and which was used in the construction of many of Cornwall's churches and larger houses. **All Saints Parish Church**, built in 1821 (but with a south wall that is Norman), is a good example of a church built in Pentewan stone. It was also a china clay port, but the silting up of the harbour led to the village's decline. Today it is another popular holiday destination with the harbour now playing host to sailing boats and pleasure craft.

Inland from the village lie the famous **Lost Gardens of Heligan**, one of the country's most interesting gardens - or, more properly, series of gardens. Situated at the heart of one of the most mysterious estates in England, Heligan Manor was the seat of the Tremayne family for more than 400 years. It was a huge estate, of over 1000 acres, and had its own brewery, farms, saw mills, orchards, gardens, brickworks and flour mill. In many ways it was self-supporting, and had a staff of 20 'inside' and 22 'outside'. In World War I many of them were killed, and the Tremaynes eventually moved away, and the beautiful gardens were neglected.

These world famous gardens were originally laid out in 1780 but they lay undisturbed before being rediscovered in 1990 and thereafter restored on a shoestring budget by a small band of enthusiasts that has grown to a large working team. Following one of the largest garden restoration projects in the world, the gardens, after spending years under brambles and ivy, have been restored to their original beauty and Heligan is a real living museum of 19th century horticulture covering 80 acres, where the main focus is an exploration of man's relationship with the land.

There are walled gardens, a formal Italian garden, a New Zealand garden, hothouses and a subtropical jungle garden to be found here, as well as many others, that all benefit from the mild Cornish climate. Snacks and meals are served in the Picnic Basket and Licensed Restaurant, and the shop holds a wide-ranging stock that includes books, woodland products, honey and preserves, kitchen and garden related goods, and locally grown plants and seeds relating to the collections in the gardens. A delightful place that will interest many more than just keen gardeners, Heligan is a treat not to be missed. On the wider estate, Lost Valley comprises lakes, wetlands and ancient broad-leaved woodland, and the ancient practices of coppicing and charcoal-burning take place again; Horsemoor Hide is a new wildlife interpretation centre; and the Farm Walk offers access through permanent pasture, where hedgerows have been re-laid and the Heligan herd grazes the grassland slopes.

From the village, a charming walking and cycling trail leads up the beautiful **Pentewan Valley** which follows the course of the White River. Taking in both woodland and wetland, there is plenty to see and the trail is relatively flat, thus aiding both walkers and cyclists.

Mevagissey

5 miles S of St Austell on the B3273

Mevagissey Harbour

Once aptly known as Porthilly, Mevagissey (from the Cornish Meva ag Issy, 'ag' meaning 'and') was renamed in the early 14th century after the Welsh and Irish saints, Meva and Issey, **St Peter's Parish Church** was once dedicated to these two saints, and the font is Norman. In the 17th century the tower was allowed to decay, and the bells were sold to pay for its demolition. The largest fishing village in St Austell Bay, Mevagissey was, like many Cornwall fishing villages, once an important centre of the pilchard industry and in the 19th century catches of over 12,000 tons a year were landed here. The catching and processing of the fish employed nearly everyone in the village and, as well as smoking, salting and packing the fish, there were boatbuilders, net makers, rope makers, coopers and fish merchants. Some pilchards were exported to southern Europe or supplied to the Royal Navy - the sailors used to refer to the fish as 'Mevagissey Ducks'. The need to process the catch within easy reach of the harbour created a labyrinth of buildings separated by steeply sloping alleyways,

TREGONEY HOUSE

Tregoney Hill, Mevagissey,
Cornwall PL26 6RD
Tel/Fax: 01726 842760
e-mail: young.mevagissey@btinternet.com

Located on one of the narrow, steep streets within the popular village of Mevagissey, you will find the charming **Tregoney House**. Dating back to the mid-1800's, this attractive Grade II listed terraced property, which was built as a Sea Captain's house, has recently been taken over by Dianne and Lee Young. Moving here from London, the couple are continuing to run this as a bed and breakfast offering three comfortable en-suite rooms. Although evening meals are not served, there are numerous eating places within easy reach.

some of which were so narrow that the baskets of fish sometimes had to be carried on poles between people walking one behind the other.

Mevagissey's **Inner Harbour** as it appears today dates from the 1770s, when an Act of Parliament of 1774 allowed the construction of the 'new' pier and jetties. The original pier, where the East Pier now stands, dated back as far as 1430. Many of the buildings around this area of the town date from the late 18th century when stone cottages and warehouses were built in place of the town's original cob cottages. The **Outer Harbour** was built so that the size of the port could be increased to cater for the needs of the growing fishing fleets. However, it was destroyed in the Great Storm of 1891 and it was not finally finished until 1897.

As well as still being an interesting place from which to watch the boats, the harbour here is also home to **Mevagissey Museum**. Housed in a museum piece itself (the building dates from 1745), the museum has a broad collection of artefacts that cover not only the pilchard industry but also old agriculture machinery, a collection of 19th and 20th century photographs depicting village life and the story behind Pears soap. In 1789, Andrew Pears, a young Cornish barber, went to

TREWINNEY FARMHOUSE

Mevagissey, Cornwall PL26 6TD
Tel: 01726 844332
e-mail: trewinneyfarm@aol.com
website:
www.mevagisseybedandbreakfast.co.uk

Trewinney Farmhouse is a typically cornish, stone built farmhouse dating from the 17th century, and well hidden along a charming country road. Everything here speaks of tradition and history - the furniture, the building itself and the quality of the welcome from the owner, Stephanie Fleig. There are three rooms on

offer - one with a four poster, a double and a twin, all sharing. The attention to detail is meticulous and the rooms are all comfortable and beautifully furnished in period style.

There is a choice of breakfasts, including freshly baked farmhouse bread. The full English is a treat in itself, though lighter options, as well as vegetarian choices, are also available. Plus, of course, plenty of tea, or coffee to accompany it!

Stephanie believes in old style standards, such as Cornish hospitality and value for money, so you' re sure to find everything at Trewinney to your liking. Dogs can also be accommodated but the owners have animals and the local farm animals need to be taken into consideration

You won't find many B&Bs like Trewinney. It is the perfect base from which to explore Cornwall, from the Lost Gardens of Heligan and the Eden Project to Land's End, and from The Lizard to Tintagel and its Arthurian connections. And of Course, Mevagissey itself is right on your doorstep, with its restaurants, quaint pubs and typical Cornish ambience.

THE RISING SUN INN

Portmellon Cove, Mevagissey,
Cornwall PL26 6PR
Tel: 01726 843235
e-mail: cliffnsheila@tiscali.co.uk
website:: www.risingsunportmellon.co.uk

The Rising Sun Inn is one of the best-kept secrets in this delightful part of Cornwall and a gem worth seeking out. Located on the water's edge, this glorious whitewashed inn was built around 1681 and was originally owned by Lord Gordon, of Gordon's gin fame. To one side is a small patio, while inside you will find exposed beams, wood panelling and an open fire. Professional chefs prepare the superb menus, with an emphasis on seafood, as befits the coastal setting, which can be enjoyed in the 50-seater restaurant. Also seven en-suite guest rooms.

London where he began to groom the rich and influential. His customers' complaints about the harshness of the available soap led Andrew to experiment and develop a softer soap that was more gentle on the skin - the still popular Pears soap.

Another attraction found around the harbour is the **World of Model Railway Exhibition** in Meadow Street, which houses a fascinating display of over 2,000 models and over 40 trains; the detailed scenery through which the trains run is exceptional, as are the many moving accessories. A well-stocked model shop caters for everyone from the enthusiast to the complete beginner, and those interested in Thomas the Tank Engine will also not be disappointed. The old lifeboat station that was built on the quayside in 1897 to allow for quick and easy launching has now become **The Aquarium**, with all the money from the entrance fees being used to maintain the harbour. The lifeboat station closed in the 1930s after

THE ANCHORAGE

Portmellon Road, Near Mevagissey,
Cornwall PL26 6PH
Tel: 012726 844412
e-mail: lee@anchorage4u.co.uk
website: www.anchorage4u.co.uk

The Anchorage is one of the best B&Bs in the Mevagissey area and owners Pat and Dermot Lee offer you a very warm welcome. The beautifully proportioned, late 18th century house, was originally built by a sea captain and has splendid views out over the sea. There are three rooms - two en suite and one with private facilities, and all are spacious, elegant and full of character. The traditional English breakfast includes delicious home-made bread and preserves. Only a short distance from the picturesque port of Mevagissey, it makes a wonderful base from which to explore an area of Cornwall that is rich in history, beauty and heritage.

this original building had sustained regular and repeated storm damage.

Today, all but a handful of inshore fishing craft have gone and, in common with most of Cornwall's coastal communities, the local economy relies greatly on tourism. Thankfully though, the annual influx of visitors, which has given rise to a proliferation of cafés and gift shops, has not seriously diminished the port's essential character. In the 1750s, when John Wesley first came to Mevagissey to preach at the Market Square, he was greeted by a barrage of rotten eggs and old fish and had to be rescued from the crowd and taken to safety. In return for their hospitality, Wesley gave his hosts, James and Mary Lelean, his silver shoe buckles. Visitors to Mevagissey today need not fear such a welcome.

Like a lot of Cornish places, Mevagissay has featured in many films, including *Dracula*. And in 1906, while staying in the village, George Bernard Shaw wrote his play *The Doctor's Dilemma*.

Gorran Haven
7 miles S of St Austell off the B3273

Once a community with a history to rival that of Mevagissey, Gorran Haven is now a cluster of fishermen's cottages with a sheltered sandy beach that connects, at low tide, with the longer **Great Perhaver Beach** to the north. To the southeast, the land rises into the impressive headland of **Dodman Point**, which marks the southern point of St Austell Bay and is owned by the National Trust. Sometimes known locally as Deadman Point, this headland, which stands over 370 feet above sea level, was the site of a substantial Iron Age coastal fort.

One mile inland is **St Gorran Parish Church**, which has 53 beautifully carved ancient pews ends. The tower dates from 1606, when the medieval steeple collapsed. And in the village itself is the **Church of St Just**, which was originally a chapel-of-ease dating mainly from the 15th century. After the Reformation, it

CAERHAYS CASTLE GARDENS
Gorran, Nr St Austell, Cornwall PL26 6LY
Tel: 01872 501310/501144
Fax: 01872 501870
website: www.caerhays.co.uk

Caerhays is an informal 60-acre woodland garden on the coast by Porthluney Cove. The garden can be traced back to the end of the 19th century, and many of the plants and shrubs to be seen today were introduced by Chinese plant hunters. The garden is best known for its huge Asiatic magnolias, which are in their prime in March and April, and is the holder of the NCCPG National Magnolia Collection. It is also home to the x williamsii

camellia hybrids and to many varieties of rhododendron. The house, built in the gothic style by John Nash between 1805 and 1807, is open for conducted tours on certain days.

was abandoned and used to store fish nets. It was restored as place of worship in the 19th century, and is now well worth visiting.

St Michael Caerhays

7 miles SW of St Austell off the B3287

This small place is mentioned in the *Domesday Book* as Carrioggel. **St Michael's Parish Church** is well worth visiting. Close to the village lies the **Caerhays Castle and Gardens** (see panel opposite), one of only a few remaining examples of a castle built by John Nash, with, surrounding it, 100 acres of woodland gardens. Most of the plants were collected in China at the beginning of the 20th century. The gardens are at their best in March, April and May, and are only open during these three months.

Truro

This small elegant city has grown to become the administration, commercial and tourism centre for Cornwall. It nestles in the valley of three rivers - the Kenwyn, the Allen and the Truro which branches off from the River Fal at Tolverne. Much of the city dates back to the Georgian era and there are some handsome examples of architecture still to be found in the cobbled streets. Lemon Street is

considered to be the finest example west of Bath.

2002 was an important year in the history of Truro, as it commemorated, with great celebration, the 125th anniversary of the charter that made it a city. Its site, where there are pleasant walks beside the river, has been occupied for thousands of years, but it was not until mineral extraction in the area began in earnest in the medieval age that the settlement started to expand into a place of importance. In 1305 Truro became a stannary town, and huge quantities of smelted tin and other metals were brought here for assaying, taxing and exporting. A number of picturesque alleyways, or 'opes', have survived from Truro's days as a port and many have colourful names such as Tippet's Backlet, Burton's Ope and Squeezeguts Alley.

Although the river around Truro had begun to silt up and Falmouth was taking over as the main seagoing port of the area, the increase in mineral prices

Truro Cathedral

ADMIRAL BOSCAWEN

7 Richmond Hill (beneath railway station),
Truro, Cornwall TR1 3HS
Tel 01872 278941

Sitting on Richmond Hill, this inn was once called the Exeter Inn until its name was changed to the **Admiral Boscawen** in the late 1960s. It has everything a local pub should have - bags of character, great service, friendly locals and real value for money. The landlord is Ken Carlyon, who used to be one of its most faithful regulars, so he has a fondness for the place that is reflected in the way he runs it, retaining most of its olde worlde character. It has open fires, for instance, and sells a range of keg bitters, as well as lagers, wines and spirits. It is open all day every day, and has three letting rooms available all year round.

during the 18th century saw a revival of Truro's fortunes. Wealthy merchants and bankers moved into the town and Truro became fashionable within high society, its reputation rivalling that of Bath.

The arrival of the railway in 1859 confirmed Truro's status as a regional capital and, in 1877, it became a city in its own right when the diocese of Exeter was divided into two and Cornwall was granted its own bishop. Many places were originally put forward as the site of a new cathedral, including Bodmin, St Columb and St Germans, where Cornwall's cathedral had stood up until the 10th century, when the diocese was suppressed and combined with that of Exeter. Three years later, the foundation stone for **Truro Cathedral**, the first Anglican cathedral to be built on a new site in England since Salisbury was built in 1220, was laid by the future Edward VII. The site had originally been occupied by the 13th century St Mary's Parish Church, and St Mary's Aisle survives from that building. Before work could begin, however, many old buildings to the north of the cathedral had to be demolished, creating a small cathedral close.

The next 30 years saw the construction of this splendid Early English style building, designed by architect John Loughborough Pearson, it was finally completed in 1910. The stained glass in the Cathedral is considered to be one of the finest collections in England. Other treasures include two 14th century statues from Brittany given to Bishop Frere in 1929, the Bath stone reredos behind the high altar, and the terracotta panel *Way of the Cross* by George Tinworth. The cathedral has three organs, the one in St Mary's Aisle originally dating from 1750. Lunchtime recitals on the famous 'Father' Willis organ take place every Friday from mid-March to the end of October.

The **Royal Cornwall Museum**, housed in what was the Truro Savings Bank building, explores the history of the county from the Stone Age right up to the present day, whilst the art gallery is the home of works by Constable and Lowry as well as paintings by the Newlyn School of Artists.

The city has an excellent shopping centre which comes to life at Christmas with the City of Lights lantern procession, now an established tradition in Truro.

Along with the elegantly planned streets, Truro has **Victoria Gardens** beside the River Kenwyn, and **Boscawen Park**, named after Admiral Edward Boscawen, the younger son of Lord Falmouth, both of which offer tranquility away from the busy city centre. One of the city's best-known landmarks is a column commemorating the Lander brothers, Richard and John, who were born in Truro in the first decade of the 19th century. In 1830 Richard was commissioned to go to Africa to try to discover the source of the River Niger, and in 1832 he was awarded the first gold medal of the Royal Geographical Society.

Bosvigo, a small garden surrounding a private house on the outskirts of the city, is beautifully planted with summer herbaceous borders to give the impression of moving from one room to another. Truro's theatre, **The Hall for Cornwall**, can be found at Back Quay, in the heart of the city. A lively programme of events is offered throughout the year.

Around Truro

Probus

4½ miles NE of Truro off the A390

The granite tower of **St Probus's and St Grace's Parish Chuch** is the tallest and grandest in all of Cornwall, being 125 feet high. The saints to whom it is dedicated are also unusual, in that they were husband and wife. During renovation, male and female skulls were discovered buried near the altar, and it is thought that they were of the two saints.

Just to the west of the village lies a place that will be of great interest to gardeners - **Trewithen House and Gardens**. An early Georgian house whose name literally means 'house of the trees', Trewithen stands in glorious woods and parkland. The house was built in the 1730s by Philip Hawkins, with later additions in 1763. It is filled with paintings, furniture and other artefacts collected over the years by the Hawkins family

The garden was laid out in the early 20th century by George Johnstone, and the outbreak of World War I led to his finest creation - 300 beech trees were felled to be used as props in the trenches - allowing him to plant the great glade that stretches out from the front of the house. The gardens are planted with many rare species of flowering shrubs, among them magnolias and rhododendrons, and a notable camellia collection that includes *x williamsii*, a cross between *camellia saluensis* and *camellia japonica*. The nursery and café at Trewithen complete the facilities at this world renowned garden.

St Clement
1½ miles E of Truro off the A390

Though little more than a suburb of Truro nowadays, this hamlet should be visited to see the 14th century **St Clement's Parish Church**. The place has long been a favourite with painters and photographers, perhaps because it has an unusual lych gate, with an upper room that was reputedly once used as the village school.

Evidence of previous inhabitants of the area can be found on a stone near the church porch that is dedicated to Isniocus Vitalis, a 3rd century Roman, but which also bears inscriptions in the ancient Ogham alphabet of the Celts.

Tregony
6 miles E of Truro on the B3287

Often referred to as the 'Gateway to the Roseland Peninsula', this village was, in the 14th century, a busy river port long before Truro and Falmouth had developed. Built on the wealth of the local woollen trade, the surrounding mills produced a rough serge known as Tregony Cloth; the silting up of the river left Tregony's quayside unusable though parts of it can still be made out today. Tregony and St Mawes both used to return two members of parliament, being so-called rotten boroughs that were common before the Reform Act.

The **Roseland Peninsula** is the name given to the indented tongue of land which forms the eastern margin of the Fal estuary which is always known by its Cornish name - Carrick Roads.

Ruan Lanihorne
4 miles SE of Truro off the A3078

Situated on the old main coaching route

KINGS HEAD

Ruan Lanihorne, Near Truro,
Cornwall TR2 5NX
Tel: 01872 501263
e-mail: andrew@law1601.fsnet.co.uk

With its bright, colourful exterior, the **Kings Head** is a real gem of a traditional Cornish pub. Even though it's well hidden off the B3078, tourists should seek it out for its warm welcome, its cosy, traditional atmosphere and its superb food and drink.

It is renowned for its food, which has earned quite a reputation in the area, and the locals eat here frequently - always a good sign! It uses only fresh local produce, and the cuisine combines tradition and innovation, creating a wonderful menu. And a quiet drink

is a must - it serves Skinners real ales, as well as a wide range of wines and spirits. So come and experience one of Cornwall's best kept secrets. You won't be disappointed!

from London to Penzance, this now quiet village is a bird lovers' paradise as the creek is a haven for waders and waterfowl. **St Romon's Parish Church** dates mainly from the 14th century, and is dedicated to a saint who is alo the patron saint of Tavistock in Devon. In Brittany he is known as St Ronan. He is said to have been a royal prince who lived the life of a hermit in Ireland until he was consecrated bishop.

Veryan
6 miles SE of Truro off the A3078

This charming village, set in a wooded hollow, is famous for its five **Round-** **houses** which lie at the entrances to Veryan. Built in the early 19th century for the daughters of the local vicar, Jeremiah Trist, the whitewashed cottages each have a conical thatched roof with a wood cross at the apex. It was believed that their circular shape would guard the village from evil as the Devil would be unable to hide in any corners.

Portloe
7½ miles SE of Truro off the A3078

Portloe is one of the most attractive and unspoilt villages in Cornwall, with stone cottages surrounding the tiny

POLSUE MANOR

Ruanhighlanes, Truro, Cornwall TR2 5LU
Tel: 01872 501270 Fax: 01872 501177
website: www.polsuemanor.co.uk

Set in nine acres of mature grounds, **Polsue Manor** is a traditional country house that appeals to people who appreciate gracious living and the finer things in life! It has three fully en suite rooms that are comfortable and spacious, each one individually styled in the traditional manner to make your stay a pleasurable one, with colour TV, direct dial phones and tea and coffee making facilities. There are beautiful views of the surrounding Cornish countryside from each room, which is a bonus for those who appreciate the peace and quiet of the countryside!

The guest drawing room is elegant and comfortable, just right for a quiet read of the paper or a book after a hectic day touring the delights that are within easy driving distance of this exclusive guest house. Polsue Manor is on the Roseland peninsula, midway along the south coast of Cornwall, and within easy distance of fine, sandy beaches, stunning countryside with old inns and churches, and one of the county's hidden gems - the King Harry ferry, that takes you across the River Fal. And the gardens in the area are a delight! The warm Gulf Stream allows many exotic plants to grow here, and you could spend most of your time just going round them and admiring the bright colours if it wasn't for the fact that there's so much else to do as well!

The warm and friendly atmosphere coupled with the elegant décor make many people return year after year to this beautiful guest house! Try it - you'll end up doing the same!

Portloe

beach to Carne and back again by the public footpath. During World War II Cornwall's first above-ground aircraft reporting post, made of wood and containing obvservation and plotting equipment, was sited at Carne Beacon, though many local people objected strongly to such a historic site being used.

harbour, which is overshadowed by the steep cliff. In stormy weather, it is impossible for boats to fight their way against the wind and waves through the narrow gap into the safety of the harbour.

Carne

6½ miles SE of Truro off the A3078

Overlooking Gerrans Bay on land owned by the National Trust stands **Carne Beacon**. One of the largest Bronze Age barrows in the country, this ancient burial mound is thought to be the grave of King Geraint, who, in the 5th century, is said to have rowed across the bay in a golden boat with silver oars. He is reputed to have been buried in full regalia, but recent excavations have failed to confirm this story. An interesting 2-mile geological trail runs from the car park at Pendower along the

Portscatho

7 miles SE of Truro off the A3078

This pleasant and unspoilt fishing village, with its sandy beach on Gerrans Bay, is well worth a visit and may appear familiar to anyone who watched the television drama, *The Camomile Lawn*, as it was used as the filming location. Nowadays it and the neighbouring village of Gerrans have almost joined to form one village. In the 18th century, a lot of smuggling was carried out. The villagers placed lookouts on the two headlands either side of the bay to watch for revenue cutters.

St Anthony

9 miles S of Truro off the A3078

This little hamlet lies towards the bottom of the Roseland Peninsula and, from **St Anthony Head,** there are splendid views across Carrick Roads to Falmouth. At the foot of this squat headland stands **St Anthony Lighthouse**, which was built in 1834 and replaced a coal beacon that for centuries had warned sailors off the infamous Manacles rocks.

This headland, which guards the entrance into Carrick Roads, has had a strategic importance for many years and, on the cliff top behind the lighthouse, are

St Anthony Head

the remains of **St Anthony Battery**. In military use right up until the 1950s, this was a significant World War II observation post and the old officers' quarters, which like the headland are now in the hands of the National Trust, have been converted into holiday cottages.

St Mawes

7½ miles S of Truro on the A3078

A popular and exclusive sailing centre in the shelter of Carrick Roads, St Mawes is a charming small town with a

safe anchorage and good beaches. From here ferries take passengers across the river to Falmouth and, during the summer, a boat also takes passengers down the river to the remote and unspoilt area of Roseland around St Anthony. The town is dominated by its artillery fort, **St Mawes Castle**, which was built between 1539 and 1545 as part of Henry VIII's coastal defences. Guarding the entrance into Carrick Roads, the castle stands opposite Pendennis Castle with which it shared the duty of protecting Falmouth and the river. A favourite walk goes from the Castle to St Just in Roseland and back (or one way on the bus).

The parish church for St Mawes stands in St Just in Roseland, though at one time a small chapel dedicated to St Mawes, or Mandatus, stood in the town along with his 'holy chair' and 'holy well'. Not a stone from any of them now remains.

St Mawes

St Just in Roseland

6 miles S of Truro on the B3289

This enchanting hamlet has the exquisite 13th century **St Just Parish Church**, which lies in one of the most superb settings in the country. . St Just is said to have been a son of Geriant of Anglesey, after whom Gerrans Bay is named. Concealed in a steep wooded tidal creek of the Percuil River, the church, which has been described as one of the most beautiful in England, is surrounded by gardens that contain many subtropical trees and shrubs, including African fire bush and Chilean myrtle. A.V. Morton, in his book *In Search of England*, called the churchyard 'one of the little known glories of England'. Unfortunately, the interior of the church does not live up to expectations as it underwent a clumsy Victorian restoration. There is a tradition that when Joseph of Arimathaea brought Jesus to Britain, they landed in St Just Creek.

St Just in Roseland

ROUND HOUSE BARN COTTAGES & B&B

St Just in Roseland, Truro, Cornwall TR2 5JJ
Tel: 01872 580087/38 Fax: 01872 580067
e-mail: kim@roundhousebarn.co.uk
websites: www.a-bed-in-cornwall.co.uk
 & www.a-cottage-in-cornwall.co.uk

Set in the unspoilt Roseland Peninsula, close to the beach at Carrick Roads, **Round House Barn Cottages and B&B** are situated in a beautiful rural/marine location close to St Just in Roseland. It has three, high quality, well equipped and decorated, cottage/apartments, designed for couples only. All have internet access and two are equipped with Sky TV. in addition, there are two en-suite B&B rooms decorated and furnished to a high standard. There is an extensive breakfast menu using local produce and includes locally smoked haddock and salmon, as well as an extensive choice of coffees and teas.

SMUGGLERS COTTAGE

Tolverne, Philleigh, Nr St Mawes,
Cornwall TR2 5NG
Tel: 01872 580309
website: www.tolverneriverfal.co.uk

Smugglers Cottage is a lovely old thatched building in a glorious location on the River Fal. During the summer months the cottage and terraces are open for morning coffee, drinks and home-cooked lunches, cream teas and early evening pasty suppers. Tolverne was closely involved with the D-Day landings, when thousands of American troops left for Normandy and Eisenhower visited the cottage. The Newman family, here since 1934, have assembled a fascinating collection of memorabilia of that period. Three sailings a day, on their pleasure boat, leave from the cottage for the 45-minute trip to Falmouth.

Tolverne

4 miles S of Truro off the B3289

During World War II, this quiet village was taken over by the American army and was used as an embarkation point for Allied troops during the D-Day landings. On the shingle beach the remains of the concrete honeycomb mattresses that covered it in the 1940s can still be seen. While in the area, General Eisenhower stayed at the thatched, 500-years old **Smugglers Cottage** and, today, this simple dwelling is home to a large collection of memorabilia from that period.

Trelissick

3½ miles S of Truro off the B3289

Situated on a promontory that is bound by the River Fal and two creeks, the **Trelissick Estate** is a private 18th century house that is surrounded by 25 acres of beautiful gardens and 500 acres of park and farmland from which there are marvellous views over Carrick Roads. Several miles of paths lead around the National Trust estate, which takes in rolling parkland and dense woodland, and visitors will see an abundance of subtropical trees and shrubs that live happily alongside native plants. The estate's Cornish apple orchard is another

Trelissick Gardens

Mid Cornwall South

interesting feature here and it was created to preserve many traditional apple species. Various of the house's outbuildings have been converted to take visitors and, in the stables, there is a display of saddlery while another building is home to Trelissick Gallery, a showcase for the work of artists and craftsmen working in Cornwall. The shop sells gifts, souvenirs, books and plants, and light refreshments and lunches are served.

Close to the estate is the landing point of the **King Harry Ferry** which takes cars and passengers across the narrow, yet deep, stretch of water on the River Fal between Feock on the west bank and Philleigh on the Roseland Peninsula. There has been a ferry crossing at this point for centuries; the present ferry was built at Penryn in 1974 and is one of only five chain ferries at work in Britain. River trips can be taken in summer from either Truro or Falmouth across to the new pontoon at Trelissick.

Feock
4 miles S of Truro off the B3289

The charming collection of whitewashed thatched cottages that make up this tiny hamlet, along with its glorious position, have lead to Feock being considered one of the most attractive little villages in the county. A pleasant creekside walk to the west of the village follows the course of an old tramway which dates from the time when this area was not as peaceful and tranquil as it is today but

was a bustling port serving inland Cornwall. To the south of Feock, a country lane leads to the tip of **Restronguet Point** and, at the mouth of Restronguet Creek, stands the Pandora Inn. A typical whitewashed and thatched 17th century inn, it was known as the Passage House until 1850, when its name was changed to the present one. Some claim that the new name comes from the ship which was sent out to capture the mutineers from the *Bounty*, while others claim it was named after a small schooner which regularly sailed between Truro and Plymouth carrying drink. Certainly, the inn was once owned by the man who brought the mutineers to justice.

Mylor
5½ miles SW of Truro off the A39

The two attractive villages of Mylor Churchtown and Mylor Bridge, on the south side of Mylor Creek, have blended into one another and, today, are popular yachting centres with a club and many watersports activities. Mylor Churchtown, at the mouth of the creek, is the larger of the two and was once a dockyard and landing place for the packet ships which carried mail throughout the world. In the churchyard of the heavily restored **St Mylor Parish Church** can be seen the graves of many sea captains as well as, close to the south porch, a round-headed **Celtic Cross** which, at over 17 feet tall, is one of the tallest in Cornwall. It now stands ten feet above the surface.

CREEKSIDE HOLIDAY HOUSES

Restronguet, Mylor, Nr Falmouth,
Cornwall TR11 5ST
Tel: 01326 372722

Restronguet is a peaceful picturesque waters edge hamlet three miles north of Falmouth and ideal for an 'away from the crowd' holiday. Peter Watson owns and lets his three properties comfortably sleeping two to eight people and will be pleased to talk on the telephone or send his brochure. The house, cottage and flat all have shrubbed gardens and facilities for your boats, shared use of a dinghy too with outboard motor. Footpath walks along the creekside give opportunity for bird and boat watching and walking your dogs who are welcome. The thatched Pandora Inn is nearby and Mylor Bridge (1 mile) has a full compliment of shops.

Dating from the 10th century, it was rediscovered during restorations in Victorian times after having been used for centuries as a flying buttress against the south wall of the church. Some people have speculated that at one time it may have marked St Mylor's grave.

Flushing

7 miles S of Truro off the A39

This small village, which is another popular yachting centre, was built by settlers from Vlissingen in Holland in the 17th century and still retains a Dutch appearance. A prosperous port in the 17th and 18th centuries, Flushing's narrow streets are home to some fine Queen Anne houses, many of which were built to house sea captains and naval officers.

Falmouth

8 miles S of Truro on the A39

In Britain's Western Approaches and guarding the entrance into Carrick Roads, Falmouth is a spectacular deep-water anchorage that is the world's third deepest natural harbour. The place was originally called *Peny-cwn-cuik*, which very soon became Anglicised as 'Pennycomequick'. Although a settlement has existed here for hundreds of years, it was not until the 17th century that the port was properly

Falmouth Harbour

TUDOR COURT HOTEL

55 Melville Road, Falmouth,
Cornwall TR11 4DF
Tel/Fax: 01326 312807
e-mail: enquiries@tudor-court-
hotel.freeserve.co.uk
website: www.hotels-falmouth.com

The **Tudor Court Hotel** has nine comfortable and spacious rooms for discerning guests who demand the very best in accommodation. Eight are fully en suite and one has a private bathroom. Once a manor house, it dates from the 1800s and is now one of the best family hotels in the bustling port of Falmouth · one which has a friendly and welcoming atmosphere. It is set in mature gardens which have won "Britain in Bloom" awards, has ample parking and is ideal for a long or short stay, business or pleasure.

developed. However, in the 16th century Henry VIII sought to guard this strategically important harbour from attack. Standing on a 200-foot promontory overlooking the entrance to Carrick Roads, Henry's **Pendennis Castle** is one of Cornwall's great fortresses and, along with St Mawes Castle on the opposite side of the river mouth, it has protected Britain's shores from attack ever since its construction. Its low circular keep has extremely thick walls and it stands within a 16-sided enclosure - the outer curtain wall was added in response to the threat of a second Spanish Armada in Elizabethan times. One of the last Royalist strongholds to fall during the Civil War (in 1646), and then only after a grim five month siege from land and sea, Pendennis Castle remained in use up until the end of World War II

In the 17th century, the arrival of the packet boats at Falmouth, which sailed between Britain, Europe and the Americas carrying mail and goods, saw the development of the port. During its heyday, in the early 19th century, Falmouth was the base for almost 40 such sailing ships, but, a few decades later, the introduction of steam-powered vessels heralded the end of Falmouth; by

BISTRO DE LA MER

28 Arwenack, Falmouth, Cornwall TR11 3JB
Tel: 01326 316509
e-mail: bistro.delamer@aol.com

Bistro de la Mer in Falmouth is more than a restaurant · it is an outstanding eating experience where the food has become well known even outside of Cornwall! The reason? Attention to detail!

Only the finest and freshest of local produce is used, and the menu is imaginative and trendy yet with a traditional feel. The whole ambience of the place speaks of quality and comfort, with the staff being friendly and knowledgeable about the dishes on offer. Being in Falmouth, seafood is a speciality!

When in the town, you can't afford not to eat here!

Tall Ships Race, Falmouth

and history of the dockyard. Promising an experience 'as rich as the sea', the **National Maritime Museum Cornwall** on Discovery Quay is home to Cornwall's Maritime Heritage and the National Small Boat Collection, and special exhibitions include a Tidal Gallery and a Meteorology Gallery. Pirates and smugglers too were attracted to Falmouth and, on **Custom House Quay** stands an early 19th century brick-built incinerator and chimney known as the **Queen's Pipe**. It was here that contraband tobacco seized by Falmouth's customs men was burnt.

the 1850s, the packet service had moved to Southampton. Despite this, the town has maintained its maritime links and today it plays a dual role as a commercial port and holiday centre. The docks continue to be used by merchant shipping but the town's traditional activities are being overshadowed by its increasing popularity as a yachting and tourist centre. During the summer there are regular bus tours around the wharves, workshops and dry docks, with an explanation of the day-to-day activities

As well as carrying commercial cargoes around the world, the ships coming into Falmouth also brought exotic plants from such places as China, Australia and the Americas. Many of the subtropical trees and shrubs ended

CAVENDISH COFFEE HOUSE

Market street, Falmouth, Cornwall TR11 3AC
Tel: 01326 319438
e-mail: cavendish-coffee@aol.com

Everyone is made welcome at the **Cavendish Coffee House**, right in the heart of historic Falmouth.

It serves the best teas and coffees in town, plus the food is outstanding. From snacks and simple sandwiches to home-cooked roasts, beef, lamb and pork, you'll find everything beautifully cooked and all at reasonable prices.

The décor inside is charming, and the staff are a "little bit special" · warm, friendly and highly efficient. Make this your first stop for a tasty lunch or a refreshing tea or coffee with cakes!

up in private gardens but the town's four central public gardens, **Fox Rosehill**, **Queen Mary**, **Kimberley Park** and **Gyllyngdune** are also packed with such plants as magnolias and palms which all benefit from the mild climate. Gyllyngdune Gardens have a splendid centrepiece in the shape of a Victorian bandstand; a grotto walkway links the formal gardens to the seafront area.

Visitors here can also find fine sandy beaches, including Gyllyngcase beach with its Blue Flag status, while for those looking for a wilder time there is the **Ships and Castles Leisure Pool** complete with its rapid river run and wave machine. For those keen to explore the upper reaches of Carrick Roads by boat, a number of pleasure trips depart from Prince of Wales pier, as do the passenger ferry to St Mawes and several others along the coast. A short distance from the pier is the tree-lined square known as the Moor, where the town hall and Falmouth's **Art Gallery** can be found. A little way outside town is **Swanpool Nature Reserve**, a brackish lagoon that is home to a wide variety of wildlife. Over 100 species of birds have been recorded at this Site of Special Scientific Interest, and one creature is unique to Swanpool: this is the Trembling Sea Mat, which belongs to the primitive group *Bryozoa*. Many tiny animals link up to form a colony which attaches itself to plants and stones under the surface. To feed, each animal extends a crown of tentacles lined with tiny hairs to trap food particles.

It was from Pendennnis Castle that Charles I's wife, Henrietta Maria, fled the country between 1642 and 1645. The place was staunchly Royalist, and at the Restoration in 1660, local landowner Sir Peter Killigrew sougth permission to found a proper town and church at Falmouth. In 1660 Charles II granted it a town charter, and the following year it bacame a parish in its own right. Not long after **King Charles the Martyr Parish Church** was built on its main street.

Penryn

7 miles SW of Truro on the B3292

Mentioned in the *Domesday Book*, this ancient town at the head of the Penryn River was, before Falmouth's rise to prominence in Tudor times, the controlling port at the mouth of Carrick Roads. During medieval times it was also the home of **Glasney College**, an important collegiate church which survived until the Dissolution of the Monasteries in 1539. Now only a portion of wall and an arch survives of what was at one time one of Cornwall's most important ecclesiastical foundations. It had been founded in 1265 by Bishop Bronescombe of Exeter, and indeed much of the college was modelled on Exeter Cathedral.

At one time, granite quarried close by was shipped from here all over the world and it has been used in places as far apart as the Thames Embankment and Singapore harbour. The availability of

CROSSKEYS

Church Road, Penryn, Cornwall TR10 8DA
Tel: 01326 373233 Fax: 01326 327738

The **Crosskeys** is a fine old English pub that is loved by locals and visitors alike. It dates from the 1800s, and you get a real sense of tradition here, with an interior that is both welcoming and comfortable. It has recently undergone a modernisation that has improved it even further, and now its food · good, honest pub grub that is beautifully cooked and represents great value for money · is gaining an enviable reputation. It is served all day and every day, and you're sure of hearty portions. There is live music every Friday and Saturday evening, so why not come along and make a great night of it?

the stone has also left its mark on Penryn as there are many fine Tudor, Jacobean and Georgian houses to be seen here which, now restored, can be found in the town's conservation area. An fascinating collection of objects offering an insight into the local history can be found at the town musuem, located under the town hall.

Another reminder of the town's maritime past is the sad story that forms the basis of the play, *The Penryn Tragedy*, based on a popular pamphlet published in the reign of James I of which not one single copy now exists. After years at sea, a young sailor from Penryn returned home to his parents' inn and, as a joke, he disguised himself as a rich man but not before telling his sister of his plan. His parents, overcome with temptation on meeting this rich stranger, murdered the young man for his money. Next morning, the sister came in search of her brother and the full horror of their crime caused her parents to commit suicide. Whether the events ever happened or not is another matter, as the same story can be found all over Europe.

Mid Cornwall South

PLACES TO STAY, EAT AND DRINK

● Denotes entries in other chapters

6 The Helford River & The Lizard Peninsula

This area of Cornwall is often called Poldark Country after the series of successful novels by Winston Graham (1910-2003), set in the county's tin and copper mining region, became popular following their appearance on television. At the centre of the industry are the twin towns of Camborne and Redruth, which now form Cornwall's largest conurbation, and where most of the mines were found. Although the industry closed down in the early 20th century, unable to compete against the great mineral finds in South Africa, Australia and the Americas, there is plenty to see in the region from those days.

For visitors wishing to find out more of the lives of the miners and the industry itself will find that the staff at the Poldark Mine Heritage Complex will be able to answer most questions.

As well as being mining country this is also land that has been settled for centuries, and Carn Brea, to the southeast of Camborne, is the site of the earliest known Neolithic settlement in southern Britain. Another curious feature of this landscape is Gwennap Pit, a large natural amphitheatre, probably created by a collapsed mine shaft, that was used on many occasions by John Wesley, the founder of Methodism.

A famous literary association with the area is Daphne du Maurier, who based her novel *Frenchman's Creek* on the Helford River and surrounding countryside. To the south lies the Lizard Peninsula, the southernmost point of mainland England. An area of contrasts - there are beautiful secluded wooded inlets around the Helford estuary, areas of bleak moorland and dramatic cliffs -

Kynance Cove

exploration of the peninsula is very worthwhile. Warmed by the Gulf Stream, the Lizard is home to some of the county's most interesting and most exotic gardens, including Trevarno, where there is also a Gardening Museum.

Camborne

Once the capital of Cornwall's main tin and copper mining area, Camborne and neighbouring Redruth have combined to form the largest urban centre of population in the county. In the mid 19th century, the area surrounding Camborne was the most intensely mined in the world and the district is still littered with evidence of this lost era. In the 1850s, Cornwall had well over 300 mines, which together produced some two thirds of the world's copper and tin. This was when the area round the town enjoyed its greatest area of prosperity, with Cornwall employing over 50,000 people in the mining industry. However, from the middle of the 19th century until the early 20th century most of the mines had to close when the discovery of extensive mineral deposits in the Americas, South Africa and Australia rendered the local industry no longer economically viable.

Before the mining industry took off in the 18th century, Camborne was a small village surrounded by moorland, and the results of its rapid expansion at the time can still be seen in the numerous terraces of 18th and 19th century miners' houses. Contrasting with these densely populated streets and alleyways, the **Literary Institute**, built in 1829 in granite, has a grand, Tuscan style. A **Town Trail** now guides visitors around this historic former mining town, introducing the many interesting buildings that could easily be missed among the bustle of Camborne's busy town centre.

As the town's, and indeed the area's, livelihood depended on mining for several hundred years it is not surprising that Camborne was once home to the **School of Mines,** (now at Penrhyn). One of the specialists in mining

CORNISH CHOUGHS INN

Treswithian, Camborne, Cornwall TR14 7NW
Tel: 01209 712361
e-mail: sjzmorris@hotmail.com

The **Cornish Choughs Inn** dates from 1627, and since it was taken over in 2004 by Sue and Andy Morris, it has become one of the most popular pubs in the area. Inside it is traditional yet spacious, with a lovely little bar, a games section for pool and darts, and a separate restaurant that serves everything from sizzling steaks with all the trimmings to mixed grills and snacks. There's also a great

selection of Real Ales and drinks, including soft drinks if you're driving. If it's the real Cornwall you're looking for, you'll find it in the Cornish Choughs Inn!

Richard Trevithick Statue

up Camborne Hill on Christmas Eve 1801. **Trevithic Cottage**, where he was born is owned by the National Trust, and can be visited. Though a genius, Trevithick died penniless and was buried in an unmarked grave in Dartford, Kent. The town still celebrates the achievements of its great son on April 26 each year, his birthday, with the **Trevithick Day Festival** .

Around Camborne

Godrevy Point
5 miles NW of Camborne off the B3301

Marking the northern edge of St Ives Bay, the low cliffs here lead down to a

education, Robert Hunt, is remembered here in the school's impressive **Geological Museum and Art Gallery**, which displays minerals and rocks from all over the world. The School of Mines is now part of the University of Exeter.

Outside the town's library is a statue to a **Richard Trevithick** (1771-1833) who, as an accomplished amateur wrestler, became known as the Cornish Giant. Trevithick was also an inventor and he was responsible for developing the high pressure steam engine, the screw propeller and an early locomotive which predated Stephenson's Rocket by 12 years. He also invented a high pressure steam carriage known as the 'Puffing Devil', the forerunner of the motor car, which completed a test run

Godrevy Point

sandy beach on the eastern side of the headland. Godrevy Point is a well known beauty spot that, along with **Navax Point** where seals can be sighted off shore, is owned by the National Trust. A short distance from the point lies **Godrevy Island** on which stands a Lighthouse that provides a useful landmark from both sea and land and is also featured in Virginia Woolf's *To the Lighthouse*.

Portreath

3½ miles N of Camborne on the B3300

Now a thriving holiday centre, Portreath developed in the 18th century as a port from which copper was exported and into which coal was imported, mainly to and from Wales. Prior to the quay being constructed by the Bassett family in 1760, copper ore from the mines around Redruth had to be loaded on to ships from the beach which was not only a slow job but also a dangerous one. Some years later, in 1809, the new **Harbour** was connected to the mines by the first railway in Cornwall.

The remains of the inclined plane, on which the ore-laden wagons were lowered down the steep gradient to the quayside, can still be seen as can the

CLIFF HOUSE

The Square, Portreath, Cornwall TR16 4LB
Tel: 01209 843847
e-mail: cliffhouseportreath@ btinternet.co.uk

Cliff House is an old, whitewashed cottage dating back over 200 years and situated in the heart of the village. The rooms are all comfortable and spacious, and the breakfasts range from traditional Cornish to lighter options. Owned and personally managed by Gail and Paul Mackenzie, this establishment represents surprising value for money with its friendly welcome and the many thoughtful extras that make it such a delight to stay in, such as information packs in each room which contain discount vouchers for local amenities, and even an emergency laundry service! You get a real Cornish welcome at Cliff House!

BRIDGE INN

Bridge, Near Portreath, Redruth, Cornwall TR16 4QW
Tel: 01209 842532
website: www.downourlocal.com/thebridgeinn

A well run, friendly pub is always a great find and there are not many as well run and as friendly as the **Bridge Inn**, the oldest pub in the village of Bridge. It dates to the 17th century when it was a hunting lodge, and has many original features, giving it the look of a real Cornish hostelry. Here lovers of traditional pubs will feel right at home, with a wide range of ales, wines and spirits, and good, honest, home-cooked food that is served at lunchtimes and in the evenings. There is plenty of parking, a beer garden and a children's play area.

white conical daymark that stands on the cliffs above the harbour. Built in the 19th century, the locally nicknamed Pepperpot still guides ships safely into the harbour. During the 19th century, this now quiet village was at its busiest with over 100,000 tons of copper passing through the port and equally vast quantities of coal were received here from the coalfields of South Wales.

A popular destination with surfers and families, the village also marks the starting point of the **Mineral Tramway Walks** while, just to the south, lies the 250-acre **Tehidy Country Park**, which is mainly woodland with about nine miles of woodland walks. It once belonged to the same Bassett family which first developed Portreath as a port. At Tolgus Mill, near Portreath, **Cornish Goldsmiths** has the largest collection of gold jewellery in the West Country and many gold artefacts and other attractions, including Tolgus tin, the Pot of Gold pottery, Tutankhamun regalia and James Bond's Aston Martin DB5 from the film *Goldfinger*.

Pool
2 miles NE of Camborne on the A3047

Pool is one of several villages which have been consumed by the Camborne and Redruth conurbation. Very much in the heart of Cornwall's mining area, here can be found **Cornish Mines and Engines**, where the secrets of the county's dramatic landscape can be discovered, and where Trevithic's mighty steam engines are

explained. At the **Cornwall Industrial Discovery Centre** you can see Michell's Whim, a winding engine now operated by electricity. The world of Cornish mining is explained through the displays and guided tours and there are specially designed activities for children.

St Day
4 miles E of Camborne off the 3298

A **Heritage Trail** around this village and the adjoining Lanner and Carharrack takes in the historic sites which are all that remain from the time when, in the 19th century, St Day was known as the richest square mile in the world due to the number of copper and tin mines in the area.

Gwennap
4 miles E of Camborne on the A393

The mysterious **Gwennap Pit**, found just to the southeast of Redruth, is a round, grass covered amphitheatre 114 feet in diameter that is thought to have been created by the collapse of a subterranean mine shaft. Used as a cock pit, this curious theatre is sometimes referred to as the 'Methodist Cathedral', as it was here that John Wesley preached on many occasions from 1743 onwards. In 1806, the seating terraces were cut into the banks and, the following year, a Whit Monday service was held which has continued and is now the annual focus for Methodist pilgrimage from around the world.

The **Museum of Cornish Methodism**, nearby, was opened in the 1980s and provides an interesting and informative series of displays and exhibits on the religion and its founder.

Redruth

2 miles E of Camborne on the A393

This market town was once, along with much of the surrounding area, at the centre of the county's mining industry and, as such, was a prosperous town. Some pockets of Victorian, Georgian and earlier buildings still remain and, particularly at Churchtown, there are some attractive old cottages and **St Uny's Parish Church**, mainly Georgian with a 15th century tower. The lychgate has an unusually long coffin rest that was built to deal with the aftermath of mining disasters. Redruth was also the home of the Scottish inventor William Murdoch (1754-1839) who was responsible for such innovations as coal-gas lighting and the vacuum powered tubes that were once a common feature in department stores. His house, the first in Britain to use gas lighting, can still be seen.

The countryside immediately to the south of Redruth is dominated by dramatic **Carn Brea** - pronounced Bray - which rises some 750 feet above sea level. The summit of this windswept granite hill is crowned with a 90 feet monument to Francis Bassett, a benevolent Georgian land and mine owner who did much to improve the lot

PENVENTON HOTEL

West End, Redruth Cornwall TR15 1TE
Tel: 012909 203000 Fax: 01209 203001
e-mail: inspire@penventon.com
website: www.penventon.com

The **Penventon Hotel** is a gracious Georgian mansion standing in its own grounds close to Redruth, and enjoying all the privileges and amenities of a fine three-star hotel. Under the personal supervision of the Pascoe family, who have been here since the 1960s, it has enjoyed a reputation that places it among the best hotels of its kind in Cornwall.

Swim and be pampered in the Aphrodite's Health and Leisure Complex in the grounds; dine on one of the 100 classic French, Italian and English dishes served in the elegant restaurant; visit many of the historic sites that are a only a short distance away from the hotel. You'll find it all here at the Penventon - and a whole lot more besides. There are ten chefs dedicated to preparing only the finest food from the freshest of local produce. The staff are friendly and knowledgeable about what to do and see in the area. Tours to all the major attractions of Cornwall, from St Michael's Mount and the St Ives Tate Gallery to the world-famous Eden Project or Falmouth's Maritime Centre can be personally arranged by the staff.

The guest rooms are extremely well appointed, as you would expect, and all are en suite, with bath or shower facilities. All rooms have colour TV, direct dial phones, controllable central heating and tea/coffee making facilities. Suites have one or two bedrooms and a lounge area, and some even have patios.

So if it's pampering and comfort you're after, it must be the Penventon Hotel for you!

SPORTSMANS ARMS

Four Lanes, Redruth, Cornwall TR16 6LR
Tel: 01209 313724

Owned and personally managed by Roger Barbery and his daughter Sara, the **Sportsman's Arms** on the B3297 is undoubtedly the most popular pub in the Four Lanes area - and it's not difficult to see why. Formerly a coaching inn, it retains all the warmth and cosiness of a well-run, friendly establishment that puts customers first. There is a wide range of ales, cider, wines and spirits to choose from at it's well stocked bar, and the food is good, simple, reasonably priced pub fayre that is beautifully cooked and presented by Sara. There is a 50 cover function room for that special occasion and live music on Saturday evenings.

of poor labourers. It was built in 1836. Also to be found on Carn Brea, on the lower eastern summit, is a small castle, a part medieval building that was once used as a hunting lodge and has since been restored. However, this land has been occupied for centuries and Carn Brea is also the site of the earliest known Neolithic settlement in southern Britain. It was also the site of an Iron Age fort, and possibly a Romano-British mining settlement called *Durocornavium*.

Each year, in June, Carn Brea sees the Midsummer Bonfire ceremony, a pagan ritual in which the lighting of a fire on the summit of the beacon is the signal to light further fires that stretch across the county from Land's End to the River Tamar. Each fire is blessed by a clergyman in Cornish and, after burning flowers and herbs, young people leap across the dying embers to ward off evil and bring good luck. Another attraction south of Redruth is the **Shire Horse & Carriage Museum** (see panel below) at Lower Gryllis, Treskillard. Here you can see the magnificent shire horses at rest, play and work, along with the biggest collection of horse drawn buses in Britain.

THE SHIRE HORSE & CARRIAGE MUSEUM

Lower Gryllis, Treskillard, Nr Redruth, Cornwall TR16 6LA
Tel: 01209 713606

The Shire Horse & Carriage Museum offers a variety of attractions but pride of place goes to the magnificent Shires, Clydesdale and Suffolk Punch horses, which can be seen at work and at rest. Also on site are wheelwright's and blacksmith's shops, and in the museum an impressive array of private and commercial wagons includes the largest collection of horse-drawn buses in the United Kingdom. Among smaller exhibits are farming implements and hand tools of bygone days. Guided tours enable visitors to get the most out of the farm

and museum, and a visit can end with a scrumptious home-made cream tea.

FOX AND HOUNDS

Comford, Lanner, Cornwall TR16 6AX
Tel: 01209 820251

The **Fox and Hounds** must be one of the most picturesque pubs in this part of Cornwall. Set on the B393 road between Falmouth and Redruth, it is a former 18th century coaching inn, whitewashed and aflame with flowers in the summer months. This is a real pub lovers' pub - for those more mature people who appreciate tradition, warmth and a friendly Cornish welcome. The interior is crammed with period features, such as stone floors and low, beamed ceilings. It serves beers, wines and spirits, and there is a separate dining area where real Cornish food is served from fine, local produce. This is a gem of a pub that just cannot be missed!

Tuckingmill
1½ miles E of Camborne off the A3047

While most places in this area devoted their energies to the mining industry, Tuckingmill was home to a fuse factory (the last fuseworks closed in the 1960s) that went on to become world famous for the production of safety fuses. Invented in 1830 by William Bickford, the fuses were used widely in Hollywood films and, most notably, as dynamite fuses in *Mission Impossible*.

Stithians
5½ miles SE of Camborne off the A393

This quiet rural village is home to the second largest agricultural show in Cornwall, which takes place every July. The 300-acre **Stithians Reservoir**, just to the west of the village, is a watersports centre and also home to a bird sanctuary. The **Parish Church of St Stithians** is medieval, with a Victorian chancel.

Troon
1½ miles S of Camborne off the B3303

Though not as famous as the golfing town of the same name in Scotland, Troon in Cornwall should still be visited for the restored **King Edward Mine and Mining Museum,** on the northern edge of the village. Here you can see the old tramways and the mines they served, and find out about the area's mining history.

Treverna
8 miles SE of Camborne off the A394

To the north of this village is the **Argal and College Water Park**, which offers watersports and course fishing. A mile and a half to the southeast is **Penjerrick**, a ten acre garden created by the Quaker Fox family in the 19th century. It features rhododendrons, magnolias, camellias and tree ferns.

Mawnan Smith

10½ miles SE of Camborne off the A39

Just to the west of this pretty village, which overlooks the River Helford, lies **Glendurgan**, a marvellous jungly valley garden owned by the National Trust (the house is private). Set in a wooded valley that drops steeply down to the hamlet of Durgan and the shores of the Helford estuary, this subtropical garden was first laid out at the beginning of the 19th century, again by the Fox family, and includes many exotic trees and shrubs. The famous **Heade Maze**, created in 1833 from laurels, and the **Giant's Stride** - a maypole - are two features that are particularly popular with younger visitors to this beautiful and secluded garden. Also on site are a tea room, shop and plant sales.

Carwinion, also near Mawnan Smith, is an 18th century manor house set in 12 acres of Victorian gardens overlooking the Helford Estuary.

Mawnan

11½ miles SE of Camborne off the A39

Its elevated position, above this hamlet, has led to the 15th century **St Mawnan Parish Church**, and particularly its tower, to have been used as a landmark by sailors for centuries. Built on a spur at the mouth of the River Helford, this tower is an excellent viewing point not only for those wishing to in this

sweeping coastline but it was also used as a lookout post during times of war and potential invasion. St Mawnan himself was an Irish bishop who seems to have had a particularly bad temper. When St Maelruain refused to absolve him for some minor misdemeanour, Mawnan is supposed to have cursed him, adding that the time will come when women will get above themselves, the poor will lack reverence to their betters, and churches will be poorly attended.

Durgan

11 miles SE of Camborne off the A39

This tiny hamlet, which today is owned by the National Trust, was, for centuries, a fishing village whose daily catch was transported to Falmouth by donkey. Now a peaceful backwater, with cottages overlooking a sand and shingle beach on the River Helford, Durgan is also home to **Trebah Garden** - often dubbed the 'garden of dreams', and often rated among the top 80 gardens in the world. The ravine in which the garden has been created was long ago owned by the Bishops of Exeter and in the 1830s the land was bought by the Fox family.

The Quaker Charles Fox set out to create a garden of rare and exotic plants and trees that were collected from all over the world.

Reaching maturity some 100 years later, Trebah came to be regarded as one of the most beautiful gardens in Britain. At the outset of the Second World War the house was sold and the estate was split up, and the gardens left to become submerged under weeds, ivy and other creepers. In 1980 Trebah was bought by the Hibbert family, who inaugurated a massive restoration programme that returned the garden to its original impressive state.

The 25 acres of the garden fall down to a secluded private beach on Helford River and here visitors can discover glades of subtropical shrubs and trees, 100 year old rhododendrons, waterfalls and ponds of giant Koi carp. This is a garden for all the family, and children will be enthralled by the Gunnera Passage, a tunnel of giant rhubarb 16 feet high. The purpose-built visitor and education centre includes exhibition space, a lecture theatre, tea house and gift shop.

Trebah Garden, Durgan

Helford Passage

11 miles SE of Camborne off the A39

Situated on the opposite bank of the estuary from Helford, this hamlet is a popular mooring point, with sailing and motor boats for hire, and also a sand and shingle beach. During the summer a ferry runs from here across the estuary, as it has since the Middle Ages; until the early 20th century, while a cart was allowed on the ferry the horse, led by a rope, had to swim alongside the boat.

Helston

Dating back to Roman times, when it was developed as a port, Helston is the westernmost of Cornwall's five medieval stannary towns. During the early Middle Ages, it was an important inland port that sat on the tidal River Cober. Tin was brought here for assaying and taxing before being shipped from the once busy quaysides. However, in the 13th century a shingle bar, the **Loe Bar**, formed across the mouth of the River Cober, preventing access to the sea, and goods were transported to the newly formed harbour at Gweek. The shingle bar turned what was a small tidal creek into Cornwall's largest lake, the **Loe Pool**, a mile south of the town. At one time local people used to cut a channel from the Loe pool to the sea to allow excess water to drain away, and the resultant slick of silt and debris reached the Scilly Isles. A culvert now takes the overflow from the lake to the sea.

Forming part of the Penrose estate (which is now owned by the National Trust) Loe Pool is a haven for sea birds as well as waterfowl and is surrounded by the woodlands of the old estate. A Cornish folk tale links the Pool with the Arthurian legend of the Lady of the Lake: like Bodmin Moor's Dozmary Pool, a hand is said to have risen from the depths of the water to catch the dying King Arthur's sword. Another local story connects Loe Bar with the legendary rogue, Jan Tregeagle, who was set the task of weaving a rope from its sand as a punishment.

FITZSIMMONS ARMS

Coinagehall St, Helston, Cornwall TR13 8EQ
Tel:01326 574897

Situated in the heart of the small town of Helston you will find one of the best and most historic pubs in Cornwall · The **Fitzsimmons Arms**.

Named after a famous local boxer, the place is cosy yet spacious, with a wonderfully intimate atmosphere that is typically Cornish. The food is excellent, and all home cooked to perfection. There are plans to upgrade the pub without it losing any of its special character, so you are sure of a warm welcome and the best of hospitality if you pay it a visit!

Helston's long and colourful history has left it with a legacy of interesting old buildings: **The Blue Anchor Inn** was a hostel for monks in the 15th century while 16th century **Angel House** was the former town house of the renowned Godolphin family. In the 1750s, the Earl of Godolphin rebuilt **St Michael's Parish Church** in Georgian style, and, in the churchyard of this unusual granite structure, lies a memorial to **Henry Trengrouse**, the Helston man responsible for inventing the rocket propelled safety line which saved so many lives around the British coast. Trengrouse devoted himself to its development after the frigate *Anson* ran aground on nearby Loe Bar in 1807 and 100 people lost their lives unnecessarily. He was not much feted in Britain, but was presented with a diamond ring by the Tsar of Russia; the inventor was later forced by penury to pawn the ring and he died penniless in 1854. Another of the town's famous sons was the boxer **Bob Fitzsimmons**, who was the first boxer to hold the world middleweight,

light heavyweight and heavyweight championship titles. In one bout he fought against Tom Sharkey in San Francisco in 1896 and was disqualified for punching below the belt by the referee, who was none other than Wyatt Earp, sometime deputy marshal of Tombstone, Arizona. He died in Chicago in 1917, three years after he retired from the ring.

Helston has a surprising number of Georgian, Regency and Victorian buildings which all help to give it a quaint and genteel air. By the traffic lights is the Victorian **Guildhall**, and housed in one of the town's old market halls close by is Helston's **Folk Museum**. Covering local history, the displays here include trades associated with Helston such as fishing, agriculture and mining, along with exhibits depicting domestic life. The cannon which guards its entrance was taken from HMS Anson, which was wrecked on the Loe Bar in 1807 with much loss of life.

Still very much a market town today, and serving much of the Lizard

Peninsula, Helston has managed to escape from the mass tourism that has affected many other Cornish towns. However, what does draw people here is the famous Festival of the Furry, or **Flora Dance**, a colourful festival of music and dance. The origins of the name are unclear but it could have been derived from the Middle English word 'ferrie' which suggests a Christian festival or from the Celtic 'feur' which means holiday or fair. As it is held im May, this would suggest that the festival has connections with ancient pagan spring celebrations. There are various stories and legends surrounding the Furry Dance and one tells how the Devil, flying across Cornwall carrying a large stone to block the gates of Hell, was intercepted by St Michael. During the ensuing encounter, the Devil dropped the boulder and the place where it fell became known as Hell's Stone, or Helston. The people of Helston took to the streets dancing to celebrate St Michael's victory and this is said to be the original Furry Dance which takes place on the nearest Saturday to St Michael's Day (8 May). The Helston Town Band leads dances throughout the day, and in the principal dance the participants wear top hats, tails and dress gowns. Not only do they dance through the streets, they also weave in and out of houses and shops.

Two miles northwest of the town lies **Trevarno Estate and Gardens**, a beautiful and rare estate that has a long history that stretches back to 1246 when Randolphus de Trevarno first gave the land its name. Over the centuries the gardens and grounds have been developed and extended, and in 1995 it was put up for sale for the first time in 120 years in 33 lots. However, the estate was saved, and today, Trevarno has become known as one of the finest gardens in the county and one that displays a great gardening tradition. From walled gardens and Victorian and Georgian gardens to mature woodlands, there are many different styles to be discovered here along with an extensive collection of rare trees and shrubs. The estate's **National Museum of Gardening**, housed in a modern purpose-designed building, complements the grounds and highlights the ingenuity of gardeners down the ages by the range of gardening implements, antiques, memorabilia and ephemera on display. Also at Trevarno is a unique range of craft workshops, including a soap workshop, organic herbal workshop, a bee centre, a furniture-maker and a potter. Home-made refreshments are served among sub-tropical plants in the delightful fountain garden conservatory.

To the east of the town lies another interesting attraction that will keep all the family amused for hours - **Flambards Victorian Village** (see panel on page 172). With its re-creation of a lamp lit Victorian street where over 50 shops and domestic situations have been authentically furnished and equipped, a visit to Flambards is like taking a step back in time. However, there is much

FLAMBARDS THEME PARK

Clodgey Lane, Helston,
Cornwall TR13 0QA
Tel: 01326 573404
website: www.flambards.co.uk

An intriguing and unique attraction, **Flambards** has been entertaining visitors of all ages for more than 30 years with its

award-winning exhibitions, exciting rides, family shows and glorious gardens. At the centre of the complex is the Victorian village, a faithfully re-created collection of lamplit streets and alleyways where visitors can peer into over 50 shops, watch traders at work and see how life both above and below stairs was carried on more than a century ago.

Each of the lifelike characters is authentically dressed in genuine Victorian costume, and the houses and shops are equipped and furnished with thousands of antique items. The famous chemist shop time capsule is particularly intriguing with its old medicines and cures that give a unique glimpse of

dispensing long before the NHS. These fascinating displays are augmented by an audio tour that tells about the magic and misery of life in Victorian times.

Another top attraction here is an undercover life-size re-creation of a World War II blitzed street, avowed chillingly authentic by those old enough to remember those dark days and a source of wonder for others. This remarkable exhibition was opened by Dame Vera Lynn in 1984.

'Wedding Fashions Down the Years' features a romantic assembly of changing styles, a collection of wedding dresses and wedding cakes from 1870 to 1970.

Rides and slides that range from the gentle to the adventurous keep the youngsters happy, and for older children and adults the figure-of-eight karting circuit offers the opportunity to put driving skills to the test. Some of nature's less cuddly creatures · birds, snakes and large spiders · can be seen close up at the Creepy Crawly Show, and among the other attractions · the list is almost endless · are boats and bumper cars, fun buggies for toddlers and a science centre, and after all the excitement a stroll round the lovely gardens and the plant centre is the perfect way to end a visit.

more to see and do here: Britain in the Blitz, for instance, a re-created bombed street from World War II; the award winning gardens and the country's most southerly rollercoaster.

Close to Flambards is the Royal Navy's land and sea rescue headquarters at **Culdrose**, one of the largest and busiest helicopter bases in Europe. Aircraft from here have been responsible for a great many successful search and rescue operations since the base was commissioned in 1947 as *HMS Seahawk*. There are guided tours and a special public viewing area from which the comings and goings of the helicopters can be observed.

Around Helston

Wendron
2 miles N of Helston on the B3297

Close to this bleak village is one of the many mines that have been worked in this area since the 15th century. Now reopened as the **Poldark Mine Heritage Complex**, it is one of Cornwall's most interesting attractions. The guided underground tours which take visitors into the mine's tunnels are an adventure not to be missed, and there are many other interesting things to see, including demonstrations of candle making, wood turning, pottery and the manufacture of tin and pewter jewellery, a museum, shops, cafeteria, toddlers' play room and amusement arcade. The complex is laid out with award winning gardens and both young and old will find there is

plenty here to keep them amused.

St Wendron's Parish Church is mainly 14th and 15th century, though it was heavily restored in Victorian times. The lychgate, which has a room above, dates from the 17th century.

Gweek
3 miles E of Helston off the A394

Situated at the westernmost branch of the River Helford, Gweek was once an important commercial port that grew up after nearby Helston harbour became silted in the 13th century. The same fate befell Gweek many years later and today it is a picturesque village that has replaced it's cargo vessels with small pleasure craft. However, the village has maintained links with it's maritime past and the rejuvenated harbour now plays host to such delights as craft shops and small boatyards. A short distance from the centre of Gweek, on the picturesque reaches of the Helford Estuary, is the **National Seal Sanctuary** (see panel on page 174), Europe's leading marine animal rescue centre. It was the brainchild of a retired Welsh miner, Ken Jones, who moved to Cornwall in the 1950s to set up a café on the Cornish coast. He found an abandoned seal pup on the beach, and decided to care for it until it recovered. Since then the centre has cared for many sick, injured and orphaned seals as well as being home to a community of seals and sea lions which are unable to fend for themselves. Visitors to the sanctuary can not only witness the antics of the seals at feeding time but also have a look at the new otter facility, which highlights the conservation work being undertaken by local environment groups. Close by is an ancient coppiced wood.

Constantine
4 miles E of Helston off the A394

St Constantine Parish Church dates mainly from the 15th century, apart from the chancel, which is Victorian. St Constantine was the son of King Patrenus of Cornwall who had a misspent youth until he turned to Christianity. He travelled north and evangelised the Scots, founding a monastery in Govan, now part of Glasgow, on his travels. He died a martyr's death in AD 598 when pirates cut off his right arm and let him bleed to death.

THE NATIONAL SEAL SANCTUARY

Gweek, Nr Helston, Cornwall TR12 6UG
Tel: 01326 221361
e-mail: seals@sealsanctuary.co.uk
website: www.sealsanctuary.co.uk

The National Seal Sanctuary is set in the picturesque Helford Estuary, by the beautiful village of Gweek, in Cornwall. It started in 1958 when Ken Jones, who lived with his wife just one hundred yards from the beach, found a baby seal, only a few hours old, washed up at St Agnes. He took it home and so began the rescue centre for seals and oiled birds. As news of his work spread, he found that he needed more room to be able to care for the increasing number of seals being rescued around the Cornish coast and in 1975, moved to Gweek where the Sanctuary has been gradually expanding ever since.

The Sanctuary now has nursery pools, convalescence pools and resident pools, as well as a specially designed hospital, which includes isolation pools and treatment areas.

Many seals have been rescued over the years and most are returned to the wild when they are well enough, but some who would not survive back in the wild now live at the Sanctuary.

As well as the Common and Grey seals, there are Californian and Patagonian sea lions at this busy centre. The Sanctuary also provides a haven for a variety of other animals including otters, ponies and goats. Occasionally the facilities and expertise here are called on in the rescue of other marine creatures such as dolphins and turtles.

Lizard Peninsula
Area SE of Helston on the A3083

Physically separate from the main part of Cornwall and with a unique landscape, the Lizard Peninsula, parts of which are a National Nature Reserve, has been designated an Area of Outstanding Natural Beauty. Much of the coastline around this most southerly part of mainland Britain is in the hands of the National Trust and the **South West Coast Path** winds around the peninsula providing beautiful scenery for walkers of all ages and abilities. From the luxurious greenery of the Helford River to the dramatic cliffs around Kynance, Mullion and Lizard Point, there is a variety of landscape that is matched only by the vast range of both rare and common plants and many species of birds that make this their home. **Lizard Point**, and not Land's End, is the most southerly point on the British mainland.

The Lizard is also known for its unique Serpentine rock, a green mineral that became fashionable in Victorian times when ornaments were, and still are, made as souvenirs and objets d'art. Several shops near Lizard Point sell souvenirs made from it, though at one time it was mined on a commercial scale.

Mawgan
3½ miles E of Helston off the B3293

This small village lies beside a creek in the Helford estuary that inspired the setting for Daphne du Maurier's novel *Frenchman's Creek*. An isolated inlet

The Lizard Peninsula

THE OLD COURT HOUSE

Mawgan, near Helston, Cornwall TR12 6AD
Tel:01326 221240
e-mail:
contact@theoldcourthousemawgan.co.uk
website: www.theoldcourthousemawgan.co.uk

Everyone is made welcome at **The Old Court House** in the picturesque old village of Mawgan. It was once a coaching inn dating from the 18th century, and still retains some of its original features, giving a cosy, attractive ambience to the place. It serves three rotating real ales, as well as a fine selection of beers, wines, spirits and soft drinks. It prides itself on its good, honest "pub grub" which is always beautifully cooked and presented, and should satisfy the heartiest of appetites. The bar, the cosy snug and the lounge are the perfect places to unwind after a hard day exploring the area. And you'll get to meet the resident parrot, "Nibbles", who will keep you entertained!

that is overhung with trees, the creek is more reminiscent of the Amazonian rainforest than Cornwall and many local people down the ages have believed that the area is haunted. The village is more properly called Mawgan-in-Meneage, as this part of the county, lying just north of The Lizard, is called Meneage, meaning 'monklands'.

Trelowarren House, in the village, is an impressive part-Tudor country mansion that has been the home of the Vyvyan family since the 15th century. It sits in 1,000 acers of woodland, which is open to the public. On the estate are to be found the **Halliggye Fogou**, which are mysterious Iron Age underground chambers. **St Mawgan Parish Church** is 15th century, but was sympaheically restored in Victorian times.

Helford

6½ miles E of Helston off the B3293

This picture postcard village stands on the secluded tree lined southern bank of the Helford estuary and it must be one of the most attractive settings in the whole of the county. Once the haunt of

Helford

smugglers, who took advantage of the estuary's many isolated creeks and inlets, the series of deep tidal creeks in the area are rumoured to be the home of **Morgawr**, the legendary Helford monster. The first recorded sighting of this sea serpent was in 1926 and, ever since, there have been numerous other sightings of this "hideous, hump-backed creature with stumpy horns". It is said to look like the Loch Ness Monster, and indeed some video footage recorded in 1999 by someone who formerly worked for the Natural History Museum reveals a creature that looks remarkably like Nessie.

Now a popular sailing centre, this charming and relaxed village is linked during the summer to Helford Passage by a ferry across the river.

St Anthony
8 miles E of Helston off the B3293

This small and remote hamlet, on the northern bank of the Gillan Creek, is little more than a cluster of old cottages and a church. Said to have been founded by shipwrecked Norman sailors grateful that they had reached dry land, the Church of St Anthony does, in some ways, verify this claim as it is built of a stone that is not found in Cornwall but in Normandy.

A path from the church leads to **Dennis Head**, from which there are views across Falmouth Bay to St Anthony Head, and the hamlet has its own small beach of sand and shingle that is also used by sailing boats and sailboarders. **St**

Anthony's Parish Church is mainly 15th century, though a Norman church preceded it. A legend says it was built by Normans who had been blown off course crossing over from France and landed up in the local creek. Dennis is a corruption of the Cornish 'dinas', meaning a fort, so a Celtic fort or settlement may have stood here at one time.

St Keverne
9 miles SE of Helston on the B3293

This pleasant village, which is something of a focal point for this part of the Lizard Peninsula, has a handsome square, an unusual feature in a Cornish village. St Keverne's elevated position, on a high plateau, has led to its church spire long being used as a landmark for ships attempting to negotiate the treacherous rocks, **The Manacles**, which lie just offshore. The name comes from the Cornish 'maen eglos', meaning 'church rocks'. In the churchyard are some 400 graves of those who have fallen victim to the dangerous reef and, as well as a stone marking the graves of nearly 200 emigrants who drowned in 1855 on their way to Canada in *The John*, there is a large granite cross marking the mass grave of the 106 passengers and crew who lost their lives when *The Mohegan* foundered on the rocks in 1898. Because of the number of wrecks lying there, The Manacles is now a favourite spot for divers.

Just outside St Keverne, a statue commemorates the 500th anniversary of

THREE TUNS

The Square, St Keverne, Cornwall TR12 6NR
Tel/Fax: 01326 280949
e-mail: lisa@stkeverne.co.uk
website: www.threetunsstkeverne.co.uk

Within the picture-postcard village of St Keverne you will find one of the best pubs in Cornwall - the **Three Tuns**. It is situated a short distance from some magnificent rocky coastline, and is a popular place with sea divers. The hostelry is built from warm, local stone and has that warm, traditional interior that makes visiting a real pleasure. Of the six comfortable rooms, three are fully en suite, and all will soon be refurbished to an extremely high standard while still retaining great value for money. The food is all home cooked, using local produce (especially fish!) wherever possible. The Three Tuns is a real discovery for lovers of traditional inns!

the **Cornish Rebellion** of 1497 and, back in the church, is a plaque in memory of the executed rebel leaders. At the head of the rebellion was the village's most famous son, **Michael Joseph**, a blacksmith. When King Henry VII imposed heavy taxes to raise money for a war against Scotland, Joseph led 40,000 rebels on a march to London. They were crushed by the King's forces at Blackheath, and Joseph and the other protagonists were hanged, drawn and quartered.

While the sea has dominated the life of St Keverne for centuries the village also has an agricultural heritage and the ancient custom of Crying the Neck lives on. Dating back to pagan times, when it was believed that the corn spirit resided in the last wheatsheaf cut, on the last day of harvest, the last wheatsheaf, or neck, is taken to the farmhouse where it is plaited and hung over the fireplace until the spring, when it is ploughed back into the ground.

St Keverne's Parish Church is one of the few Cornish churches to have a spire. In 2003 it was voted the 'Best Church to Visit' in Britain. It dates mainly from the 15th century and earlier, though the spire was rebuilt in 1770 after being struck by lightning. It is thought that a church of some kind has stood here since about AD 600, when the area was settled by Celtic monks.

Porthallow
10 miles SE of Helston off the B3293

A small, unspoilt village known locally as 'Pralla'. It was once renowned for its pilchards, and one of the biggest events of the year is the Fishing Festival, usually held in June or July. The biggest is the Beach Party on the third Wednesday in August, with gig racing, live music, a barbecue, bonfire and fireworks. At **Nare Point**, north of the village, is an abandoned observation point for a torpedo range that operated here until 1994.

THE PARIS HOTEL

Coverack, Helston, Cornwall TR12 6SX
Tel: 01326 280258
e-mail: info@pariscoverack.com

Overlooking the picturesque fishing harbour at Coverack on the Lizard Peninsula, **The Paris Hotel** is a small, intimate establishment that places great emphasis on comfort, high standards of friendly service and value for money. Named after a liner that ran aground on the Manacle Rocks, it is popular with both visitors and tourists alike. The Harbour Bar is where you will meet the locals and enjoy their lively conversation, while the Oceanview Restaurant has an outstanding reputation for fine food, with fish (locally caught of course) predominating. There are four en suite rooms, all with TV and hospitality tray, and all with gorgeous sea views. An outstanding small hotel in an outstanding part of Cornwall!

Coverack

10 miles SE of Helston on the B3294

This old and unspoilt fishing village, where crab, mullet and monkfish are still landed at the small harbour, has a sheltered, sweeping beach of sand and shingle. Once the haunt of smugglers, Coverack was, for many years, home to an RNLI station because of its proximity to The Manacles.

Goonhilly Downs

5½ miles SE of Helston off the B3293

This area of windswept granite and Serpentine heathland is littered with prehistoric remains including some large Neolithic standing stones that are thought to have been erected to aid communication with the heavenly gods. Rather more up-to-date communications can be explored at the **Earth Satellite Station** (see panel on page 180) whose giant dishes can be seen from many miles away. The largest such station in the world, the Earth Station was opened in the 1960s and, since then, there have been few world events that have not been

Coverack Harbour

The Helford River & The Lizard Peninsula

GOONHILLY EARTH SATELLITE STATION

Goonhilly Downs, Helston,
Cornwall TR12 6RQ
Tel: 0800 679593
website: www.goonhilly.bt.com

Goonhilly has over 60 dishes on site and is the largest satellite earth station in the world. With the ability to transmit to every corner of the globe via space, and through undersea fibre optic cables, Goonhilly simultaneously handles millions of international phone calls, e-mails and TV broadcasts.

The downland surrounding Goonhilly was purchased by the Nature Conservancy Council (now known as English Nature) in 1976, as Cornwall's first nature reserve. BT works closely with English Nature to preserve the natural character of that part of the downland for which we are responsible.

Just outside the Goonhilly site, there's a standing stone called a menhir which has been there for more than 6,000 years, weighs about 15 tonnes and, judging by the rock type, they say it must have been dragged here from at least 20 miles away!

The purpose-built visitor centre offers a unique insight into the world of

communications and has a variety of interactive displays. A licensed cafe and gift shop will make your trip complete.

transmitted or received through here. It handles millions of telephone calls, radio broadcasts, television broadcasts and emails by satellite and fibre optic cables laid in the ocean bed. The guided tour around the station, which takes in all manner of telecommunications including the internet and videophone links, is a fascinating and rewarding experience.

Poltesco

8½ miles SE of Helston off the A3083

Just a few minutes walk from this pretty National Trust owned village lies the deserted **Carleon Cove** which was, until the early 19th century, a busy pilchard fishing and processing harbour. However, with the rise in interest in Serpentine stone, the processing buildings were converted into a factory to work the stone and the pilchard cellars were extended to house steam engines. The finished articles, from ornaments to shop fronts, were carried to the waiting ships on flat bottomed barges at the start of a journey that could lead half way across the world. All now that remains of the stone works is the ruined warehouse.

Cadgwith

9 miles SE of Helston off the A3083

This minuscule and very picturesque fishing village, with its cluster of pastel coloured thatched cottages and two shingle beaches, is, perhaps, everyone's idea of the typical Cornish village. However, in the 19th century this was a busy pilchard fishing centre and it is recorded that in 1904 the fleet from Cadgwith landed a record 1,798,000 pilchards over just four days. Lobster and crab fishing is still carried on, albeit on a small scale, and the boats can still be seen drawn up onto the beach.

Separating the main cove here from Little Cove is **The Todden**, a grass covered mushroom of land. A walk to Little Cove to the south also leads to the curiously named **Devil's Frying Pan**, a collapsed sea cave that is filled with water at high tide.

Lizard

10 miles SE of Helston on the A3083

The most southerly village in mainland Britain, Lizard is a place of craft shops, cafés, art galleries and an inn, all clustered around the village green. Following a visit to Cornwall by Queen Victoria in the 19th century, when she ordered many items made from Serpentine stone for her new house on the Isle of Wight, Osborne, this richly coloured green stone has been popular and Lizard is a centre for it's polishing and fashioning into ornaments.

To the south of the village lies **Lizard Point**, the tip of the Lizard Peninsula,

Cadgwith

THE CAERTHILLIAN GUEST HOUSE

The Lizard, Lizard Peninsula,
Cornwall TR12 7NQ
Tel: 01326 290019
e-mail: hpeake@caerthillian.fsnet.co.uk
website: www.thecaerthillian.co.uk

Visitors to the most southerly point in mainland Britain will find a warm welcome from owners Don and Helen Peake at the **Caerthillian Guest House**. A fine Georgian house cheerfully painted white and light blue, it has four guest bedrooms, all of a very generous size and well furnished, with en suite facilities and some with sea views. Over an excellent English breakfast guests can relax and plan their day in this wonderful part of the country-starting perhaps with a walk to the Lizard Lighthouse half a mile away.

whose three sides of high cliffs are lashed by the waves whatever the season. There has been a form of lighthouse on Lizard Point since the early 17th century but the present twin-towered **Lighthouse**, which warns ships away from the treacherous cliffs, was built in 1751 despite protests from the locals fearing that they would lose a regular source of income from looting ships wrecked around the point. Another feature are the twin horns of the fog horn, which still boom out over the waters once every 30 seconds when the weather is bad. The whole place is now open to the public.

Kynance Cove
9 miles S of Helston off the A3083

A famed beauty spot, now owned by the National Trust, Kynance Cove has a marvellous sandy beach and dramatic offshore rock formations. The name 'Kynance' comes from the Cornish word

REGENT RESTAURANT & GIFT SHOP

The Square, Lizard, Cornwall TR12 7NZ
Tel: 01326 290483

At mainland Britain's most southerly village you will find the **Regent Restaurant & Gift Shop**, a delightful place stocked with many items that would make great gifts or souvenirs, including a wide range of serpentine, a rock for which The Lizard is famous. Plus there's a spacious and modern 60-seat licensed restaurant that sells wonderful home-cooked food · everything

from a tasty lunch to a snack or even just a Cornish cream tea. This family run business is committed to offering outstanding value for money and it succeeds admirably. When visiting The Lizard be sure to pay a visit.

The Old Lifeboat Station, The Lizard

'kynans', meaning a deep ravine, and the place has been occupied since at least the Bronze Age. A favourite destination with wealthy Victorians, including Tennyson, after a visit here by Prince Albert and his children in 1846, one of the giant rocks on the beach became known as **Albert Rock**.

Out to sea is **Asparagus Island**, where, at one time, wild asparagus grew. The cove is also the site of the largest outcrop of Serpentine rock, the rock unique to the Lizard, that is dark, mottled and veined with green, red and white. The caves to the west of the cove can be explored around low tide and these include the **Devil's Bellows**, a cave that, at high tide, becomes a dramatic blowhole. On **Rill Point** is an old coastguard lookout post, from where in 1588 watchers spotted the Spanish Armada several miles offshore. The fleet of 130 galleons announced its imminent arrival with a mass broadside fire, but, alerted by beacons and runners, the English fleet under Sir Francis Drake was waiting.

Mullion Cove
6 miles S of Helston on the B3296

The pretty, weather worn harbour here is overlooked by a few ancient buildings and huge walls of Serpentine rock. Much of the land surrounding this secluded cove of white sand, as well as the harbour and offshore **Mullion Island**, is owned by the National Trust and the views from here extend westwards, across Mount's Bay, to Penzance and Newlyn. The island is home to colonies of sea birds, including fulmars, guillemots and kittiwakes.

A mile inland lies the village of **Mullion**, the largest settlement on the Lizard Peninsula and an ideal base from which to explore this remarkable part of the county. **St Mallenus Parish Church**, dedicated to the French saint Malo (or Mellane of Rennes), has some interestingly carved bench ends - one of them depicts Jonah in the belly of the whale - and there is also a 'dog door' in the south door that was used by sheepdogs who were allowed to attend church with their masters but who were made to leave if they became unruly. This sturdy 15th century building, the roof of which was completely rebuilt in the 1980s, also has a tower built of granite and Serpentine rock.

Mullion Cove

Inland are the remains of the **Wheal Unity** copper mine, which closed in 1919. A large boulder containing copper was dug out of the mine and given to the Natural History Msueum in London.

Poldhu Point

5 miles S of Helston off the A3083

A memorial on the cliffs above the popular sandy beach of Poldhu Cove commemorates the work of Guglielmo Marconi, the radio pioneer who transmitted the first wireless message across the Atlantic from here in 1901. His Morse signal, the letter 's' repeated three times, was received in St John's, Newfoundland, quelling the doubts of the many who said that radio waves could not bend round the earth's curvature. In 1903 Marconi received a visit from the future King George V and his wife, and in 1905 a daily news service for ships was inaugurated, and in 1910 a message from Poldhu to the SS *Montrose* led to the arrest of the murderer Dr Crippen. Marconi had chosen this lonely spot a year earlier and had gone on to build one of the largest wireless stations in the world, the pylons and aerials of which survived until 1937. The small granite obelisk, the **Marconi Monument**, was unveiled by his daughter after the inventor's death.

Gunwalloe
4 miles S of Helston off the A3083

This place is one of the unsung delights of Cornwall, and though not well known by visitors, is a favourite Sunday haunt for locals out walking, even on a winter's day. A tiny fishing hamlet with a charming cove, in 1526 a treasure ship belonging to the King of Portugal sank off **Chuerch Cove**. Many attempts were made to recover the booty on board, but no one ever succeeeded. In 1785 a ship carrying a consignment of gold coins ran aground, making this place still popular with treasure hunters who comb the sands with metal detectors hoping to unearth more coins from the two ships.

The 15th century **St Winwaloe's Parish Church** is dedicated to the Breton missionary St Winwaloe, and lies protected in the sand dunes behind the rounded cliffs of Castle Mound, with the sea pounding away outside (the church is often called the Church of the Storms). Its bell tower was, unusually, built separately right into the rock. Many ships have met their end in the stormy seas in this area, among them the *James & Rebecca*, driven into the nearby Halzephron cliffs by a gale in November 1807. Many lives were saved by local people using a rope chair, but 40 of those on board, including troopers of the 9th Light Dragoons returning from Buenos Aires, were drowned. Only one crew member survived - a young boy. The victims were buried in a common grave on Halzephron Cliff.

Porthleven
2 miles SW of Helston on the B3304

This pleasant fishing town, the most southerly port in mainland Britain, first came into prominence in 1811, when work began on the construction of a harbour in the sweep of Mounts Bay to meet the demand for coal and supplies for the mines and to provide a refuge for the growing

Porthleven

fishing fleet, which reached 100 boats at one time. Trade steadily increased, so from the 1850s a boat-building industry developed, and up until the 1970s clippers, schooners, trawlers and yachts were launched from the slipway. The fishing industry also expanded rapidly, and on a single day in 1834 2,000 54-gallon barrels of pilchards were landed.

Boats still fish from the harbour, mainly now for crab, lobster and crayfish. A number of the small town's old industrial premises have been converted into handsome craft galleries, restaurants and shops and the charming old harbour is overlooked by an assortment of attractive residential terraces and fishermen's cottages. One street is named after Guy Gibson, wartime commander of 617 Squadron, the Dam Busters. He visited the town on holiday with his parents.

When the tide is out, it is possible to walk from Porhtleven to the Loe Bar (see Helston), though great care must be taken.

Sithney
2 miles W of Helston off the A394

This small village, no more than **St Sidinius Parish Church** (consecrated in 1497 and having a 67-feet high tower) and a few cottages, has one unique feature - the **Sithney Treacle Mine**. This miniature folly, sited in the small patch of village green, raises many a smile when people passing through the village see it.

Breage
4 miles W of Helston off the A394

Pronounced Braig, this village is noted for the superb 15th century wall paintings that were discovered in **St Breaca Parish Church** in the 19th century. The building too dates from the same time and this remarkable set of murals, which feature such subjects as St Christopher and Christ blessing the trades, lay beneath a layer of whitewash until the 1890s. In the north aisle there is a rare Roman milestone from the 3rd century AD that provides evidence that tin was extracted here for use by the Roman occupiers. St Breaca is said to have been an Irish saint to who came to Cornwall around AD 460 with her brother St Germoe, an Irish king.

The whole area surrounding the village became one of the richest mining districts in Cornwall, and in 1840 had a population of over 6,000, most of them dependant on the industry.

Praa Sands
6 miles W of Helston off the A394

Two headlands and high dunes enclose the mile long crescent of sand that have helped to build Praa Sands reputation as one of the finest family beaches in Cornwall. An ideal place for bathing and surfing, the beach here never gets too crowded and the village provides a variety of accommodation that is suitable for a small family resort.

THE GARDENS

Tresowes, Ashton, Helston TR13 9SY
Tel: 01736 763299

Owned and personally managed by Moira
Cattell, **The Gardens** is the ideal B&B for
people who prefer a quiet retreat while
holidaying in the lovely county of Cornwall. It
has three comfortable rooms, two en suite and

one with private bathroom, all stylish and
reflecting the history of the house, which
started off life as three 18th century miners'
cottages. It is now extremely picturesque,
nestling within gardens that are a riot of colour
in summer. The breakfasts are all home-
cooked, and you can choose from a hearty full
English or a lighter option if required.

Germoe

7 miles W of Helston off the A394

This small rural village is home to **St
Germoe's Parish Church**. St Germoe, or
St Germochus, was an Irish king and
missionary who was the brother of St
Breaca. Dating from the 12th century,
the present church contains a
remarkable Celtic font that is carved
with a mysterious human head. In the
porch are strange carvings of long-tailed
monkeys, which were said to ward off
evil. Built into the churchyard wall is **St
Germoe's Chair**, a curious covered seat.
Some beleieve that St Germoe lies
buried beneath it; however, the chair has
been dated to Norman times.

Rosudgeon

7 miles W of Helston on the A394

A narrow, winding lane from the
village leads to **Prussia Cove**, a clifftop
settlement that was named after a
notorious 18th century smuggler, John
Carter, who modelled himself on
Frederick the Great. One story
surrounding this unsavoury man tells
how he used a cannon mounted on the
cliffs to scare off revenue officers. The
smugglers' wheel tracks can still be seen
in the steep stone slipway leading up
from the water's edge. Small scale
fishing is still carried out here, and old,
picturesque fishing huts can still be
seen.

Logan Rock

St Ives

Gwithian

131 A3

125 126

127 B3306 129

137 128

138 133 132 134

Treen 130 135

Zennor Lelant Hayle

Pendeen Leedstown

151

B3311

St Just Penzance

150 141 139 145

Newbridge 140 136

142 144 Marazion A394 124

143

Newlyn

146 Mousehole Breage

Sennen 149 A30

Land's End 147 B3315 Porthleve

Land's End Lamorna

148

Porthcurno Mount's

Meathe Bay

PLACES TO STAY, EAT AND DRINK

● Denotes entries in other chapters

7 St Ives, Penzance and Lands End

This, the most southwesterly area of mainland Britain - a region often referred to as Penwith - juts out into the Atlantic and the warm waters of the Gulf Stream and, as a result, experiences a mild climate. The area has been settled for over 4,000 years and numerous prehistoric relics are dotted around the lonely and sparsely populated countryside. The Iron Age village of Carn Euny, the Merry Maidens standing stones and Zennor Quoit are just some of the ancient remains that are well worth visiting.

First fishing and then the tin and

The Tate Gallery, St Ives

PLACES TO STAY, EAT AND DRINK

● Denotes entries in other chapters

economic mainstay of this region and, while many of the little seaports have now become picturesque holiday villages, Newlyn (now more or less a suburb of Penzance) is still one of the busiest fish landing ports in the country. Reminders of the days of mining abound and, near Pendeen, the Geevor Tin Mine and Heritage Centre and the Levant Beam Engine at Pendeen give an excellent insight into what was, until the beginning of the 20th century, a vast industry in southwest Cornwall.

This area has also, since the 1880s, become a place for artists, attracted by the clear, natural light as well as the spectacular scenery. St Ives and Newlyn both still have large communities of painters and sculptors and, as a result, there are numerous commercial galleries as well as the superb modern Tate Gallery and Newlyn Art Gallery displaying their works.

However, it is Land's End, one of the most famous places in Great Britain, that brings most visitors to this extreme tip of the kingdom. The dramatic series of steep granite cliffs, the most westerly point in England (but not the most southerly), are a great pull and, as well as providing an unforgettable view out into the Atlantic, the area around Land's End has a series of exhibitions that are connected with the people and surrounding area. Plus there's the open air Minack Theatre, where watching drama played against the backdrop of the Atlantic ocean, is an unforgettable experience. While a visit to this point is a must on everyone's itinerary, other places equally worthy of visiting for their beauty alone are the almost perfect fishing village of Mousehole, and Marazion, from where the spectacular granite island of St Michael's Mount, sitting out in Mount's Bay, can be seen and visited.

St Ives

With its five sandy beaches, maze of narrow streets and picturesque harbour and headland, this beautifully situated old fishing town still retains much of its charm despite being deluged with

THE SHEAF OF WHEAT

Chapel Street, St Ives, Cornwall TR26 2LS
Tel: 01736 797130 Fax No: 01736 796089
e-mail: info@sheafofwheat.co.uk
website: www.sheafofwheat.co.uk

Situated right in the heart of St Ives, **The Sheaf of Wheat** is an extremely popular pub with an enviable reputation for the quality of its food and drink. It serves two real ales and a selection of lagers, ciders, wines and spirits in its newly refurbished lounge bar. The food is outstanding, and served in an elegant lounge restaurant. In the summer you can eat in the beer garden. There is a wide variety of meals to suit all tastes, with curry night on

Thursdays and a popular carvery (where it is advisable to book!) on Friday, Saturday and Sunday evenings, plus Sunday lunchtime. Children are welcome and there is a large sports TV screen as well as pool and darts.

Barbara Hepworth Museum, St Ives

Known locally as The Island, St Ives Head was also the spot from where a lookout would scan the sea looking for shoals of pilchards. One of the most important pilchard fishing centres in Cornwall, until the industry declined in the early 20th century, St Ives holds

tourists for much of the late spring, summer and early autumn. The original settlement of St Ives took its name from the 6th century missionary, St Ia, who is said to have landed here having sailed from Ireland on an ivy leaf. The 15th century **St Ia's Parish Church**, near the harbour, bears her name, along with those of the two fishermen Apostles St Peter and St Andrew. The 80 feet high tower is built of granite brought by sea from quarries at Zennor, a few miles south. Nearby on **St Ives Head**, stands another ecclesiastical building, the mariners' **Chapel of St Nicholas**.

a record dating back to 1868 for the greatest number of fish caught in a single seine net. On catch days, the streets of St Ives would reek of the smell of pilchard oil as the fish were pressed before being salted and packed ready to be despatched throughout Europe. A local speciality, heavy or hevva cake (so called because the Cornish word for a shoal of fish is 'hevva'), was traditionally made for the seiners on their return from fishing.

As well as providing shelter for the fishing fleet, St Ives' harbour was developed for exporting locally mined

TATE ST IVES

Porthmeor Beach, St Ives, Cornwall TR26 1TG
Tel: 01736 796226 Fax: 01736 794480
website: www.tate.org.uk

St Ives has attracted artists of renown for well over a century, and among early visitors were Turner, Whistler and Sickert. That tradition continues in **Tate St Ives**, housed in a superb modern three-storey building backing directly into the cliff face. The gallery offers a unique introduction to contemporary and modern art, and many works can be viewed in the surroundings that inspired them. Apart from the permanent and changing exhibitions, Tate St Ives stages regular special events and talks. It also manages the town's Barbara Hepworth Museum and Sculpture Garden.

HALSETOWN INN

Halsetown, St Ives, Cornwall TR26 3NP
Tel: 01736 795583

The **Halsetown Inn** dates from 1832, and is a friendly, warm local with five B&B rooms on offer. It has an elegant, Regency façade, and is soon to undergo a complete refurbishment, which will improve the service and value for money even further, and add to its many charming amenities. It sells a wide range of beers, including Courage Best, and during the season serves good, honest pub food every day from 12 - 2 pm (3 pm on Sundays) and 6 - 9.30pm. Out of season, food is served on

Fridays, Saturdays and Sundays. If you're in the area, you can't afford to pass the Halsetown Inn by!

ores and minerals and the sturdy main pier was built by John Smeaton, the 18th century marine architect who was responsible for designing the famous Eddystone Lighthouse. The town's two industries led to the labyrinth of narrow streets and alleyways to become divided into two communities: Downalong, where the fishing families lived, and Upalong, a district of mining families. In fact, **St Ives Museum** is housed in a building belonging to an old mine and here can be seen a wide range of artefacts that chronicle the natural, industrial and maritime history of the area. There is also a display dedicated to the exploits of one of the town's most colourful people, **John Knill**. Mayor of the town in 1767 and a customs officer by profession, it was widely rumoured that Knill was an energetic smuggler himself and that the tall monument he built to the south of the town, now known as the **Knill Steeple**, supposedly as his mausoleum, served to guide ships carrying contraband safely to the shore. Though buried in London, Knill left a bequest to the town so that, every five

years, on July 25, they could hold a ceremony in his honour when a procession, led by a fiddler, two widows and 10 young ladies or children from fishing and mining families, dances its way from the town centre to his monument to sing the 100th Psalm. The first such ceremony took place in 1801, and John himself took part, as he didn't die until 1811.

As both the fishing and mining industries declined in the late 19th century, St Ives developed as an artists' colony. Since the 1880s, the town has attracted many diverse painters, brought here by the special quality of the light, and they have included such talents as Turner, Whistler, Sickert, Munnings and Hepworth. Many of the old pilchard cellars and sail lofts were converted into studios and a 'St Ives School' quickly became established which gained an international reputation.

Art still dominates the town and, as well as the numerous private galleries there is the **Tate Gallery**, overlooking the beach of Porthmeor, where the work of 20th century painters and sculptors is permanently on display. It was officially opened by HRH Prince Charles in 1993. A short walk away, and managed by the Tate, is the **Barbara Hepworth Sculpture Garden and Museum** at Trewyn Studio on Barnoon Hill, where she lived and worked until her death, in a fire, in 1975. As well as the many pieces of her work displayed in the garden, visitors can also see the little summerhouse where Barbara used to rest in the afternoons and her workshop, which has been left untouched since her death. The garden was designed by Barbara Hepworth herself and the South African composer Priaulx Rainier. The Old Mariners Church is home to the **St Ives Society of Artists**, whose 50 members display and sell their work in two galleries.

However, it is not only artists who have been inspired by the beauty of St Ives and the surrounding area. As a child in the late 19th century, Virginia Woolf holidayed in the town, staying at Talland House overlooking St Ives Bay. Said to be the happiest time of her life, she recaptures the mood of those days in her novel *To the Lighthouse*.

Rosamunde Pilcher was born close to St Ives in 1924, but she had moved away long before publishing her two novels *The Day of the Storm* and *The Shell Seekers*, which both have Cornish settings. One of the most delightful ways of seeing the Cornish coast and countryside is to take the train that runs on the branch line from St Ives to Penzance. The branch, like so many others, was scheduled for closure in the 1960s, but was reprieved by the Transport Minister of the time, Barbara Castle. The journey passes through Carbis Bay, Lelant and St Erth (junction with the main line) before reaching the opposite coast at Marazion and thence to Penzance. The section of the line between Lelant Church to Carbis Bay is part of the 12-mile St Michael's Way walk that leads to Marazion and St Michael's Mount.

Around St Ives

Carbis Bay
1 mile SE of St Ives off the A3074

The sheltered beach here is ideal for

presented to your taste. It is open all day in the season, and really keeps up a very high standard in a town that is one of the best holiday resorts in Cornwall.

Carbis Bay

the 19th century, the famous Providence copper and tin mines employed hundreds of men, women and children.

Lelant
2½ miles SE of St Ives on the A3074

A thriving seaport in the Middle Ages, until the silting up of the Hayle estuary caused traffic through here to divert to St Ives, Lelant is now a popular holiday village with a golf course and a scenic rail link to St Ives. Though little remains from the heyday of the port here, **St Uny's Parish**

families as it is safe for children and there are various watersports available. Easy to reach on foot from St Ives, there is a footpath along the cliffs; at low tide the more adventurous may like to walk along the exposed sands to Lelant. In

THE CARBIS BAY HOTEL

Carbis Bay, Nr St Ives, Cornwall TR26 2NP
Tel: 01736 795311 Fax: 01736 797677
e-mail: info@carbisbayhotel.co.uk
website: www.carbisbayhotel.co.uk

Right by the sea, overlooking the beach and the bay, the **Carbis Bay Hotel** is a handsome, traditionally styled hotel set in its own attractive grounds.

Built in 1894 by the noted Cornish architect Sylvanus Trevail, the hotel is everything a fine seaside hotel should be, offering comfort, peace, relaxation, excellent food and personal service orchestrated by long-time owners Stephen Baker and his family.

Each of the bedrooms has its own individual appeal, and all have bath/shower, radio, telephone, hairdryer, tea & coffee making facilities, room service and baby listening; most enjoy sea views. Two comfortable lounges provide ample space for relaxing or planning the day's activities, and when the sun shines the terrace is a perfect

spot for tucking into a Cornish cream tea.

In the AA Rosetted dining room, the head chef and his team have built up a great reputation for their cuisine, which features local seafood, seasonal game and desserts made with that luscious Cornish cream. Morning coffee, afternoon tea and light meals are available in the stunning conservatory.

The hotel is also strong on entertainment, with snooker and pool tables, live cabaret dancing, a pianist to accompany dinner on some nights, and children's entertainers. The owners also offer a choice of holiday apartments, bungalows and beach houses.

THE TYRINGHAM ARMS

Old Coach Road,
Lelant Downs,
Near St Ives,
Cornwall TR26 3EZ

Tel: 01736 740434

PUBLIC HOUSE
FAMILY RESTAURANT
& CARVERY

A truly family orientated Restaurant and Carvery situated on the Old Coach Road between Lelant and St Ives.

Pub and Restaurant open daily. Carvery evenings and Sunday lunchtimes.

Daily specials, bar menu, beergarden with play area.

Ample parking.

Church, which overlooks the golf course, dates from the 15th century and it is dedicated to a Celtic saint said to be the brother of St Ia. The village used to be called Lantana, meaning 'Anta's Church', as a chapel to St Anta used to stand north of the present parish chruch.

Overlooking the saltflats of the Hayle estuary, Lelant is another place of particular interest to ornithologists, who come here to view a wide variety of wildfowl and waders; nearby in Ryans Field, a short distance from Quay House, is an RSPB hide.

Merlin's Magic Land is a children's fun park with a mini roller coaster, electric motor bikes and other attractions.

Gwithian
4 miles E of St Ives on the B3301

This ancient village of thatched cottages and houses, surrounded by sand dunes to the south of Godrevy Point, remains unspoilt. The high dunes, known as **The Towans**, back the long stretch of sandy beach that forms the eastern side of St Ives Bay and they have numerous

RED RIVER INN

Gwithain, Near Hayle, Cornwall TR27 5BW
Tel/Fax: 01736 753223
e-mail: redriverinn@hotmail.co.uk
website: www.redriverinn.co.uk

Once an old coaching inn dating from the 17th century, the **Red River Inn** is an attractive, stone built inn that still retains much of its character and atmosphere. The décor is cosy and traditional with wooden floors and polished tables and speaks of great standards of service. The bar sells a range of drinks, including real ales such as Doom Bar, and the food is all home-cooked using only fresh local produce where possible. The inn has

accommodation and is only minutes walk to the Coastal Path, Godrevy Lighthouse and a three mile sand beach.

footpaths running through them that provide perfect picnic areas. A sizeable prehistoric settlement is said to lie buried beneath the Towans, along with a 7th century oratory founded by the Irish missionary, St Gothian.

Tin was still being extracted from the sand around the village after World War I, the ore being taken by buckets suspended from a cableway over the sand to a firmer collection point.

Godolphin Cross
8 miles SE of St Ives off the B3302

To the northwest of the village lies **Godolphin House**, an exceptional part Tudor, part Stuart house that still retains its original Elizabethan stables (which now house a collection of unrestored local wagons). The home of the Godolphins until the 18th century, a prominent Cornish family who made their fortune through mining, the house is noted for its splendid King's Room, fine Jacobean fireplaces and the unique north front which was completed shortly after the Civil War and incorporates an impressive granite colonnade. The Entrance Hall has a fine 16th century chimney piece, and the Dining Room has some superb linen-fold panelling.

Outside, the gardens still retain traces of their original ancient raised walks and the carp ponds. The Godolphin family itself is of great interest: one Godolphin, Sidney the poet, was killed during the Civil War while supporting the king; Sidney, the 1st Earl was a Lord High Treasurer; and it was the 2nd Earl who imported the famous Godolphin Arabian, one of the three stallions from which all British thoroughbreds are descended. A painting of this magnificent horse, by John Wootton in 1731, hangs in the Dining Room. Used as a location for the *Poldark* television series, Godolphin House is open in sections for visits as major work is undertaken. Car parking is shared with the National Trust, which owns the estate and hill, over which there are extensive walks that reveal important archaeological and mining remains.

Hayle
3 miles SE of St Ives on the B3302

Established in the 18th century as an industrial village where copper was smelted and foundries made industrial machinery, Hayle was also a seaport with a harbour in the shelter of Hayle estuary. It was here, in the early 1800s, that the great Cornish inventor, Richard Trevithick built an early version of the steam locomotive and, not long afterwards, one of the first railways in the world was constructed to carry tin and copper to the town from Redruth and the mines in between. At the height of the foundry industry in Hayle, in the 19th century, steam powered engines built by the famous company, Harveys of Hayle, were being used in the majority of Cornwall's mines and beyond. Richard Trevithic married the founder's daughter, Jane Harvey.

WESTWOOD PARK

1 Caroline Row, Hayle, Cornwall TR27 4EQ
Tel: 01736 753086
e-mail: westwoodpark@btinternet.com

Westwood Park is set on beautiful St Ives Bay, and is one of the best small chalet and caravan parks in Cornwall. The chalets come fully equipped for a comfortable and enjoyable holiday, as do the large, well appointed caravans. All have TVs, cooking facilities, refrigerators, and many other extras that add that certain something to a holiday in this sunny part of the county. Set in one acre of

carefully tended gardens, it boasts semi tropical plants such as bamboo and palm trees. There is so much to do and see in the area, and the site itself is a safe, secure haven for children to play as the adults relax and enjoy the sunshine.

CORNISH ARMS

Commericial Street, Hayle,
Cornwall TR27 4DJ
Tel: 01736 753237

The **Cornish Arms** is a whitewashed, attractive inn that brims with olde worlde character and charm. It is an old coaching inn that dates from the 18th century, and is set at the top of this busy coastal town. It serves a great selection of St Austell Ales, as well as wines, spirits and soft drinks if you're driving. The excellent menu has food to suit every taste, and everything is cooked to perfection

using only the finest local produce wherever possible. This pub represents great value for money and if you're looking for a quiet drink or a meal, you shouldn't miss it!

On the southern outskirts of the town is **Paradise Park Wuildlife Sanctuary**, the award-winning wildlife park that is home to some of the world's rarest and most beautiful birds, as well as various other animals such as otters and squirrels. It is also involved in the programme to reintroduce the Cornish chough into the wild in the county, where it was extinct for the last 50

ANGARRACK INN

12 Stemares Hill, Angarrack,
Cornwall TR27 5JB
Tel: 01736 752380
e-mail: david@peake0401.freeserve.co.uk

Dating to 1755, the **Angarrack Inn** is a handsome, well-proportioned inn that offers all that is best in Cornish hospitality. It has a fine range of St Austell real ales, and a great selection of bottled beers and, of course, ciders! It is owned and personally managed by Jackie and David Peake, who have made it a popular venue for visitors and locals alike. You

can even drink in a beer garden that has a trout stream running past it! Jackie and David offer a wide range of home cooked meals, and even boast that if you want it, they'll cook it (within reason!)

ROYAL STANDARD INN

50 Church Town, Gwinear, Near Hayle,
Cornwall TR27 5JL
Tel/Fax: 01736 850080
e-mail: theroyalstandard@aol.com

The **Royal Standard Inn** sits just off the A30, about two and a half miles east of Hayle. It is a freehouse, with mine hosts being Rob Taft and Kevin White, who have created a hostelry full of character. There's always a warm welcome here, and you'll appreciate the good, honest pub fare that is served in the restaurant, all home cooked by Rob. It is served each day from 12 noon - 2 pm and 7 pm until 9 pm. And don't forget - Monday night is curry night, Friday is carvery night and also the Sunday lunch carvery! There is a well stocked bar, so you're sure to find something to suit your taste, and the inn also offers three B&B rooms with shared facilities - making this the perfect base from which to explore this part of Cornwall.

years. Set in wonderful gardens and with something new to see on a regular basis this is a superb place for all the family. Daily events include penguin and otter feeding, and visitors can buy a pot of nectar for the rainbow lorikeets in their walk-through aviary. The Hayle estuary and sands around the town are an ornithologist's delight.

Perranuthnoe
7 miles S of St Ives off the A394

From the village a steep flight of steps lead down to **Perran Sands**, a rocky, sandy beach off which a sand bank sometimes forms that can make swimming hazardous. Overlooking Mount's Bay, to the southeast, the cliffs lead to the jagged **Cudden Point**, where many ships have foundered, and which is now owned by the National Trust. The **Parish Church of St Piran** was originally erected in the 13th century, with an aisle being added in Tudor times. It was restored in 1883. The village's pub, the **Victoria Arms**, is reckoned to be the oldest in Cornwall, and was even mentioned in the *Domesday Book*.

To the north of the village is **Goldsithney**, whose name means 'Sithney Fair'. The yearly fair was moved from the

THE CROWN

Goldsithney, Penzance, Cornwall TR20 9LG
Tel: 01736 715494
e-mail: woodkencrown@aol.com

The **Crown** is situated about three miles east of Penzance, off the A394. It is an old coaching inn dating from 1761 and is all that an English pub should be - a homely interior with a roaring fire in the winter and many period features. There is a well stocked bar, and the traditional-style restaurant serves beautiful meals that are all cooked to perfection. There is always a good choice,

including daily specials, and the fresh fish and beef are especially popular. People come from near and far to sample the hospitality and if you pay it a visit, you're sure to return!

village of Sithney, six miles east, to here in the 12th century. A legend tells of a wrestling match in which the prize was a glove, and as well as the glove, the village from which the winning team came was allowed to collect all the market dues. Sithney won it year after year, until it was won by the wrestlers of Goldsithney, who refused to give up the right to hold the fair each year.

Marazion
6 miles S of St Ives off the A394

A port as long ago as the Bronze Age and for many centuries the most important settlement around Mount's Bay, Marazion is one of Cornwall's oldest chartered towns (the first charter was granted by Henry III in 1257 and reaffirmed in 1595 by Queen Elizabeth I). Its long history, through which the port continued to prosper with the export trade in tin and copper, has left a legacy of fine old inns and residential houses which overlook the fine expanse of sandy beach. **Marazion Town Museum** is housed in the town hall in the small Market Square, in what was once the fire brigade HQ and a jail. A typical cell of the period has been reconstructed within it. Another

house in the square was where Charles II hid after his defeeat at the Battle of Naseby in 1646. To the northwest of the town is **Marazion Marsh & RSPB Reserve**, an extensive area of wetland and reed beds behind Marazion Beach on the Penzance road. Over 450 plant species have been recorded here, and the area is home to many nesting and roosting birds, including herons, reed and sedge warblers, and Cetti's warbler. Guided tours with an RSPB warden are available from May until September each year. The beach, long favoured for its sunny aspect and safe bathing, is also a well-known windsurfing venue and the location of national and international surfing and sailing championships. **Chapel Rock**, on the beach, used to have a small chapel on it dedicated to the Virgin Mary, where pilgrims would stop to pray before continuing on to St Michael's Mount in Mounts Bay.

Mounts Bay, Marazion

St Michael's Mount
6½ miles S of St Ives off the A394

Situated a third of a mile offshore and connected to Marazion by a cobbled causeway that is exposed at low tide, **St Michael's Mount** is a remarkable slate and granite outcrop that rises dramatically from the seabed. The steep sided islet has been inhabited since prehistoric times and its Cornish name, 'Carrick luz en cuz' (meaning 'the ancient rock in the wood'), suggests that, at one time, the coastline here was covered in trees. Indeed, the fossilised remains of a forest that once covered the land around St Michael's Mount can be seen at low tide.

It has been an important place since ancient times, and some people claim that it is 'Ictis', the island where the ancient Greeks and Romans traded for tin and other metal ores. A Greek historian, in the 1st century AD, wrote of miners bringing the ore in woooden wagons to an offshore island that was exposed at low tide. There they traded with the Greek and Roman merchants.

The rock is named after the Archangel St Michael, who,

according to legend, appeared to a party of fishermen in a vision in the 5th century. A place of pilgrimage for centuries, it was Edward the Confessor who, in 1044, founded a priory on the mount. It was Robert Mortian, Earl of Cornwall and William the Conquerer's half-brother, who gave the priory to the Benedictine monks of the famous Mont St Michel in Normandy. The monastery was fortified after the Dissolution in 1539 and in 1660 it became the home of the St Aubyn family, who donated it to the National Trust in 1964. The marvellous battlemented **St Michael's Mount Castle** shows differing architectural styles from the 17th century through to the 19th. The house contains some impressive medieval remains, including the Chevy Chase

St Michael's Mount

Room which was the original monks' refectory, and there are other interesting details here such as the Strawberry Hill Gothic plaster work in the 18th century Blue Drawing Room, the artefacts in the Map and Museum Rooms and paintings and portraits by artists including the Cornishman John Opie. The beautiful **Chapel of St Michael** is 15th century, and has a small tower which was used to guide ships in and out of local ports.

Zennor
4 miles W of St Ives on the B3306

This delightful village, situated between moorland and coastal cliffs, is one of only a few settlements along this stretch of the north Cornish coastline. In this ancient community, where evidence has been found of Bronze Age settlers, the 12th century **St Senara's Parish Church** is famous for a bench end that depicts a local mermaid holding a comb and mirror and resembling the Greek goddess of love, Aphrodite. A famous local legend tells of a mysterious young maiden who was drawn to the church by the beautiful singing of a handsome chorister, the squire's son Matthew Trewhella. An enchanting singer herself, one night she lured him down to nearby Pendour Cove where she was swimming in the calm waters. He swam out to join her and disappeared. She was a mermaid, and her name, it is said, was Morveren. On a warm summer's evening it is said that their voices can be heard rising from beneath the waves.

By the porch is a memorial to John Davey, who died in 1891, stating that he was the last person to have any great knowledge of the native Cornish language, Kernewek. It is said that he remained familiar with the language by speaking it to his cat. There has recently been a revival of interest in the language and it is estimated that anything up to 3,500 can now speak it. A campaign has been launched to revive Cornish GCSE, which was scrapped in 1996 after a decade in which only 42 candidates sat the exam. Visitors to Cornwall who chance upon a Kernewek speaker can impress him by asking *'Plema'n diwotti?'*

Tinners Arms

Zennor, St Ives, Cornwall TR26 3BY
Tel: 01736 796927

Dating from the 15th century, the **Tinners Arms** is a cosy, stone built inn that is full of period character. It has everything you would expect to find in a country pub, with pine bench seating, heavy wooden tables and open log fires. Comfortable accommodation is also available at this fine inn, and the food is outstanding. The kitchens use only the finest and freshest of local produce wherever possible, making it popular by both locals and visitors. It has a great selection of beers,

ciders, wines and spirits, making it a place that just cannot be missed!

WAYSIDE FOLK MUSEUM

Zennor, Nr St Ives, Cornwall TR26 3DA
Tel: 01736 796945

It was in the 1930s that Colonel 'Freddie' Hirst started a collection of relics peculiar to Zennor. That collection was the basis of the **Wayside Folk Museum**, a privately owned museum which portrays the lives of ordinary people in the area through its displays of artefacts, stories and photographs. Although it appears small from the outside, the museum has something of the tardis about

it, and the 16 display areas contain more than 5,000 items, from maps and archaeological exhibits to blacksmith's and wheelwright's equipment, a cobbler's shop, an 18th century kitchen, relics of local mining and quarrying and early agricultural implements.

In 1997 the old piggery was incorporated into the museum and contains displays on 'Childhood Memories', 'The Sea' and ' Village Dairy'. 'People of Past Zennor' is an exhibition of photographs and text depicting the lives of its inhabitants. In the grounds are two waterwheels from the mining industry and a unique collection of corn grinding querns and stone tools dating back as far as 3000 BC. Bridge House Gift & Book Shop specialises in things Cornish as well as providing light refreshments.

and with any luck being directed to the nearest pub. Another useful entry in the Cornish phrase book is *'Fatell yu an pastyon yn gwerthji ma? A wrons i ri dhymn drog goans?'* which means 'What are the pasties like in this shop? Will they give me indigestion?' Or how about *'Ass yu teg an penty mal A allaf vy y brena rag chy haf?'* - 'What a delightful cottage! Can I buy it for a second home?' Recognising a fellow Cornish speaker can be tricky, but an identifying badge can be bought, featuring a black frog - after Dolly Pentreath of Mousehole's favourite insult to someone she didn't like.

Behind the church is a stone where it is said that the Giant of Zennor would sit. He was not a typical Cornish giant as he

was fond of people and liked their company. One day he patted a human on the head in a friendly way but inadvertently fractured the poor man's skull. The giant was so full of remorse that he died of a broken heart soon afterwards. For an insight into the history of Zennor and the surrounding area, the **Wayside Folk Museum** (see panel above) has numerous exhibits that tell of the region's industrial past. Cornwall's oldest private museum houses a collection of over 5,000 items covering local mining and quarrying, agriculture, archaeology and domestic history. In the delightful grounds are two waterwheels from the mining industry and a collection of corn-grinding querns and stone tools dating as far back as 3,000 BC.

The tin mining heritage is also referred to in the name of the local inn, The Tinners Arms. It was at this pub that DH Lawrence spent many hours while living with his wife Frieda in the village during World War I. Originally intending to set up a farming cum literary commune, the couple rented a cheap cottage at Zennor for five pounds a year and while here, under police surveillance, he wrote *Women in Love*. However, eventually his pacifist tendencies and Frieda's German heritage (her cousin was the flying ace the Red Baron) caused them to be 'moved on' in October 1917.

Just to the southeast of Zennor, on the granite moorland, lies the Neolithic chamber tomb, **Zennor Quoit**. One of many such ancient monuments to be found in this area, the tomb has a huge capstone that was once supported on five broad uprights, with two standing stones marking the entrance to the inner chamber. Another is **Mulfra Quoit**, two

miles to the south east of the village. The whole thing has partially collapsed, with the five-ton capstone lying against the uprights at an angle.

Penzance

Penzance comes from the Cornish 'pen sans', meaning 'holy headland', as an ancient chapel dedicated to St Mary used to stand on the headland to the west of the present harbour. For centuries, it was a remote market town which made its living from fishing, mining and smuggling and, today, it is not only popular with holidaymakers looking to stay in the area but also for those taking the ferry or helicopter from here to the Isles of Scilly. Along with nearby Newlyn and Mousehole, Penzance was sacked by the Spanish in 1595, destroying most of the town and the ancient chapel. Between 1646 and 1648 it suffered a similar fate as it had supported the Royalist cause. A major port in the 19th century for the

ALEXANDRA INN

Alexandra Road, Penzance,
Cornwall TR18 4LY
Tel: 01736 365165
e-mail: alexamdrainn@btopenworld.com

Situated close to the seafront in the west end of Penzance, the **Alexandra Inn** (known affectionately as the "Alex") is one of the town's most popular pubs, and for good reason! It has achieved entry status in the CAMRA Good Beer guide for 2004 and 2005, selling five real ales as well as cider, lager and Guinness. It has three guest rooms, all with TV and tea/coffee making facilities. There is an excellent selection of meals available, all home cooked on the premises by "Pierre the chef", such as dinosaur ribs (beef really!) and chicken rosemary. A beer festival is held here every March, and the "sub tropical" garden is a sun trap at all times of the year. With a 10ftx5ft scaletrix available for customer use in the public bar, this is one pub you can't afford to miss!

Penzance Harbour

exporting of tin, the fortunes of Penzance were transformed by the arrival of the railway in 1859. Not only could the direct despatch of early flowers, vegetables and locally caught fish to the rest of Britain be undertaken with ease but the railways also brought a great influx of holidaymakers and boosted the town's fledgling industry. In 1851 a housewife from neighbouring Newlyn had a novel way of advertising the area. She walked from Penzance to London dressed as a fish wife, and sought an audience with Queen Victoria.

She managed to get one, and presented Her Majesty with half a pound of tea as a present from the town.

In 1879 another event took place that put the town firmly on the tourist map. In that year, the premier of Gilbert and Sullivan's opera *The Pirates of Penzance* took place, not in London, but in Paignton, Devon, followed, next day, by a performance in New York. The London premier had to wait until 3rd April 1880. This, as well as the coming of the railway, turned it into a holiday resort.

A bustling town and harbour today and home to Cornwall's only promenade, which stretches to Newlyn, Penzance has plenty to offer the visitor. Along the promenade lies the **Jubilee Swimming Pool**, a wonderful open-air seawater pool that still has its original art deco styling.

TARBERT HOTEL

Clarence Street, Penzance,
Cornwall TR18 2NU
Tel: 01736 363758 Fax: 01736 331336
e-mail: reception@tarbert-hotel.co.uk
website: www.tarbert-hotel.co.uk

Built in the 1830s the **Tarbert Hotel**, once a sea captain's house, is set in a late Georgian terrace. Now a small and comfortable family run hotel situated right in the heart of the town, it makes everyone feel welcome,. There is a choice of family, double and twin rooms, all en suite and all boasting TV, hair dryer, shaver point and tea/coffee making facilities. There is a fully stocked bar and the food is outstanding. The spacious restaurant is open to non residents, and has an excellent menu of delicious home-cooked food, all made from fresh, local produce. The Tarbert is two star and makes an excellent base from which to explore all of southern Cornwall!

Egyptian House, Penzance

Most of the town's most interesting buildings can be found on Chapel Street, which leads down from the domed **Market House**, built in 1836, to the quay. Outside the Market House is a statue to Penzance's most famous son, **Sir Humphry Davy** , the scientist who is best remembered for inventing the miners' safety lamp. He was born on 17th December 1778, knighted in 1812, and three days later got married. He died in 1829 in Geneva. One of the more exotic buildings along this narrow thoroughfare is the **Egyptian House**, built in the 1830s and restored by the Landmark Trust. It is an amazing confection of paned windows, painted walls and elaborate mouldings. Behind the Georgian façade of **The Union**

SABEGO GUEST HOUSE

61 Morrab Road, Penzance,
Cornwall TR18 4EP
Tel: 01736 365560
e-mail: info@sabego.com
website: www.sabego.com

The **Sabego Guest House**, in the beautiful old town of Penzance, is the ideal base for a great holiday in Cornwall. It sits within easy reach of Penzance train station, the ferry terminal for the Scilly Isles, and all the historical and scenic amenities for which the county is famous.

This 'adults only', no smoking establishment offers excellent accommodation at

surprisingly realistic prices, and has six comfortable rooms that are beautifully furnished and decorated. There is a choice of breakfast · everything from a full English to a Continental, as well as vegetarian. For a quiet, relaxing holiday, this is the place to stay!

CROWN INN

1 Victoria Square, Penzance,
Cornwall TR18 2EP
Tel: 01736 351070
website: www.thecrownpenzance.co.uk

The **Crown Inn** is a friendly pub that sits behind Penzance's busy main street, and is well worth seeking out! It dates from the late 1800s, and has many period features, such an open fire in the winter months. You are assured of a warm welcome here, and there is a great selection of real ales, including a rotating guest ale. The pub is also the perfect place for a beautifully cooked pub lunch or an evening meal. The food is all home cooked, having French, Italian and English influences. In fact, it is claimed that the inn's cuisine is the talk of Penzance!

Hotel opposite is an impressive Elizabethan interior where, from a minstrels' gallery in the assembly room, the first mainland announcement of the victory of Trafalgar and the death of Lord Nelson was made.

Further down is Chapel Street, which was the childhood home of Marie Branwell, the mother of the Brontë sisters. Down around the harbour on Wharf Road lies the **Trinity House Lighthouse Centre**, where the interesting story of lighthouse keeping is told. Opened by Prince Andrew in 1991, the centre has amassed what is probably the largest and finest collection of lighthouse equipment in the world. Outside are some of the buoys which down the years were repaired and maintained in the building. Elsewhere in Penzance, local history and the work of the Newlyn School of artists can be seen at the **Penlee House Art Gallery and Museum**, where paintings by Walter Langley can be seen, and where the county's long association with the mining industry led to the foundation of the Royal Geological Society of Cornwall in 1814.

Anyone who saw the television adaptation of Mary Wesley's novel *The Camomile Lawn* will recognise Penzance

TURKS HEAD

Chapel Street, Penzance, Cornwall TR18 4AF
Tel: 01736 363093
e-mail: turks@gibbard9476.f/sworld.co.uk

Long regarded as the oldest and best pub in Penzance, the **Turk's Head** dates back to the 13th century, and is full of character and atmosphere. The original building was destroyed by the Spanish in the 16th century, but there's still plenty of history here. There's a range of real ales, including Doom Bar and a rotating guest ale. The food is outstanding, and as you would expect, seafood predominates. There's a huge blackboard choice, from 'lite bites' to full dinners. Try the inn's speciality · monkfish special. It is truly outstanding. There's also a sunny garden at the rear where you can relax in absolute comfort.

CARLTON INN

The Promenade, Penzance,
Cornwall TR18 4NW
Tel/Fax: 01736 362081
e-mail: carltonhotelpenzance@talk21.com

If it's first class holiday accommodation in Cornwall you're looking for, then the **Carlton Hotel** is the answer! It is a small, friendly, family-run hotel that sits right on the prom, with views across to St Michael's Mount. There are nine en suite bedrooms, three with shared facilities, and all are comfortable and well furnished, with TV, radio, hairdryer and tea/coffee making facilities. The residents' lounge has lovely sea views, and a full English breakfast is served to guests, though there are no evening meals. Children are most welcome, and the hotel is open all year round.

as the town was the place to which the three main characters, Calypso, Walter and Polly, came for their annual summer visit.

Two miles west of Penzance on the A30 towards Land's End, **Trewidden Garden** is best known for its camellias, with a collection of over 300 varieties built up over many decades from places as far afield as China and India. Other highlights include a superb magnolia x veitchii that is believed to be the largest specimen in the British Isles, and which overshadows a pond. There are also several remnants of the tin mining industry and a bomb crater formed in World War II when a series of parachute bombs exploded in the area.

A **Penzance Heritage Trail** has been laid out taking visitors around most of the historic sites and attractions that can be seen.

Around Penzance

Newlyn
1 mile SW of Penzance on the B3315

The largest fish landing port in England and Wales, Newlyn has long been associated with fishing. Its massive jetties were built in the 1880s to enclose

MOUNT VIEW HOTEL

Long Rock, Penzance, Cornwall TR20 8JJ
Tel/Fax: 01736 710416

With five well appointed rooms, three of which are fully en suite, the **Mount View Hotel** is undoubtedly one of the best in the Penwith area. Dating back to 1894, it sits off the A30 close to the shore between Penzance and Marazion. It·is a small, family-run hotel that prides itself in value for money, and has a cosy bar and a separate restaurant that seats 18 in comfort. The extensive menu includes many firm favourites, with vegetarian choices. The rooms all have TVs and hospitality trays,

and the atmosphere is friendly and informal · just right for a relaxing holiday in this picturesque part of Cornwall.

Newlyn Harbour

transfer to wooden boxes. The pilchard (*Sardina pilchardus*) contains high amounts of Omega 3 oils that are well known for promoting good health. The museum and factory are open for visits on weekdays from Easter to the end of October.

some 40 acres of Mount's Bay and they also embraced the existing 15th century harbour. The whole fishing industry, like other industries, was spurred on by the arrival of the railways - at Newlyn in 1859 - which allowed the swift transportation of fresh fish and seafood to London and beyond. Today, it is the base for around 200 vessels, which vary greatly in size, and whose valuable catches are now shipped around Britain and Europe in massive refrigerated lorries. Before the coming of railways, the pilchards had to be salted to preserve them, and you can still see the processes involved in the **Pilchard Works Museum and Factory**, the only place in Britain where the process is still carried out. It offers a unique insight into the fascinating history of the industry in Cornwall. You can see the process step by step, from the layering with salt of the freshly caught fish to the pressing to get rid of excess water and oil when they are cured and the

Fishing is not the only reason for visiting Newlyn. Drawn here by the exceptionally clear natural light, Stanhope Forbes came here to paint outside rather than in a studio in the 1880s. He was soon joined by other artists keen to experience the joys of working here and the **Newlyn School** of art developed with the help of artists such as Lamorna Birch, Alfred Munnings, Norman Garstin and Laura Knight. The town is still a favourite place for artists, and the **Newlyn Art Gallery**, founded in 1895 by the Cornishman Passmore Edwards, shows the paintings of those living and working here today.

Recently, a **Newlyn Heritage Trail** (smiliar to the one in neighbouring Penzance) has been laid out around the town, with bronze plaques at all the interesting sites and attractions. It is just under one and a half miles in length. Like Penzance, the town was sacked by the Spanish in 1595.

KINGS ARMS

Paul Churchtown, Penzance,
Cornwall TR 19 6TZ
Tel: 01736 731224

Paul is situated off the B3315 south of Penzance, and it is here that you will find the charming **Kings Arms**, a pub packed full of character. Dating from the early 1700s, it has hardwood tables, oak beams and slab flooring, making for an olde worlde ambience that ensures a friendly welcome. The bar sells a wide range of drinks to suit everyone's taste, including Cornish Real Ales and the pub has three comfortable en suite guest rooms which are let on a B&B basis - a double and two singles. The food is honest, home-cooked Cornish dishes, such as steaks and seafood, served during lunchtimes and in the evenings.

Mousehole

2½ miles SW of Penzance off the B3315

Dylan Thomas married Caitlin Macnamara, from County Clare in Ireland, in nearby Penzance Registry Office in July 1937, against the wishes of his parents. The pair honeymooned in Mousehole, which Thomas described as "the loveliest village in England". Mousehole (pronounced Mowzel) is indeed the epitome of a Cornish fishing village. Certainly visited by Phoenician tin merchants in around 500 BC - it is thought that the village's name is derived from the Phoenician word for 'watering place' - Mousehole has a long and sometimes disturbing history. Some 2,000 years after these first known visitors, the Spanish arrived and ransacked the village in 1595, leaving only the former manor house, now known as **Squire Keigwin**, in Keigwin Street relatively unscathed. However, this attack was not totally unexpected by the villagers as they saw it as the fulfilment of a prophecy made by Merlin that can be seen inscribed on **Merlin's Rock**, near the quay. The stone bears these words:

> *"There shall land on the Rock of Merlin*
> *Those who shall burn Paul, Penzance and*
> *Newlyn."*

Paul is the village above Mousehole,

Mousehole

where stands the parish church. The village was rebuilt and went on to become an important pilchard fishing port until the stocks of fish dwindled in the early 20th century. Every year just before Christmas, a **Stargazy Pie** (see also Newquay) - a local speciality made with whole fish whose heads stick up through the pastry crust - is made in commemoration of Tom Bawcock, a local fisherman who saved Mousehole from starvation by setting sail in a storm and bringing home a large catch of seven varieties of fish.

Less fortunate were the eight man crew of the Penlee lifeboat, *Solomon Browne*, who were lost in hurricane conditions while attempting to rescue the last four crew members from the coaster *Union Star*, in December 1981. Every member of the lifeboat crew was a Mousehole man. The **Penlee Lifeboat Disaster Memorial** commemorates those who lost their lives. On the cliffs at Raginnis Hill is the **Mousehole Wild Bird Hospital & Sanctuary**, founded by Dorothy and Phyllis Yglesias in 1928, run for some time by the RSPCA and now run as a charity. The hospital treats about 1,500 birds a year, and about 100 are permanent residents in the sanctuary. The hospital was at its busiest at the time of the *Torrey Canyon* disaster, when over 8,000 oil-affected birds were treated. Dolly Pentreath, the last Cornish person to speak only the Kernewek, died in 1777 aged 102 and lies buried in Paul churchyard. The **Dolly Pentreath Memorial** in the churchyard wall marks her grave (see also Introduction and Zennor).

Offshore is the small rocky **St Clement's Island**, where it is said a hermit once lived, and along the coast is a cave which is said to have given the village its name - 'Mouse Hole'. The truth is, no one really knows where the name came from, and it's local pronunciation clearly shows it had nothing to do with mice.

Lamorna
4 miles SW of Penzance off the B3315

This isolated hamlet is set in the craggy **Lamorna Cove** that was immortalised by the artist 'Lamorna Birch' (real name Samuel John Birch) and author Derek Tangye, who were among several artists to be attracted to this area between 1880 and 1910. Birch died in 1955, and Tangye, who wrote the immensely popular 'Minack Chronicles', died in 1996. Once only licensed to sell beer, Lamorna's pub, The Wink, got its name from the old custom of winking to the landlord to obtain something stronger from under the counter.

To the west of the hamlet, amid excellent walking country, is the exceptional Bronze Age stone circle known as the **Merry Maidens**. The standing stones are said to be all that remains of 19 young women who were turned into granite for daring to dance on the Sabbath. The circle is also known as Dawn's Men, a corruption of the Cornish 'dans maen', meaning 'stone dance'. **The Pipers**, two large menhirs in a field to the north east, are thought to be the musicians who suffered the same fate for providing the dancing music.

St Buryan

5 miles SW of Penzance on the B3283

This village is home to one of the finest churches in the county, **St Buryan's Parish Church**. The first church was built by King Athelstan in the 10th century. Having subdued the Scilly Isles, he returned to the mainland and founded a collegiate church, i.e., a church with a college of priests rather than monks, and dedicated it to St Buriana, said to be the virgin daughter of an Irish king who landed at St Ives in the 5th century. The church is packed with interesting features, such as misericords, a fine font, a chancel screen and a 14th century tower that dominates the landscape and provides a daymark for shipping around Land's End. Apart from the Celtic crosses beside the porch, the most interesting feature in the

graveyard is a stone that reads:

> "Here lie John and Richard Benn
> Two lawyers and two honest men.
> God works miracles now and then."

To the north of St Buryan is the **Boscawen-Un Stone Circle** which, though not the most impressive in the country, certainly has much appeal; the circle is in fact an oval made up of 19 stones, and its central standing stone - an attractive eight feet tall leaning pillar of sparkling quartz, was deliberately placed so that it leaned at an angle, its tip only being six feet from the ground.

Treen

6½ miles SW of Penzance on the B3315

Sheltered from the worst of the weather as it is situated in a shallow valley, Treen is an unspoilt hamlet that lies only a short walk away from the spectacularly sited Iron Age coastal fort, **Treryn Dinas** - found on the headland that also bears this name. Despite having been constructed over 2000 years ago, the earthwork defences on the

Logan Rock, Treen

landward side can still be made out.

Also on the headland is the famous **Logan Rock**, a massive 60-ton granite boulder that was once so finely balanced that it could be rocked by hand. The rock was a popular tourist attraction until 1824, when Lieutenant Hugh Goldsmith (the nephew of the poet and playwright Oliver Goldsmith), egged on by some Royal Navy colleagues, pushed the stone on to the beach below. After many complaints by the locals, the naval officer was instructed to replace the rock - an extraordinary feat of engineering in itself - at his own expense but the fine balance the rock once had has never returned. This act of misadventure is recorded in the local inn.

In 1959 the poet John Jetjeman bought a house at Trebetherick in Treen, and it was his home until he died in 1984.

Porthcurno
7½ miles SW of Penzance off the B3315

Overlooking one of the most dramatic and atmospheric coves in southwest Cornwall, Porthcurno's triangle of beach, made up of crushed sea shells, is sheltered by **Gwennap Head** to the west and **Cribba Head** to the east. It was from here, in 1870, that the first telegraph cable was laid, linking Britain to the rest of the world, and this little bay soon became known as 'the centre of the universe'. The **Porthcurno Telegraph Museum** (see panel opposite) explains the technology that has been developed, from Victorian times to the present day, to make global communications possible. The museum is housed in a secret underground wartime bunker, with some of the equipment still being in good working order. This interesting and picturesque village is also the home of the **Minack Theatre**, an open air amphitheatre cut into the high cliffs, that was founded by Rowena Cade, the daughter of a textile tycoon who was born in Derbyshire, grew up in Cheltenham and finally moved to Lamorna when her father died, where her mother rented a house. Rowena eventually built them a house of their own, and bought the Minack headland for £100. Rowena, who was interested in the theatre, did a lot of

PORTHCURNO TELEGRAPH MUSEUM

Eastern House, Porthcurno,
Penzance TR19 6JX
Tel: 01736 810966
website: www.porthcurno.org.uk

This unique museum stands in the beautiful valley of Porthcurno. The first cable station here was built in 1870, and from that time an increasing number of undersea cables were laid, creating a communications network, which connected the village with remote and exotic parts of the world.

By the start of the Second World War, there were 14 cables and it had become the most important cable station in the world, so it was considered necessary to build bomb-proof tunnels to protect the station from attack. These tunnels now house the major part of the museum, where regular demonstrations show working telegraph equipment from throughout the era, as well as giving a taste of the social changes that took place.

The sights, sounds and smells here are evocative of times gone by, and there is something to interest every member of the family. There are many hands-on exhibits, as well as special activities for children, a local history exhibition and an exhibition about Brunel.

entertaining, which usually had something to do with drama. The first production staged at this classical Greek style theatre was *The Tempest* in 1932 (lit by car headlights and a feeble power cable led down from Minack House) and a summer series has continued ever since in the 750-seat auditorium. The theatre is well worth a visit even when there isn't a performance, for the stunning views over Porthcurno Bay to the Logan Rock, the thriving sub-tropical plants and the Visitor Centre telling Rowena Cade's remarkable story.

Porthgwarra
8 miles SW of Penzance off the B3315

Minack Theatre, Porthcurno

This quaint old fishing hamlet lies just

northeast of high cliffs of Gwennap Head from which there is a spectacular coastal walk to Land's End although walkers should be aware that the terrain is sometimes rugged. A tunnel runs from the slipway up to the road at Porthgwarra, and some people claim it was dug and used by smuugglers. A more likely explanation, however, is that it was excavated to allow farmers to bring seaweed from the beach to their fields to use as fertiliser.

The small and cosy cove, with its sandy beach and backdrop of steep cliffs, was once known as **Sweetheart's Cove** as this is where, many years ago, Nancy, a prosperous farmer's daughter from the village, said goodbye to her forbidden lover, William, who had been a farmhand on her father's farm. Nancy's parents had objected to the marriage, considering William not to be good enough, but then relented, and said that before any marriage could take place, William had to go to sea for three years to make his fortune. Three years passed, and there was no sign of William, much to the parents' delight. Nancy watched constantly from the shore for her lover's return, and her parents eventually became worried by her peculiar behaviour. One evening Nancy's Aunt Prudence heard voices coming from Nancy's room and she eavesdropped, clearly hearing William say 'Waken up and come to the shore, my love, where I await you'.

Nancy went to the shore, and the aunt followed, only to see Nancy safe in the arms of William by the shore. However, a sudden wave engulfed them both and they were swept out to sea. A few days later word reached the distraught parents that William had indeed been returning home on that fateful night, and that he had climbed the mast to get his first look at Porthgwarra where Nancy awaited him. Alas he fell from the mast, and was swept overboard and drowned. Neither him nor Nancy were ever seen again.

Land's End

9 miles SW of Penzance on the A30; 874 miles SW of John O'Groats

A curious mix of natural spectacle and man-made indulgence, Land's End, England's most westerly point, is

Lands End

certainly one of the country's most famous landmarks. Notwithstanding the commercialisation and the dubious tourist trappings, it is still a spectacular place. It is here that the granite on which most of Cornwall stands finally meets the Atlantic Ocean in a series of savage cliffs, reefs and sheer-sided islets that provide some of the most awe-inspiring scenery in the country. Known to the Romans as Belevian, or Seat of Storms, from this headland can be seen **Longships Lighthouse**, which protects shipping from the Longships reef just offshore and **Wolf Rock Lighthouse**, some seven miles away.

Naturally, this place has given rise to numerous legends over the centuries and one claims that Land's End was once the entrance to Lyonesse, the fertile kingdom that stretched from here to the Isles of Scilly some 28 miles to the southwest. With great cities and 140 churches, a great wave is said to have engulfed it on 11th November 1099, taking with it all the fine buildings and all its inhabitants bar one man - Trevilian, who escaped from Lyonesse riding a white horse. The Trevilian family crest still depicts a horse rising from the waves.

For many years afterwards, sailors would tell of hearing bells ringing beneath the waves, and fishermen would claim that doors, furniture and pottery had been brought up in their nets. In the 1930s a journalist actually claimed he had heard the bells in the night, and people still say that occasionally they have made out walls and battlements beneath the waves. It goes without saying that the legend of King Arthur has been caught up in all of this.

The scenery is the amazing natural attraction here, but there's much more to interest the visitor, including tales of the sea and smuggling, the John O'Groats connection and life at Land's End in the late 18th century

Sennen
8 miles SW of Penzance on the A30

The most westerly village in England, there are superb cliff walks along the coast to Land's End and, close to the massive Pedn-men-du headland, lie the remains of a clifftop **Castle**, one of the country's earliest - this one dates from

Sennen Cove

OLD SUCCESS INN

Sennen Cove, Cornwall TR19 7DG
Tel: 01736 871232 Fax: 01736 871457
e-mail:
oldsuccess@sennencove.fsbusiness.co.uk
website: www.oldsuccess.com

The **Old Success Inn** is one of Cornwall's most delightful inns. Dating from 1691, it has 12 en suite rooms that are comfortable and spacious, plus four self-catering apartments that sleep four, and have been equipped to a very high standard. Being an old fisherman's inn and close to the sea, it has lovely views out over Whitesands Bay. It has a well stocked bar ("Charlie's Bar") and a restaurant that serves superb food. The inn also owns the "Breakers" restaurant, which should also be visited for great food superbly cooked.

300 BC. The wide sandy beach at **Sennen Cove** is ideal for both bathing and surfing, and the former windlass house of the lifeboat station has been converted into a crafts gallery. **St Sennen Parish Church** is named after a supposed Irish saint, Sinninus, who accompanied St Patrick to Rome, though a more likely explanation for the name is that Sennen comes from the Cornish 'sen nan', meaning 'holy valley'. The church dates mainly from the 15th century. There are some medieval wall paintings in the south aisle.

Brane
4½ miles W of Penzance off the A30

Just to the west of this lovely hamlet is the fascinating Iron Age courtyard village of **Carn Euny**, founded around 200 BC by an early Cornish farming community, though there is evidence that the site was inhabited long before this. By far the most impressive building here is the **Fogou**, which was first discovered by miners in the 19th century. Taking its name from the Cornish for 'cave', this underground chamber was constructed in three separate stages and this 65 feet long room was entered by a low, 'creep' passage at one end. Its purpose is still unclear although it may have been used for storage or for religious ceremonies. Immediately west of Carn Euny is **Bartinney Downs**, a large area of heathland being managed with a programme of controlled cattle and sheep grazing and cutting of scrub that will result in a high-quality wildlife area. As well as improving and extending existing wildlife habitats, the scheme will conserve archaeological sites and historic features, which include old china clay works, abandoned quarries and the ruins of **Bartinney Castle**.

Sancreed
3½ miles W of Penzance off the A30

In the churchyard of 15th century **St Credan's Parish Church** can be found five Celtic Crosses, some of the many that are scattered around Cornwall. One in particular, at nine feet high, and of the wheel-head shape, is the best example of its kind in the county. The existence of **Sancreed Holy Well** nearby and the curious circular formation of the site suggests that the church is built on much older foundations. St Sancreed, or Credan, a shadowy figure, there having been two saints by that name. One of them is suppsoed to have killed his father by accident, and as a penance lived his life as a swineherd.

In the surrounding area are two Bronze Age monuments, the **Blind Fiddler** and the **Two Sisters** and, like many Cornish menhirs, they are said to represent human beings turned to stone for committing irreligious acts on the Sabbath.

St Just-in-Penwith

6½ miles NW of Penzance on the A3071

The westernmost town in mainland Britain, St Just was one of the copper and tin mining centres of Cornwall and the area surrounding the town is littered with industrial remains. However, the mainly 15th century **St Just's Parish Church** contains some fascinating early relics, including two medieval wall paintings, and a 5th century burial stone on which is carved one of the earliest English Christian inscriptions. St Just, or Justus, was sent to England by Pope Gregory in AD 596, along with St Augustine, to convert the Saxons and Celts of the country. In AD 616 he was appointed Archbishop of Canterbury. Near the town's clock tower, at the centre of St Just, is a shallow grassy amphitheatre that is known as **Plen-an-Gwary**, which means 'playing place', where medieval plays were performed up until the 17th century and which is now the setting for an annual carnival. It is said to be the oldest still-working theatre in Britain, and it is here that the **Ordinalia**, three 500-year-old miracle plays in Cornish, are perfomed each year. St Just has become a thriving arts

centre, with several galleries and crafts shops.

A narrow road leads from the town westwards to **Cape Cornwall**, the only cape in England and Wales, from where there are views of Land's End and of Longships Lighthouse. On the way to the tip of the cape the road passes a tall chimney, all that is left of Cape Cornwall mine, the country's most westerly, which was working up until the 1870s.

On the southern side of the headland lies **Priest's Cove**, a quiet boulder strewn beach, and further along the **South West Coast Path**, which follows the clifftops, there is an unusual Bronze Age burial chamber, **Ballowall Barrow**. Cape Cornwall marks the supposed boundary between the English and St George's Channels.

Botallack
7 miles NW of Penzance on the B3306

Almost overlooking the coast lies the remains of the old engine houses of **Botallack Mine,** the underground workings of which once went out beneath the sea bed. Among the derelict buildings lies a 1908 calciner that was used to refine the tin ore

and to produce arsenic. The smell of arsenic can still be detected in the old flues.

Kenidjack
7 miles NW of Penzance off the B3306

Close to this old mining village lies **Carn Kenidjack**, a rocky outcrop with a stone circle, where one dark night two miners encountered a black-robed horseman. Inviting them to a wrestling match, the frightened miners accepted only to find that the horseman was joined by a host of fearsome demons which, as he was the Devil, he commanded. He led them to Carn Kenidajck, where, by the light of an unearthly growl, two demons were engaged in a wrestling match. During the fight, one of the demons was thrown against a rock and, overcome with Christian charity, the two miners whispered a prayer into the ear of the dying creature. Immediately the ground

Crown Mine, Botallack

View to Kenidjack Castle

trembled and the whole demonic party disappeared in a black cloud. The terrified miners hid on the carn until daylight before making their way home.

Another tale tells of a well next to Carn Kenidjack, which was used by a woman and her two brothers who lived close by. The brothers told the woman never to go near the well after sunset. However, late one evening, when the men were at their work mining, the sister ran out of water, and she decided to collect some from the well, even though the sun had set. As she approached the well she could see an old woman near it. She called out a greeting, but the woman never replied. So she dipped her bucket in the well and was surprised when she brought it back up and found it contained no water. So she lowered the bucket again, and again she couldn't draw water. Thoroughly frightened, she went home, and when her brothers arrived, told them what had happened. They told her that the old woman was called Old Moll, and that she was a witch who caused the well to dry up every night. They had seen her often when returning from the mine late at night, and didn't want to frighten her.

The carn is also known as the 'Hooting Carn', due to the strange noise the wind makes as it passes over it.

Pendeen
6½ miles NW of Penzance on the B3306

Tin has been mined in and around this village since prehistoric times and, from the 19th century, Pendeen also became a centre for copper extraction. Not surprisingly, it is this industry that dominates and to the northwest of the village there are two interesting old mines that are now open to the public. The last of 20 or so mines in the area to close was Geevor Tin Mine, where production ceased in 1990; now, extensively preserved as the **Geevor Tin Mine and Heritage Centre**, it is the largest mining history site in Britain. Also in Pendeen is the Gem & Jewellery Workshop, a private museum and enterprise selling hand-made silver and gemstone jewellery and gifts.

Nearby is the **Levant Beam Engine**,

North Inn

The Square, Pendeen, Penzance,
Cornwall TR19 7DN
Tel: 01736 788417
e-mail: ernestjohnbcoak@aol.com

The **North Inn** dates to the mid 1700s, and is full of character. It sits in the village of Pendeen, six miles west of Penzance, and is the perfect example of a welcoming Cornish pub. It won the CAMRA Cornwall pub of the Year in 2003, and serves a good range of real ales, as well as lager, cider, spirits and wines. Great food is served from 12 noon to 2.30 pm and from 6.30 pm until 8.30 pm every day. It also boasts four newly built four star B&B rooms that are both comfortable and spacious, making this the perfect base for your Cornish holiday! There is a beer garden, sea views, and the inn is also the village newsagents, with a stream of people coming in for their morning papers!

the oldest working steam engine in the country, which now stands in the engine house of the old Levant tin mine that was incorporated into the Geevor mine in the 1960s. In 1919, Levant saw a tragic accident when the 'man engine' which carried miners to the surface failed and 31 men and boys were killed.

Further to the north, on the slate promontory of Pendeen Watch stands **Pendeen Lighthouse** that has been guiding ships for nearly a century. Since all lighthouses were fully automated, Pendeen has been open for guided tours around the light and the engine house.

Madron
1½ miles NW of Penzance off the A30

The part 14th century **St Maddern's Parish Church** was once the mother church to Penzance and inside can be seen a Trafalgar Banner, placed there during the celebrations for Nelson's victory. Close to the village centre, down an overgrown path, lies the source of **St**

Trengwainton Gardens, Madron

Maddern's Well that was thought to have curative powers especially to those with rickets who tied a rag to the small thorn tree growing here. It was also used for divination, showing that the well had pre-Christian origins. Young women would tie two pieces of straw together in the form of a cross, and stick a pin in it. They would then place it on the water, the number of bubbles rising as it gradually sank indicating how many years it would be until they married. Further along the path are the remains of **St Maddern's Cell**, the place where the saint, who lived in the 6th century, was said to have baptised villagers and which was destroyed by Cromwellian soldiers in 1646.

Just to the south of the village lies **Trengwainton Gardens**, the National Trust owned woodland gardens that are particularly well known for their spring flowering shrubs, walled gardens and fine views of Mount's Bay. The walled gardens were built in the early 19th century by the then owner Sir Rose Price, the son of a wealthy Jamaican sugar planter.

The land to the north of Madron is rich in ancient monuments and, in particular, there is **Lanyon Quoit** and the granite **Men-an-Tol**, a holed stone that was originally the entrance to a tomb chamber. For centuries, this granite ring was thought to have curative powers and naked children were

Chysauster Ancient Village

passed through its centre nine times to cure all manner of diseases.

New Mill
2 miles N of Penzance off the A30

On a windy hillside northeast of the village lies **Chysauster Ancient Village**, which is looked after by English Heritage. Built around 2,000 years ago in the late Iron Age, this Romano-Cornish village was discovered during archaeological excavations in the 1860s. For all its age, the village has surpisingly modern features - neat rows of cottages, each with its own terraced garden and paved courtyard.

TOURIST INFORMATION CENTRES

BODMIN

Bodmin Shire Hall,
Mount Folly Square,
Bodmin,
Cornwall PL31 2DQ

Tel: 01208 76616
Fax: 01208 76616

e-mail: bodmintic@visit.org.uk
website: www.bodminlive.com

BOSCASTLE & TINTAGEL

Bossiney Road,
Tintagel,
Cornwall PL34 0AJ

Tel: 01840 250010 or 779084
Fax: 01840 250010

e-mail: tintagelvc@ukonline.co.uk
website: www.visitboscastleandtintagel.com

BUDE

The Crescent,
Bude,
Cornwall EX23 8LE

Tel: 01288 354240
Fax: 01288 355769

e-mail: budetic@visitbude.info
website: www.budelive.com

CAMELFORD

North Cornwall Museum,
The Clease,
Camelford,
Cornwall PL32 9PL

Tel: 01840 212954
Fax: 01840 212954

e-mail: camelfordtic@eurobell.co.uk

FALMOUTH

28 Killigrew Street,
Falmouth,
Cornwall TR11 3PN

Tel: 01326 312300
Fax: 01326 313457

e-mail: falmouthtic@yahoo.co.uk
website: www.go-cornwall.com

FOWEY

The Ticket Shop & du Maurier Literary Centre,
5 South Street,
Fowey,
Cornwall PL23 1AR

Tel: 01726 833616
Fax: 01726 834939

e-mail: info@fowey.co.uk
website: www.fowey.co.uk

HAYLE (SEASONAL)

Lethlean Lane,
Hayle,
Cornwall

Tel: 01736 754399

HELSTON

79 Meneage Street,
Helston,
Cornwall TR13 8RB

Tel: 01326 565431
Fax: 01326 572803

e-mail: info@helstontic.demon.co.uk
website: www.go-cornwall.com

LAUNCESTON

Market House Arcade,
Market Street,
Launceston,
Cornwall PL15 8EP

Tel: 01566 772321
Fax: 01566 772322

e-mail: Launcestontic1@ukonline.co.uk
website: www.visitlaunceston.com

LISKEARD

Foresters Hall,
Pike Street,
Liskeard,
Cornwall PL14 3JE

Tel: 01579 349148
Fax: 07092 399866

e-mail: tourism@liskeard.gov.uk
website: www.liskeard.gov.uk

LOOE

The Guildhall
Fore Street,
East Looe,
Cornwall PL13 1AA

Tel: 01503 262072
Fax: 01503 265426

e-mail: looetic@looetourism.freeserve.co.uk
website: www.southeastcornwall.co.uk

South East Cornwall Discovery Centre
Millpool,
West Looe,
Cornwall PL13 2AF

Tel: 01503 262777
Fax: 01503 263266

e-mail: discovery@caradon.gov.uk
website: www.southeastcornwall.com

LOSTWITHIEL

Community Centre,
Liddicoat Road,
Lostwithiel,
Cornwall PL22 0HE
Tel: 01208 872207
Fax: 01208 872207
e-mail: tourism@lostwithieltic.org.uk

MEVAGISSEY

St George's Square,
Mevagissey,
Cornwall PL26 6UB
Tel: 01726 844857
Fax: 01726 844857
e-mail: info@mevagissey-cornwall.co.uk
website: www.mevagissey-cornwall.co.uk

NEWQUAY

Municipal Offices,
Marcus Hill,
Newquay, Cornwall TR7 1BD
Tel: 01637 854020
Fax: 01637 854030
e-mail: info@newquay.co.uk
website: www.newquay.co.uk

PADSTOW

Red Brick Building,
North Quay,
Padstow, Cornwall PL28 8AF
Tel: 01841 533449
Fax: 01841 532356
e-mail:padstowtic@visit.org.uk
website: www.padstowlive.co.uk

PENZANCE

Station Road,
Penzance,
Cornwall TR18 2NF
Tel: 01736 362207
Fax: 01736 363600
e-mail: pztic@penwith.gov.uk
website: www.penwith.gov.uk

PERRANPORTH

Perranporth,
Cornwall TR6 0DP
Tel: 01872 573368
Fax: 01872 573138
e-mail: thevoice@perraninfo.co.uk
website: www.perraninfo.co.uk

ST AGNES

20 Churchtown,
St Agnes,
Cornwall TR5 0QW
Tel: 01875 554150
Fax: 01875 554150
e-mail: stagnes.tic@stagnes.com
website: www.stagnes.com

ST AUSTELL

Southbourne Road,
St Austell,
Cornwall PL25 4RS
Tel: 0870 445 0244
Fax: 01726 874168
e-mail: tic@cornish-riviera.co.uk
website: www.cornishriviera.co.uk

ST IVES

The Guildhall,
Street-an-Pol,
St Ives,
Cornwall TR26 2DS
Tel: 01736 796297
Fax: 01736 798309
e-mail: ivtic@penwith.gov.uk
website: www.go-cornwall.com

ST JUST

The Library,
Market Street,
St Just,
Penzance,
Cornwall TR19 7HX
Tel: 01736 788669
Fax: 01736 788586
e-mail: stjust.library@cornwall.gov.uk
website: www.go-cornwall.com

ST MAWES

The Roseland Visitor Centre,
The Millennuim Rooms,
The Square,
St Mawes,
Cornwall TR2 5AG
Tel: 01326 270440
Fax: 01326 270440
e-mail: manager@roselandinfo.com
website: www.roselandinfo.com

TRURO

Municipal Building,
Boscawen Street,
Truro
Coprnwall TR1 2NE
Tel: 01872 274555
Fax: 01872 263031
e-mail: truro@touristinfo.demon.co.uk
website: www.truro.gov.uk

WADEBRIDGE

Eddystone Road,
Wadebridge,
Cornwall PL27 7AL
Tel: 0870 122 3337
Fax: 01208 813781
e-mail: wadebridge.tic@btconnect.com
website: www.visitwadebridge.com

INDEX OF TOWNS, VILLAGES AND PLACES OF INTEREST

LIST OF ADVERTISERS

Travel Publishing

The Hidden Places

Regional and National guides to the less well-known places of interest and places to eat, stay and drink

Hidden Inns

Regional guides to traditional pubs and inns throughout the United Kingdom

Off the Motorway

This very popular guide follows the junctions of each of the country's leading motorways and provides detailed information on places to stop close to each junction.

COUNTRY LIVING MAGAZINE
RURAL GUIDES

Regional and National guides to the traditional countryside of Britain and Ireland with easy to read facts on places to visit, stay, eat, drink and shop

For more information:

Phone: 0118 981 7777
e-mail: info@travelpublishing.co.uk

Fax: 0118 982 0077
website: www.travelpublishing.co.uk

Easy-to-use, Informative
Travel Guides on the British Isles

Travel Publishing Limited

7a Apollo House • Calleva Park • Aldermaston • Berkshire RG7 8TN

HIDDEN PLACES ORDER FORM

To order any of our publications just fill in the payment details below and complete the order form. For orders of less than 4 copies please add £1 per book for postage and packing. Orders over 4 copies are P & P free.

Please Complete Either:

I enclose a cheque for £ [_____] made payable to Travel Publishing Ltd

Or:

Card No: [_____] Expiry Date: [_____]

Signature: [_____]

Name: [_____]

Address: [_____]

Tel no: [_____]

Please either send, telephone, fax or e-mail your order to:

Travel Publishing Ltd, 7a Apollo House, Calleva Park, Aldermaston, Berkshire RG7 8TN

Tel: 0118 981 7777   Fax: 0118 982 0077 e-mail: info@travelpublishing.co.uk

	PRICE	QUANTITY		PRICE	QUANTITY
HIDDEN INNS TITLES			**HIDDEN PLACES REGIONAL TITLES**		
East Anglia	£7.99	....	Cornwall	£8.99	....
Heart of England	£7.99	....	Devon	£8.99	....
Lancashire & Cheshire	£7.99	....	Dorset, Hants & Isle of Wight	£8.99	....
North of England	£7.99	....	East Anglia	£8.99	....
South	£7.99	....	Gloucs, Wiltshire & Somerset	£8.99	....
South East	£7.99	....	Heart of England	£8.99	....
South and Central Scotland	£7.99	....	Hereford, Worcs & Shropshire	£8.99	....
Wales	£7.99	....	Lake District & Cumbria	£8.99	....
Welsh Borders	£7.99	....	Lancashire & Cheshire	£8.99	....
West Country	£7.99	....	Northumberland & Durham	£8.99	....
Yorkshire	£7.99	....	Peak District	£8.99	....
COUNTRY LIVING RURAL GUIDES			Sussex	£8.99	....
East Anglia	£10.99	....	Yorkshire	£8.99	....
Heart of England	£10.99	....	**HIDDEN PLACES NATIONAL TITLES**		
Ireland	£11.99	....	England	£11.99	....
North East	£10.99	....	Ireland	£11.99	....
North West	£10.99	....	Scotland	£11.99	....
Scotland	£11.99	....	Wales	£11.99	....
South of England	£10.99	....			
South East of England	£10.99	....			
Wales	£11.99	....			
West Country	£10.99	....			

Value [_____]

Post and Packing [_____]

Total Value [_____]

READER REACTION FORM

The *Travel Publishing* research team would like to receive reader's comments on any visitor attractions or places reviewed in the book and also recommendations for suitable entries to be included in the next edition. This will help ensure that the *Hidden Places series of Guides* continues to provide its readers with useful information on the more interesting, unusual or unique features of each attraction or place ensuring that their visit to the local area is an enjoyable and stimulating experience. To provide your comments or recommendations would you please complete the forms below and overleaf as indicated and send to:

**The Research Department, Travel Publishing Ltd,
7a Apollo House, Calleva Park, Aldermaston, Reading, RG7 8TN.**

Your Name:

Your Address:

Your Telephone Number:

Please tick as appropriate:

       Comments ☐   Recommendation ☐

Name of Establishment:

Address:

Telephone Number:

Name of Contact:

READER REACTION FORM

Comment or Reason for Recommendation:

READER REACTION FORM

The *Travel Publishing* research team would like to receive reader's comments on any visitor attractions or places reviewed in the book and also recommendations for suitable entries to be included in the next edition. This will help ensure that the *Hidden Places series of Guides* continues to provide its readers with useful information on the more interesting, unusual or unique features of each attraction or place ensuring that their visit to the local area is an enjoyable and stimulating experience. To provide your comments or recommendations would you please complete the forms below and overleaf as indicated and send to:

The Research Department, Travel Publishing Ltd,
7a Apollo House, Calleva Park, Aldermaston, Reading, RG7 8TN.

Your Name:

Your Address:

Your Telephone Number:

Please tick as appropriate:

Comments ☐   Recommendation ☐

Name of Establishment:

Address:

Telephone Number:

Name of Contact:

READER REACTION FORM

Comment or Reason for Recommendation:

....

....

....

....

....

....

....

....

....

....

....

....

....

....

READER REACTION FORM

The *Travel Publishing* research team would like to receive reader's comments on any visitor attractions or places reviewed in the book and also recommendations for suitable entries to be included in the next edition. This will help ensure that the *Hidden Places series of Guides* continues to provide its readers with useful information on the more interesting, unusual or unique features of each attraction or place ensuring that their visit to the local area is an enjoyable and stimulating experience. To provide your comments or recommendations would you please complete the forms below and overleaf as indicated and send to:

The Research Department, Travel Publishing Ltd,
7a Apollo House, Calleva Park, Aldermaston, Reading, RG7 8TN.

Your Name:

Your Address:

Your Telephone Number:

Please tick as appropriate:

Comments ☐   Recommendation ☐

Name of Establishment:

Address:

Telephone Number:

Name of Contact:

READER REACTION FORM

Comment or Reason for Recommendation: